NO JUDGMENT

NO JUDGMENT

ESSAYS

LAUREN OYLER

HARPERONE

An Imprint of HarperCollinsPublishers

HarperCollins books may be purchased for educational, business, or sales promotional use. For information, please email the Special Markets Department at SPsales@harpercollins.com.

FIRST EDITION

Designed by Yvonne Chan

Library of Congress Cataloging-in-Publication Data has been applied for.

ISBN 978-0-06-323535-9

24 25 26 27 28 LBC 5 4 3 2 1

CONTENTS

NO JUDGMENT

INTRODUCTION: ON REVENGE

Well, well, well. The book has started. There's no turning back.

I wrote these essays over the past three years, though several were percolating for longer. All are published here for the first time. The essays on gossip, Goodreads, and vulnerability arose as many of my ideas do: from a growing agitation about what I perceived to be misunderstandings and fallacies spreading in cultural criticism and commentary, and a resulting feeling that I must say something to attempt to intervene, as futile an endeavor as that may be. The essay on spoilers has a similar origin story, but I won't ruin it for you.

The essays on expatriation, autofiction, and anxiety are more personal, though I no longer have any idea what counts as a "personal essay." They are about, among other things, me and my experiences, and they deal with the many ways we are encouraged, at this specific moment in history, to understand ourselves and our experiences, and with the ways these frameworks fail, change, and reroute us. Some of the points of departure for these essays were also things that annoy me—misconceptions, received wisdom, clichés—but because I am closer to the subjects, what might have remained mere annoyance

< 1 >

often felt like an affront. A feeling is not the truth, of course—anyone who has talked to me at a party might wonder why I don't consider an essay on the ethics of gossip as a private and increasingly public practice "personal." But that's the nature of feelings: not always rational. They pick favorites, develop complexes, fixate, concoct paranoid narratives. This tension—between thought and feeling, reason and impulse—is a feature of my own writing as well as of the conflicts and arguments I'm most often drawn to write about.

This book is called *No Judgment* because the phrase has become a discursive shield against the discomforts of these tensions. "No judgment!"—it's almost always spoken in a patronizingly casual tone, with a fake smile, the kind of thing you're supposed to say to approach awkward conversations that you know your interlocutor might not enjoy. We use it to preface advice a friend won't want to take, to soften an unflattering observation, to ease our way into difficulty. It means, sometimes, "I am not judging you harshly or negatively" or, more often, "I promise not to express the judgment I am making to your face." Regardless, it's always ironic. There is never no judgment, and certainly not in this book.

Deciding what to do with judgment is a more productive line of inquiry than worrying about what other people think. If you possess enough anxious self-awareness as a writer, you will learn a lot about yourself working on a long project. Although I intended all the pieces in this book to "fit together"—although I wanted this essay collection to cohere as a book that rewards cross-reference and highlights connections among apparently distant topics—I didn't anticipate that revenge, or its easier-going synonym *justice*, would become a theme. Upon reflection, I know exactly why I was thinking about revenge, but that is the subject of a future novel. In the meantime, I left all the little half-jokes about vengeance in; the abstract relationship between judgment and revenge isn't super hard to parse. A harsh judgment might inspire a desire for vengeance; a revenge plot, in a film or novel, implies a moral judgment of the initial act, particularly if you make it to the twist at the end. If I experience, as the title of the essay on gossip has it, "Embarrassment, Panic, Opprobrium, Job Loss, Etc.," I might seek revenge, in the form of making judgments that I distribute as gossip, or I might have been the unfortunate target of revenge, in the form of the same. The relationship between the internet commenter and the public figure, and between the critic and artist, which I discuss in "My Perfect Opinions," is often governed, or thought to be governed, by a desire for vengeance brought on by the harsh judgments of amateur and professional critics alike.

Writing is often nothing but revenge, as the critic Terry Castle is quoted saying later in the book. This revenge need not be the kind of autobiographical novel that I just suggested I'm working on myself. There are sentences and paragraphs in my essay on autofiction, "I Am the One Sitting Here, for Hours and Hours and Hours," that appeared in the first draft of my novel *Fake Accounts*, which for most of its prepublication life contained a single footnote. This footnote consisted of a jaunty 2,500-word essay about autofiction and the relationship between myself and my narrator. While a survey of preliminary readers was truly mixed on the presence of the footnote in the novel, I was encouraged by my agent to remove it for the purposes of selling the book, which I did. My revenge for this edit, about which I continue to feel ambivalent—particularly given how often comments were made about the relationship between myself and that narrator—was to make the essay much, much longer, and better, and to include it here.

The idea that the best revenge is living well is about envy, but it is also about judgment. The saying suggests that the feeling of being above or at least beyond judgment is not just a solace, or mentally healthy to cultivate; it suggests that to be unaffected by whoever or whatever has (ostensibly) painfully wronged or merely upset you can be a kind of affront itself. To live well despite past injustice is a harsh judgment; the act of living an enviable life says that whoever harmed you has no power, doesn't matter in the long run. Like "no judgment," the cliché that the best revenge is living well is the kind of thing you say to placate. "You're better than that," a friend adds, looking a little worried, a little desperate to stop whatever scheme you have in motion. "Don't stoop to his level." No one actually believes any of this, but to admit that the best revenge is patient, quiet, clever, and untraceable would mean admitting not only that we care about what other people think but also that maybe, sometimes, we should. As these essays show, that often feels very bad.

EMBARRASSMENT, PANIC, OPPROBRIUM, JOB LOSS, ETC.

heard this crazy story, and I want you to know. A person we both know, or don't, or have heard of, or whose significance must be explained, wronged another such person, or was wronged by another such person. He cheated on his girlfriend—many, many times. She got drunk and made a dramatic declaration. That guy has a problem, a problem so serious I don't know if we should really be talking about it in this flippant tone. That woman has received a scandalous amount of money, a fact she is seeking to minimize. He was cruel to interns. She was cruel to waitstaff. He still loves her. She's in denial. He's falling apart. She's going to return her dog to the adoption agency. He said something weird, at the end, that makes me wonder.

I heard this crazy story, and I want you to know. I want you to know because it's crazy, because it's weighing on me, because I don't know how to proceed, because I want someone to share the burden of knowledge I'm carrying, because I think you'll have more information, because it relates to a conversation we had about three weeks ago, because I think your reaction will be funny, because I just want something to talk about. The news might be so exciting that my motive is self-evident; my reliability, regardless, is less so. I am leaving something out, to protect myself, my interests, my political beliefs, my friends, you; I am forgetting a crucial detail, or have been given incomplete information, which I may or may not realize or disclose; I am exaggerating, fudging, ironizing, filling in, inferring, or flat out making this up. I am a reliable source. I am not at all trustworthy. I'm biased because something similar happened to me. I have literally no idea what I'm talking about.

I heard this crazy story, and I want you to know. I read it on the internet, in a tweet, in an Instagram story, in a comment. They deleted it, or they didn't, or it disappeared after the twenty-four-hour window. I have a screenshot, or I don't, or someone else has a screenshot. Yes, I saw it. No, I left just before. Someone DMed me. No, I won't ask her. I heard it last week. I heard it a long time ago. My good friend told me; she works with him. A woman I knew in New York ran into her at the grocery store. A guy I used to sleep with asked me if I knew anything about it. She told him. He told her. He's dating her best friend. She's dating his boss. He said. She said. You'll have to find out for yourself. Yes, from the source. No, but I trust her. Show it to me. I'll send it to you. I don't know who with, but I can probably find out. I told you what happened in December. I remember. I heard it, too. It didn't even seem like a big deal at the time. I can't tell you who. All right, I'll tell you. You can't tell anybody. Don't say you heard it from me. Don't get mad. I can't believe it. I always suspected. It all makes sense.

* * *

As children, we learn not to gossip, because it is bad. Lessons to this effect are plentiful, especially in the Bible. "A whisperer separates close friends," Proverbs warns, teaching us both to avoid the whisperer who

< 6 >

< 7 >

might separate us from ours and to resist the urge to dissociate others in turn. If appeals to friends aren't quite appealing enough, we should consider our own fates: "The words of a whisperer are delicious morsels; they go down into the inner parts of the body"—what seems like a special treat will add stubborn pounds to your soul. In school, we played the game "Telephone" to understand how a story changes as it is passed from one person to the next; at recess, on the bus, in the cafeteria, we practiced.

While the moral of the story was still, explicitly, do not talk behind each other's backs, we began getting conflicting information. We read Jane Austen and young adult novels and *US Weekly*; we watched daytime talk shows and teen movies and, very possibly, *Sex and the City*. On television, people who were advertised as real began telling us directly, straight to camera, what the people they were talking about weren't supposed to hear. We listened to our mothers talking on the phone. Mine, I psychoanalytically remembered while writing this essay, used to pass on to me what my friends' parents told her about their children—that is, about my friends—even when, I now have to assume, I didn't totally understand the significance: tragic pubertal developments; struggles at school resulting from mismanagement by another, worse mother.

Like a bird, my mother was scavenging for morsels, as if to feed my soul. She was trying to do several things at once by passing parental gossip onto me: to learn how to mother by talking to other mothers about it; to seek validation for her superior parenting without asking for it directly from the one person who both could and could not give it, her approximately nine-year-old daughter; to encourage me to feel thankful that I was not experiencing such a difficult puberty as one girl, or to warn me not to go down the same path as one boy; to bond. (Shared secrets are some of the best things to bond over, after shared enemies, though they're not so different.) She was also, of course, parenting unconsciously, setting me up to become, among other things, a woman who is interested (and proficient) enough in gossip that she wants to write a long essay about it. I can't remember my mother ever telling me that if I couldn't say anything nice, not to say anything at all, which is the kind of lesson you teach a child in order to shield her from the overwhelmingly complicated truth. Same goes with "You can't subtract a negative number," which has always bothered me. Of course you can. Sometimes, you must.

Academic gossip apologists make many good points. The argument tends to be that discussing other people's business helps the gossip understand the world and its threats and customs. We live in small groups governed by particular norms that may be spoken only indirectly, if they are spoken at all: a school, a department, a field; an office, an industry; a party circuit, a "scene," a subculture; even an online forum or circle of a particular social network, like fandoms or other niche communities. In the 1960s, the anthropologist Max Gluckman argued that "gossip, and even scandal, have important positive virtues . . . they maintain the unity, morals and values of social groups"; "enable these groups to control the competing cliques and aspiring individuals of which all groups are composed"; and "make possible the selection of leaders without embarrassment"—or with contained embarrassment. In the 1980s, the literary scholar Patricia Meyer Spacks established that gossip was feminized and thus unfairly maligned in her excellent book-length defense of the practice using examples from history, philosophy, psychology, literature, and her life. We use gossip to understand what is acceptable and what is not, what is possible and what has not yet been successfully tried. "Gossip may be the beginning of moral inquiry, the low end of the platonic ladder which leads to self-understanding," Phyllis Rose writes in her acclaimed and beloved 1983 book *Parallel Lives: Five Victorian Marriages*. "We are desperate for information about how other people live because we want to know how to live ourselves, yet we are taught to see this desire as an illegitimate form of prying."

We also use this information to understand our status, both among individuals and within the collective. For example: A woman you have had a couple of pleasant, if not life-changing, drinks with behaves coldly toward you at a party. You might panic that you have done something to offend her, racking your brain for the fateful faux pas, or you might ask a mutual friend: "Does she hate me?" The mutual friend might reply, "Oh my God, *no!*" followed by the description of a personal-life problem that more than satisfactorily explains the unexpected chill: a breakup, an illness, a failure. You might be reassured, or intrigued if the breakup is dramatic; you might also feel slightly closer to the mutual friend, confident she would tell you if anything were amiss. Or your doubt might linger, if instead the friend replies differently, in a stomach-churningly tentative tone, "Oh, she's never talked to me about you, but I doubt she hates you. She's probably just busy at work!" You then have to consider, again, what it is you've done, or at least what it is the recently cold woman thinks you've done. From there, you will probably worry that she is gossiping about it this very minute, given that it seems your mutual friend knows something you don't. It may be something you could never have anticipated. Or maybe the recently cold woman was right to snub you, and you knew deep down why all along.

Arguments on behalf of gossip's goodness, or its utility, or its utility-thus-goodness, supporting the idea that we should reconsider why we think talking about people who aren't there is so immoral, have always left me a little cold. Reading research studies about gossip is about as boring as the activity itself is exhilarating, because the examples used in academic literature must be stripped of their salacious, real-world content so that only their structures remain. Gossip as a lens for reading literature makes the reader want to scour biographies and archives for a novel's real-world inspirations. Yes, gossip certainly reveals the layout of our social lives; yes, it's a tool for determining position and strategy. In a high-stakes environment, such as the office or motherhood, the information we get from gossip is invaluable to the lifelong project of maintaining sanity, our own and others', as is our ability to privately complain, or bitch, about perceived slights and injustices. But do we not also love it—with a passion that exceeds logic, that drives and dictates, that is not harmless or passive?

It's a little bit nasty, the lust for gossip's mix of schadenfreude and satiation, the guilty pleasure, that comes with a new piece of extended-network information. It doesn't matter how often it happens or how many times I've read about it in novels or biographies, seen it depicted on television and in film, or contemplated doing it myself: When someone has an affair, I flip out. It's truly like Christmas. The pain infidelity causes is immaterial; I want more people to have affairs so that I may hear about them thirdhand. While I understand I do not make people I barely know have affairs by wishing they would, it still feels malicious. I know, intellectually, that the plots of the stories I hear as gossip are quotidian, evidence of the enduring sameness of human nature; in practice, the story always feels new, and I must understand how it happened. I bring the gossip to friends and, if drunk enough, acquaintances, gathering reactions and, eventually, more pieces of the puzzle, until I can put it all together. Fun—I learn more about myself as well as my confidants through these conversations, which often expand beyond the facts of who's sleeping with whom to encompass ethical questions and the stuff

< 11 >

they're now calling philosophy. Conversely, if I go too long without surprising news of other people's lives, I don't become paranoid, in need of more data, but merely depressed. Where is everyone? Did I die? Am I now a ghost? This is not a justification, but an explanation: gossip confirms not only the existence of other people but also the existence of other people *really living*—taking risks, making mistakes, committing fraud, having inner lives that expand outward, doing and saying things that don't meet the impossible expectations they set for themselves and others. Gossip confirms your suspicion that you were being lied to, that something was off, that you're not crazy.

So: Does the sense that gossip is kind of evil come from some ingrained sense of outdated propriety, pointless and oppressive? From religious morality? Is it something we should "work through" the way we had to teach ourselves that, for example, sex is not "dirty," so that when we, as enlightened adults, now engage in "dirty talk," we are always being a little bit ironic? Or is the guilt we feel on sharing a piece of confidential information a response to our having done a genuine wrong?

I've come to believe the best unfollowable advice we are given about gossip is not about gossip specifically, but about our relationship to other people in general: do unto them as you would have them do unto you. Gossip is a fact of life, but we hate the idea of being gossiped about. Balance can be achieved through elaborate guidelines about what you do and do not pass on, and to whom, based on what you would want if you were the one being gossiped about, eliminating the unrealistic option of never being spoken about in your absence at all. These rules involve an assessment of the seriousness of the topic, of whether someone has asked you to not pass it on, and of justice. Those who acknowledge that gossip is inevitable might be better prepared to become the subject in turn, and they might also adjust their behavior accordingly. This need not mean becoming se-cretive, shady, antisocial, or uninteresting; it means accepting that if you ever do anything with other people, your life is probably not as private as you might imagine it to be, and understanding that even the most upstanding behavior can be discussed without you present and interpreted in a way you might not like. Gossip is not just the sharing of information; it's the comparing and contrasting and devel-opment of interpretation. She is so nice: Is she boring? She is so nice: Is she hiding something? She lets her friends walk all over her. She is attempting to maintain a level of control over her life that is just unsustainable. I hate those fucking pants.

Is the guilty conscience really just the reasonable, self-protective fear that all these assessments will make their way back to their absent subject? "I always worry that the horrible things I say about other people will get back to them somehow," a friend told me, "but then I remember, or realize, that I have almost never, or maybe never, heard the horrible things people say about me behind my back . . . and I know it's not because they don't say them!"

She's right. The guardrails most people intuitively put in place around gossip mean that you will probably never know whether you were being gossiped about; you can only assume that you almost cer-tainly have been, and will continue to be. I have heard such things only when the other person obviously hopes that what they are saying will get back to me, and so takes measures to float their vitriol in my direction. This happens in two ways. The first is an old-fashioned strategy: a lesser character tells a mutual friend something, knowing or hoping (evilly?) that the mutual friend will deliver their message. I know this because I have been on both sides. My naughty love of gossip means I am a repository of information and tend to spread it around based on those elaborate rules I mentioned. People continue to tell me sensitive things about their lives and feelings, for some reason, even when they know I am not the most discreet confidant; my best guess is that I have one of those faces, and ask gentle journalistic questions, and can really "don't tell anyone" if asked. I worry a bit that publicly exposing myself as a relentless gossip here will discourage others from opening up to me, but I doubt it; in general people want to be known, but without having to confess themselves explicitly. I assume I have been told gossip designated for a downstream recipient at some point in my life. I have also been the subject of uncharitable interpretations by a former friend, the details of which I had to pry from the messenger's hands when I found out she had the goods. I felt justified in doing so; the former friend had betrayed me profoundly. (That the mutual friend didn't tell me *they'd had lunch!* just before the betrayal was her own possibly gossip-worthy error; I found out from someone else, who mentioned it casually, not knowing I was apparently not supposed to know.) Although the messenger said she didn't want to upset me with the horrible things the other guy had said—"It just didn't pass muster," she kept repeating, honorably and correctly—she is also much closer to me: the other guy wanted me to know. I don't think he counted on me finding his claims so risible, and disprovable, that they were less of an insult than a relief, confirmation that I was in the right. Though it's also possible my dutiful friend, resentful that I angrily forced it out of her or beholden to some unknown allegiance, left something out, or mischaracterized what was said, or lied.

The second way gossip might get back to its subject is more modern: someone posts an insult on social media, and the subject happens to see it, or someone sends it to them. Being insulted directly is not gossip—in gossip, the subject must be absent—but if I am insulted directly and tell you about it later, that transforms the event into information: you make it gossip by telling someone else. You shouldn't feel bad about it, though; the easiest kind of gossip to share is something that makes the subject look like a bad person, that indicates behavior that was not upstanding at all ("She sent a bunch of deranged messages at 2 a.m. threatening him"; "He showed up at her work"; "She contacted his boss"; "She's a TERF!"). This kind of gossip is pretending at retribution and, theoretically, might even produce a kind of observable result. Ideally, gossip would create a rollicking, only occasionally upsetting equilibrium, with everyone talking about everyone else, sometimes giving more to the chaotic mix, sometimes taking; the pressure might convince at least a few of the truly wicked not to be so flagrant, for fear of being discussed as truly wicked. As it is, that pressure is not enough. Some people are principled and do not gossip, and some people are boring and are not gossiped about. Certain people cultivate lives of the party and inundate onlookers with their antics; others are overly fearful of being talked about, or found out, and may end up becoming even bigger stories when they slip—or when someone who dislikes them inordinately, for good or bad reasons, decides they want to talk about it. The wicked persist, so flagrantly that one suspects they *want* to be discussed. For me, it is easier and more fun to be open, within reason; while I of course never do anything truly wicked, I find that by relinquishing the illusion of total control over the narrative, you can end up with more of it in the long run. "I want to tell you this," a new friend said to me, "because you're sharing so much." Did I do it strategically? No, but yes. The strategic convenience was a bonus. Something had happened, months or years ago. It came to a dissatisfying conclusion. I wanted to know what she knew. I knew she probably felt the same way.

* * *

The idea that gossip is necessary to understand social life often positions those who gossip as outsiders—observing, skeptical, distant if not exactly above. "I wanted to know everything about an industry that allowed me to live in the place whose skyline I had stenciled on my bedroom wall in childhood," Kristen Radtke writes in a 2021 *New York Times Magazine* essay in defense of gossip, "and trading information felt like an opportunity to accrue capital in a world in which we had none, providing the promise of insiderness when we were not yet inside." She is describing the joy she and a friend felt "deconstructing" New York City and its literary world as new arrivals; she does not mention the panic anyone in this position inevitably feels after the contact high wears off. The panic comes from the possibility that the higher-profile subjects of her righteous gossip somehow find out she has been talking about them and vindictively stonewall her from career opportunities. Not that this happens, ever, as I've already established, but the panic is almost always there. The reason the gossip never learns her lesson is that, rather than a hectic but loving commune, we already operate according to a policy of mutually assured destruction. Of course everyone gossips, and it's generally hard to prove it. Attempts to do so tend to make both parties look bad: paranoid, petty, and obsessed on one side, and almost certainly guilty on the other.

But not everyone is an outsider; information has to come from somewhere. The more you seek out information, the more you know; the more you know, the more you may be tempted to justify your position as a particularly canny distant observer, monitoring the foibles and hypocrisies of the object of your attention. Like a sneaky novelist—an artist!—you're merely gathering anecdota for something bigger and better than the pathetic contretemps of human relation.

We like this archetype, the quiet, somewhat furtive, but unnoticed guy in the corner, eavesdropping so that he might expose if not shift the balance of power from insider to outsider. Rarely does he actually publish his sweeping account of the scene he's been silently satirizing, and if he does, everyone gets mad: we trusted him, he was one of us. Indeed, his ability to learn all these secrets suggests he's no outsider at all.

To be in the loop is not only enlivening but empowering: if you're not really an outsider, the way you gossip may actually shape the world you purport to be merely observing, particularly if you maintain the innocent pose of the odd man out so that no one takes you too seriously. In 2002, Nick Denton launched the Gawker blog network, later known as Gawker Media, and its namesake property would advertise itself with the brilliant tagline "Today's gossip is tomorrow's news." Though not the most popular in terms of page views, Gawker.com was always the most notorious of the network's seven websites because it concerned (pun) the people who make things notorious: the media. The concept was that what journalists talked about behind the scenes was often more interesting than what they wrote in their stories, and Gawker rose to prominence by reproducing that talk for both the journalists themselves and the people who fancied themselves shrewd observers of the media. By the time Gawker stopped publishing in 2016, it was respected and reviled by those working in traditional media for having, in the words of one early collaborator, "disrupt[ed] how news was created." Gawker did this not only through prediction—by covering, teasing, or declaring what stories would become important in mainstream media, determining which gossip would tomorrow become news—but also by making the site a step in the process of news creation: the popularity of Gawker lent newsworthiness to the controversies it covered. To-

< 17 >

day's gossip is tomorrow's news, because we said so, and important people care what we say.

Denton always thought of himself as an outsider—he was the gay, Jewish child of a Hungarian immigrant attending private schools in England, as well as desperately ambitious. As a twenty-three-year-old in 1989, Denton, fluent in Hungarian because of his mother, reported on the fall of communism and the rise of Western business interests in the former Soviet bloc, and in retrospect you can see the path, from revolution to revolution. Although relations between the East and West had been warming in the months leading up to the fall of the Berlin Wall in November 1989, with crossings opening between Hungary and Czechoslovakia and the West, the actual moment the border between East and West Germany opened was an accident, the result of a series of miscommunications passed on from an ambiguous comment made by an underprepared official at a press conference. A mention of a new law permitting private trips abroad, which the official had not realized he was going to read in front of the crowd of journalists, naturally inspired questions. What about passports? When would this policy take effect? "As I understand it," the official said, frowning at the memo in front of him, rustling the papers, "it goes into effect from now on, immediately."

It was supposed to take effect the next day, according to a protocol, but journalists came to reasonable conclusions, though these were extrapolations and innocent rhetorical flourishes, and the news spread through the West German press. Running the headline "GDR Opens Frontier," one West German news program announced that "the Wall, too, should become permeable overnight"; another declared that "the gates of the Wall stand wide open." Although, as the historian Timothy Garton Ash writes in a 2023 essay for the *New York Review of*

Books, "One might even say, in the vocabulary of the 2020s, that it was 'fake news,'" neither of these statements was technically false. Interpretation, prediction, and metaphor can be used to convey a truth that isn't technically true, and not even necessarily maliciously. Who hasn't picked up a bit of ambiguous wording that they carried in the direction they were heading anyway, not even noticing that there was another route? East Germans watched and believed West German television, understood to be a reliable source. Thousands rushed to the border, where confused guards opened and closed and reopened the border crossings.

Although protests and geopolitical developments anticipated what would happen, it was still unimaginable. Today, Germans from both the East and West say they'd thought they would die before the Wall came down. Wouldn't it have been nice to be one of the only people who knew what was coming, who could have predicted it? "I'm pretty sure we have a revolution coming," Denton told the *New York Times*, predicting a shake-up in traditional media, in 2015. "It's not 100 percent guaranteed, but the existing corporate structure is looking pretty hollow."

Such proclamations are, for either a young reporter or a media mogul, inextricable from the capital you might accrue if they're right: a proven track record, of both scoops and speculations, means sources will trust you with their stories, and readers will turn to you first. A big part of Denton's "disruption" was to emphasize this aspect of news creation: the ambiguity, the possibility, the rampant speculation, everything that leads someone to start investigating a story. Traditional news outlets are bound by annoyances such as ethics and the threat of legal action; perhaps these things didn't have to matter so much, if the truth was eventually revealed to have been on your side.

< 19 >

* * *

In 1998, Denton founded Moreover.com, a news aggregator client for businesses that, according to a *Guardian* article from the time, enabled "companies to find out what is being said about them and their rivals online." (This kind of service wouldn't fully come into its own until Twitter.)* Shortly afterward, he moved to San Francisco, but he found the social scene lacking: "It's a very easy place to be the party giver or the party scene-maker." To be truly inside is boring; a little instability keeps things lively.

After Moreover, Denton initially wanted to launch a site or a service that would track analytics as blogging became more popular. "How could you figure out who was influencing whom in the blogosphere?" Christian Bailey, a tech founder and CEO, summarizes in Brian Abrams's *Gawker: An Oral History*. "Could you track the content sources and the effects of the bloggers?" The venture Denton ended up pursuing was much more sensational, though in some ways it had more of a precedent; he would found a site that charted an influential old-school social network rather than following the formation of a new one. He launched Gizmodo, a tech blog, and then Gawker.com. In a 2007 essay for *n+1*, Carla Blumenkranz described

---

* In 2022, while I was working on the essays in this book, Elon Musk purchased Twitter for $44 billion, inspiring a steady trickle of essays with the gist "What Was Twitter?" Among the disorienting adjustments he made as the site's new owner was that, in 2023, he changed the site's name to X. I have elected to keep the old name in my essays, which mostly refer to events that took place in and around the platform when it was still called Twitter and served a particular function in American culture. If you would like to understand more about that function, I recommend reading one of those essays. (My favorite is "What Was Twitter, Anyway?" by Willy Staley for the *New York Times Magazine*.) This footnote is just to let you know that I am aware that the name changed. Like many habitual Twitter users past and present, I find the whole thing bizarre, but I accept it as a blessing if the changes eventually sever my attachment to the platform once and for all.

Gawker's first (and, at the time, only) blogger, the twenty-five-year-old Elizabeth Spiers, as "a naïf new to the city," whose first posts resembled "the notebooks of young people who come to the city intent on figuring it out": quasi-anthropological lists of what to read and whom to pay attention to, evidence for the argument that gossip is a tool for understanding and situating oneself within an unfamiliar social environment. She focused especially on Tina Brown, the former *Talk* and *New Yorker* editor, and Anna Wintour, whose significance I hope I don't need to explain; at one point Spiers posed as a magazine assistant, knowingly disguised in a "wrap dress" and boots, to infiltrate the Condé Nast cafeteria, having gotten her previous information secondhand, from actual assistants. They had a salad bar with endive! She wanted a job at an actual magazine.

To care about this stuff implies you care about the structure of media, not whatever the media is producing, though of course in your sophisticated estimation the structure can't help but influence the product. It seems niche, but an insider knows that these connections and customs are really important; they determine how the news is packaged. Now an interest in what "media people" are doing is seen as myopic and sort of pathetic, the kind of thing no reasonable person would or should bother with. "Someone said to me at some point, 'I went back and read some of those original Spiers posts, and they're really pointless,'" said Lockhart Steele, who was Gawker Media's managing editor in the mid-2000s. "I'm like, 'You don't get it. That would be like picking a paragraph out of the middle of a Dickens novel. You're not getting the context of it.' So you have to be a certain kind of insider to even appreciate it."

The outsider/insider distinction corresponds nicely to the public/private distinction. Neither dichotomy is as definitive as it initially seems. If the prevailing understanding of gossip is that it is the exchange of private information between private persons—in other words, that it is not public—the act of gossiping challenges the limits of what is private; news will expand the edges of a social network until it reaches someone who doesn't care enough to pass it on. The publication of gossip might transform it into something else—unless the readership of the publication is self-regulating, composed exclusively of insiders. If only insiders care about what is being published, then what is being published is not really outside, or public, at all. Right?

Celebrity gossip, of the tabloid variety, doesn't really operate according to this principle: the idea is that the gossipmonger and her readers are so far outside the celebrity's circle that the gossip reporter doesn't even penetrate the private sphere, but at best gazes hopefully upon it through a telephoto lens. If a gossip magazine or website (or whatever) happens to come across a major scoop, the kind of revelation that will actually disrupt the celebrity's private life, the celebrity, with her professional publicity apparatus, tends to become aware of it in advance; the celebrity often tries to "take it public" herself so she can have some control over the narrative, though she must offer the threatening or competing outlet the exclusive story in exchange for this control. It is never that close, never too real. "The appeal of celebrity journalism seems to rest upon a promise," Elizabeth Hardwick wrote in 1986, "and the acceptance of the fact that the promise will again and again be unfilled."

One condition of my elaborate rules about gossip relates to whether the event took place in public. I have strong, somewhat intuitive beliefs about what is or isn't in the public sphere, which I will get to, but this policy is also defensive. What takes place in public has witnesses, any one of whom might be responsible for news of an event spreading. The drawback of being a celebrity is that the celebrity's private sphere is much smaller than the normal, unrecognizable person's private sphere; if you can walk down the street with no one noticing you, you are a "private person," even if you are not at all a "private person" because you give your thirty closest friends biweekly updates on your love life. You can walk down the street without anyone knowing you are walking down the street. Usually, celebrity gossip assumes that a broad range of people know who the subjects of its stories are, and that reasonable assumption allows individual celebrity gossip sites or reporters to spread their ethical dubiousness around: if they weren't the ones reporting that Taylor Swift was at a restaurant with a man, someone else would surely do so. Taylor Swift herself—Taylor Swift's people—might have strategically planted the news that she was at a restaurant with a man. Don't shoot the messenger.

The "insider" makes these calculations confusing. Since the 1960s, when the Norwegian sociologists Johan Galtung and Mari Holmboe Ruge proposed a set of "news factors" that determine the likelihood an event gets covered in the press, it has been made explicit that if an event involves "elite people," it is more likely to become news. If you are recognizable to only a certain kind of person in the street, whom you may or may not encounter on any given day, are you still a private person? Are you gossip, or are you news?

* * *

Within six months of its launch, Gawker was attracting five hundred thousand page views per month; for a website that mainly published a twenty-five-year-old upstart's catty musings, it was kind of a lot. But you can't write about elite endive forever. Spiers quickly got her job at an actual magazine, *New York*. The site expanded without her, gaining traction by posting often cruel and seemingly pointless celebrity sightings and, a bit later, outings. The Gawker definition of "celebrity" expanded to mean, as Blumenkranz writes, "all-but-anonymous people who, within the context of the New York media apparatus, might have seemed like the equivalent of ingénue actresses and other easy-target celebrities." This may have had something to do with the way Gawker bloggers had become bizarro fake celebrities themselves. By 2005, an anonymous disgruntled employee at Fordham University Press had started a meta-Gawker blog, *Gawkerist*, gossiping about the gossips themselves; this blogger, Chris Mohney, created an anonymous email account and "got their attention" by sending links to his subjects. He was quickly offered a job; everyone at Gawker "fell in love" with *Gawkerist*, with its vision of the site as something worth gossiping about.

While they were still "writing for people who were low- to mid-level editors inside Time Inc. or Condé Nast," according to one editor, the next era of Gawker broadened its audience by taking celebrity gossip, long a genre of media, possibly even of journalism, and making it personal; it collapsed the distinction between celebrities and those "all-but-anonymous people" by making readers feel they had about equal access to information about both, passed on through a chain of variously reliable sources, conveyed in the same really mean tone. The site's model at the time was to have a single star editor, a character in her own right, a not-at-all-anonymous xoxo Gossip Girl, who gave the reader a sense of intimacy even as the staff of Gawker Media slowly grew. "Remember Natasha Lyonne?" one post from 2006 begins. "The adorably husky actress from *American Pie* and *Slums of Beverly Hills* seemed to have skipped her DARE classes and, in the past year and a half, has threatened to molest her neighbor's dog, pissed off her landlord Michael Rappaport (who wrote about her drug den in *Jane*), and was hospitalized for all sorts of life-threatening, needle-related things." Celebrity gossip had always been cruel—invasive, ruthless, concerned with strife and physical appearance—but given the potential audience reach and the potential for reader feedback/collaboration, this kind of thing was something else. Written by "Jessica," who was Jessica Coen, the site's star editor at the time, the post refers to Gawker's own on-going coverage of Lyonne and goes on to quote several anonymous tips submitted about the struggling actress. Both Coen's tone and that of the anonymous tipsters convey a disingenuous concern that half-heartedly attempts to justify the bitchy dishing. One anonymous source concludes a disturbing sighting of Lyonne with "Poor thing!"; another notes that "she actually looked so bad I feel guilty writing this, I just know there are some people out there who like to hear she's still alive once in a while."

I first heard about Gawker when I was an intern at a small start-up in Denver in 2009, and a woman who had recently relocated to Colorado from New York bragged to me that she "knew" "Gawker Stalker." A graduate student, she must have been referring to Spiers, or a later editor, because "Gawker Stalker" was the name of the site's feature that began as a list under Spiers and eventually became an in-teractive map that tracked subjects' whereabouts using Google Maps and reader-submitted information. For this, Gawker was accused of actual stalking. It was not a good look, as we said a few years ago but don't really say now. But at the time the site was growing, hiring more employees and expanding its content, adapting to the media environ-ment it was helping to create, alongside the growth of blogging and social media. The question of stalking was incidental!

Gawker's origins as a possible influence tracker translated to a lust for web traffic and metrics that came to define the news media, whether it was online-only or an actual magazine. Now, an editor or publisher can see how a reader arrived at a particular article, what kinds of headlines and social sells generate more traffic, and pretty much any other statistic you'd find useful in order to understand who your audience is and how to make it bigger. Gawker was a pioneer of this philosophy, as Ben Smith details in his 2023 book *Traffic: Genius, Rivalry, and Delusion in the Billion-Dollar Race to Go Viral*; around 2010, the centerpiece of the Gawker office became the "Big Board" that featured live updates of the site's top-performing articles pulled from the web traffic analytics service Chartbeat. The more traffic you get, the more famous you are, of course. The more famous you are, the more traffic you get. At Gawker, you also got bonuses.

In the 2010s, Gawker's status as an actual insider couldn't really be disputed; it had outgrown the gossipy low-hanging fruit and often broke news stories and published in-depth features. "It should be said that Gawker in 2015 really wasn't very mean," Max Read, the site's former editor-in-chief, wrote in *New York Magazine* a year later. But a reputation is hard to shake—particularly if your whole thing is about establishing the importance of reputation. Gawker had always been "transparent," detailing the site's minuscule advertising revenue even at its conception and developing a tradition of goodbye posts when editors left the company, even if the split was acrimonious. The company published its own staff memos and, if relevant, unflattering instant message conversations among staff and the managing partnership, who were also known to tussle with employees in the comments sections. Denton, too. While these weren't always the best way to generate viral traffic, they did serve a purpose. They established that the workings of this company and the dramas of its staff were, like those Gawker had reported on at Condé Nast, newsworthy and public—not just private gossip, though the performance might have inspired you to tell your media friends, privately, that you thought they were all self-important and tedious.

In 2015, Tommy Craggs, the umbrella company's executive editor, and Read resigned in protest over the company's partners' decision to remove a controversial article claiming the CFO of Condé Nast had attempted to pay for a night in a hotel with a gay porn star. In the original post, which was taken down, the CFO denied all Gawker's allegations, saying, "I don't know who this individual is. This is a shakedown. . . . I have never had a text exchange with this individual. He clearly has an ulterior motive that has nothing to do with me." The post announcing their resignations was nearly 4,700 words long, consisting primarily of staff memos that had been sent during the fallout from this controversial blog post, which was significantly shorter. It is hard to imagine many people reading it all, but the effort to transcend gossip through total transparency was sort of counterproductive. The article concludes with one unflattering 2014 email that Denton sent to Jessica Coen, who'd come back to the company after editing Gawker for two years to serve as the editor-in-chief of the network's women's blog, Jezebel. Denton was taking issue with a view expressed in an article written by one of Coen's staffers, about a somewhat hard-to-follow news story. A trans woman was outed as trans by a journalist (not at Gawker) who was investigating the woman's claims to having invented a superior kind of golf club; the golf club inventor, whose degrees and credentials were fake, ended up dying by suicide in the course of being investigated. The Jezebel blogger concluded, "Don't out someone who doesn't want to be out. The end. Everyone has a right to privacy when it comes to their gender identity or sexual orientation, and beyond this, the trans status is not relevant."

Denton's response to Coen in 2014 was categorical. His email subject was "This is the opposite of our policy," and the text reads, "if the author believes this, she's working at the wrong place. And should be guided to a more congenial work environment. We're truth absolutists. Or rather, I am. And I choose to work with fellow spirits."

Truth absolutism is an ethics, certainly, but maybe not the most

< 27 >

ethical one. If your policy is "We publish everything that's true (and interesting)," it saves you from having to untangle difficult dilemmas about the possible effects of what you say and how. Beyond ethics, it's just not very strategic. Gawker's policy—that if a person is famous, or sort of famous, or an insider, or known in any kind of public way by even small, insular groups of people, that person does not have a right to privacy even regarding issues that have nothing to do with the person's ostensible fame—became, famously, its downfall.

You may already know the story, which is crazy. In 2012, Gawker posted a clip from a sex tape featuring the professional wrestler Hulk Hogan, whose real-world avatar, Terry Bollea, eventually sued the company for invasion of privacy and emotional distress. That the sex tape was filmed possibly without his consent by a friend, the Florida radio DJ Bubba the Love Sponge, and featured the wrestler having sex with Bubba's wife, with Bubba's encouragement, doesn't really matter; nor does it matter that it was ferried to Gawker's desk by a rival DJ, who is believed by both the Tampa police and the FBI to have stolen the tape from Bubba's desk drawer to embarrass Bubba in hopes of taking over his time slot. The fateful post, "Even for a Minute, Watching Hulk Hogan Have Sex in a Canopy Bed is Not Safe For Work but Watch It Anyway," did not seem as though it was going to be a huge banger to Hamilton Nolan, who is the only person who mentioned it in *Gawker: An Oral History*, which was published in 2015: "I just remember A.J. [Daulerio, the editor-in-chief of Gawker at the time] put it up, and my general thought was, 'Here is another classic A.J.-style post from A.J.' If it does bring down our company, that would be a funny way to go out, I guess." Bollea vowed to sue and did, in Florida state court, seeking $100 million in damages.

Being sued was not unusual for Gawker; the company's legal team assumed the case would result in a settlement. The trial began in early

2016 and lasted two weeks; Gawker live-streamed the proceedings. Gawker argued that the sex tape had news value; Bollea argued that his wrestling persona was completely different from his actual personality. When it was too late for the company's legal team to change its strategy, the lawsuit was revealed to have been funded by the billionaire venture capitalist Peter Thiel, meaning he could have bankrolled it forever. By August 2016, both the company and Nick Denton had filed for Chapter 11 bankruptcy protection; Gawker Media was purchased by Univision, and Gawker.com shut down. (It has been rebooted and shut down again since then.)

Thiel had had a grudge against Gawker and Denton specifically since 2007, when Gawker's tech blog *Valleywag* published a post called "Peter Thiel is totally gay, people." The writer, Owen Thomas, explained later that the knowledge of Thiel's sexuality was so "widespread" in Silicon Valley that Thomas would "never accede" that he "outed" Thiel. "He was never hiding it," Thomas said. "People just felt like somehow they could not discuss it." This was Gawker's role: discuss the undiscussed, reveal it to be discussable. Of course, if everyone in Silicon Valley knew, it doesn't follow that people felt they couldn't discuss it; they just weren't publishing articles about it. According to Ryan Holiday's 2018 book about the site's downfall, *Conspiracy*, Thiel was just as upset, if not more, about a comment Denton left on the post: "The only thing that's strange about Thiel's sexuality: why on earth was he so paranoid about its discovery for so long?"

There's nothing that purports to be factual about this rhetorical question; it is the most vicious kind of gossip, interpretation. The appeal of gawking and talking is not just about the potential access to exclusive knowledge; it's in the power granted, or maybe just implied, by remaining an observer—the knowing tone, the skeptical eyebrow. They're not really in love; she maintains a level of delusion about the functionality of her polycule that is frankly admirable; I think he needs to go on medication. "He's totally gay" is a classically 2000s topic of interpretive gossip; this was a time when people were bragging about the accuracy of their "gaydars" and it was considered, as Thomas suggests in his post, a political responsibility to come out. None of this has aged well, but I will go on record saying I think it should be acceptable to discuss such prurient and even offensive things in private, among friends. If I tell my friend, or a group of friends, or even a group of people that I consider mainly acquaintances, a piece of scandalous gossip, or speculate on an absent party's sexuality, or express my uncharitable views on an absent party's psychological issues, I am specifically not publishing this information. What I'm doing is different legally, ethically, and experientially. It may be true that among this group of acquaintances are people who might take the information public. It may be true that I have aided and abetted that process. It may be true that my behavior is in poor taste, or nasty, or representative of a self-defeatingly bitter and resentful attitude. But the act of publishing, of making public, removes gossip from the safety of mutually agreed-upon ambiguities and turns at least one into a fact: someone heard a crazy story, and they want you to know.

* * *

Often, Gawker's policy of transparency meant being explicit about what the journalists didn't know, and where they'd gotten their information. That transparency could take the form of technicalities: Gawker didn't really say anything false because of the way the site contextualized the story. The way Gawker reported gossip was similar to the way you or I might pass on a story we've heard: citing our sources, acknowledging hazy areas, ending with a request, or a hint at a request, for more information. One post from 2015, titled "Louis

C.K. Will Call You Up to Talk About His Alleged Sexual Misconduct," begins, "A few months ago we got an email from a tipster who said he was awaiting a phone call from Louis C.K., who will host the final episode of *Saturday Night Live*'s 40th season this weekend. The subject of their phone call was sexual misconduct allegations made by the tipster's friend against the comedian." The degrees of separation from the actual incident, the not-having-actually-seen-it-myself, the anonymity—none of this is untrue, I assume. "He was reluctant to go into much detail, but he said that two women he knew had been mistreated by [C.K.]. He described one of the alleged incidents, which he said had happened sometime in the second half of 2014: A female friend of his told him that C.K. had come up to her at a comedy club, grabbed her by the back of the neck, leaned into her ear, and said 'I'm going to fuck you.'"

The post ends with a kind of disclaimer, followed by a request:

> We had no means of verifying Jason's claims directly. He said the women he knew had told him they wouldn't come forward, citing C.K.'s reputation and power in the comedy world. . . . Have you been sexually harassed by Louis C.K., or do you know someone who has? Have you heard rumors of the sort? If so, please leave a comment below or contact me at jordan@gawker.com, anonymity guaranteed.

When, years after this post and others continuing the theme, women did come forward on the record to say that yes, they *had* been sexually harassed by Louis C.K., Gawker seemed to have been vindicated—not only had the site been martyred by a billionaire, setting a troubling precedent against free speech, according to its supporters, but it had tried to report the allegations against Louis C.K. Gawker

< 31 >

had seen it coming; it had tried to warn us. It was bad timing that it no longer existed when the political movement that encouraged women to come forward with their stories of sexual abuse began.

* * *

All the above takes for granted that any individual piece of gossip is probably true. This is, I think, part of the operative definition of gossip: it is a story, or set of stories, that is assumed to be at least partially true but has not been verified. A gossip may exploit this ambiguity by exaggerating or embellishing or deploying other rhetorical strategies; in disclosing what might not be true, the gossip puts the onus on the listener to interpret what she's telling them. In the traditional moral understanding of gossip, the gossip assumes some of that responsibility. It would be nice if, like literary critics, we could treat a text as just a text, and enjoy the story of any individual piece of gossip regardless of its verifiability. Most people, to say nothing of most literary critics, can't.

The end of Gawker coincided with the beginning of another media environment—chaotic, combative, aggressive in its confusion. Three months after the site filed for bankruptcy, Donald Trump was elected president, and the phrase "fake news" became something a respected historian might refer to in an otherwise unrelated article about the German Democratic Republic. Within a year of Trump's election, the kind of outlandish conspiracy theories that had been popular among what had been assumed to be a small, if dangerous, subset of his supporters revealed the extent of their influence. Claiming to be a government official with "Q" security clearance, which gives access to classified material, the notorious anonymous conspiracist(s) QAnon posted their first "drop" in October 2017. Subsequent drops laid out a "deep state" plot against Donald Trump, conveyed in language and codes that had to be deciphered. Followers of Q were said to feel a quasi-religious fervor, but to me the faith in the outlandish extremes of human relations, in the existence of unbelievable nefarious networks, and in the possibility of charting and solving the mysteries of those networks seemed secular, or just postlapsarian. One of the most prominent Q drop decoders was a former Hollywood gossip reporter. In the 2021 HBO docuseries *Into the Storm*, she says the experience taught her to "believe anything."

The particular mix of credulity and skepticism required of a gossip reporter is well suited to the parsing of conspiracy theories, which, like gossip, tend to start with some observable phenomenon and then spin out from there. One must be open to the possibility of crazy things happening—and crazy things do happen, all the time—but skeptical about any individual piece of information, or skeptical enough to want to find the necessary details to fill out a somewhat believable narrative. It helps to know one's audience, of course, but all audiences have in common that there's *something* they want to hear. Conspiracy theories and particularly QAnon exploded during the Trump administration because the country experienced a crisis of interpretation, or rather its ongoing crisis of interpretation was made clear: what was false was probably true and what was probably true, false, or at least that's how it seemed. Gossip had gone from an alternative to or side effect of public discourse to a form of public discourse—not because the *New York Times* is just a gossip rag, but rather because trust in the news media dropped and remains low, so that audiences interpret what they see and read and hear in the news as only probably or possibly true, or as some angled version of the truth. A 2022 survey conducted by Gallup and the Knight Foundation found that half of Americans believe that "most national news organizations intend to mislead, misinform or persuade the public." This is not only because of polarization and fake and Fox News, though that's part of it. The proliferation of new websites staffed by inexperienced reporters without experienced oversight—particularly those that were influenced by, achieved success during the same period as, and were Gawker—has led to what might be called a proliferation of journalistic standards. Because so many outlets now "aggregate" news reports—meaning they don't conduct original reporting or confirm other outlets' stories, but rather reword reporting from other outlets, sometimes linking to it, sometimes not—a misinterpretation of a study, a misquote, or an incorrect fact might travel far before a somewhat futile correction appears. This also happens on social media, obviously, where users as well as news outlets hoping to attract attention might sell stories in ways that require a critical eye to determine what really happened.

Also on social media, mostly, charged debates about both newsworthiness itself and the framing of newsworthy stories have led to intense scrutiny of the media on the left while the right has sought to discredit journalists altogether. It is now widely understood that all reporters are biased and that there is no such thing as "objectivity"; attempts to make more transparent the process of producing the news, via, for example, the *New York Times* public editor role, did not gain traction. (The first *New York Times* public editor, who was tasked, like a Gawker editor, with explaining to readers what happened behind the scenes of major stories, was hired in 2003; the paper discontinued the position in 2017.) Meanwhile, during the Trump administration, the use of anonymous sources became much more widespread, requiring readers to trust editors and reporters to make a set of judgments about the legitimacy of their sources, the way one might trust a well-connected friend to relay a tale of a disintegrating high-powered couple. The "anonymous Trump administration senior official" who caused a furor by writing an op-ed called "I

Am Part of the Resistance Inside the Trump Administration" for the *New York Times* in 2018 demonstrated the limits of this practice, the way it could be used to angle, when the official eventually revealed his identity: Miles Taylor, some young guy no one had heard of, who was hoping for a book deal, which he got. Meanwhile, the news, the stuff that was actually confirmed and fact-checked and well sourced, was often simply unbelievable, in a literal way, so if you didn't want to believe it or wanted to believe only one part of it—if you had something you wanted to hear—you didn't have to. There were plenty of other things to read.

* * *

As all this was happening in the media, critics began reheating the feminist idea that gossip was not bad at all, but good. A few weeks before the first QAnon drop in October 2017, the *New York Times* published its landmark investigation into the sexual harassment allegations against the movie producer Harvey Weinstein. A *New Yorker* investigation came shortly afterward. The allegations were so sweeping and stretched back so far that they ignited what was often called a "reckoning" in Hollywood and beyond. Soon, the corresponding hashtag campaign encouraging women to share their stories of sexual harassment, abuse, and assault in the workplace became ubiquitous.

The #MeToo movement coalesced around the idea of a "whisper network" as a form of power, and its proponents often drew on feminist and socialist thinking to claim that gossip was a mode of resistance for the marginalized; the idea was that women have always had these quiet, unofficial networks of talk that allow us to watch out for each other. If the whisper network became loud enough, specific pieces of information might turn into "open secrets," but the information still remained within the network, unreported due to the power

< 35 >

the subjects of rumor wielded to object or threaten or retaliate. In the context of #MeToo, these warnings might concern (the pun again) "predators" or creepy guys in whatever industry—which ones not to take private meetings with, which ones not to stay too late working for, which ones will hit on you if they get drunk.

Statistics are out on whether gossip is gendered. Some studies say men and women gossip approximately equally or within a similar ballpark; some say men gossip more quantitatively; others say that what's really noteworthy are the differences in what men and women gossip about. The men I know, in general, gossip less than the women but are also—again in my experience, again in general—significantly more clueless. This is frustrating, if you have quietly sent one on a reconnaissance mission that he couldn't execute through eye-batting and hushed, conspiratorial tones. They don't know what to look for, nor what to do with it when they find it, and they can be caught off guard when news of their exploits comes back to them via the scenic route.

The #MeToo movement didn't shy away from the notion of gossip as a woman's game but reframed it as a consequence of our position in society: we gossip because we have to, because we are "vulnerable," as many essays from the period had it. We need to protect ourselves. At this moment, however, women were encouraged to stop whispering and speak. The whisper network was acknowledged to have its limitations: it required being a kind of insider, with connections, and so excluded those not potentially in the know and those who might need it most. The power of the growing movement against sexual harassment, and of the huge wave of public support women who spoke out received, made it seem as if whisper networks could and should be accessible to everyone. Soon, the discussion of abuse in Hollywood inspired women in other industries to wonder whether they could instigate a reckoning too. What about academia? What about the media itself?

Because I was addicted to Twitter in October 2017, and because I was a member of the New York City media—a chicken-egg situation—I followed many editors and writers. I saw them tweeting, as many people were, as our "everyone" was, during the Weinstein revelations. I saw them wondering why there had been no such discussion of the sexual predators in our own backyard. Everyone knew about them. Should we not have been the vanguard movement, given that we are journalists ourselves?

Then one day, the tenor changed. I saw, sitting at the kitchen table in the one-bedroom apartment I freelanced from, multiple female editors posting tweets expressing their eagerness to see "the list," in ironically calm tones. "Someone send me the list thank you," one prominent editor tweeted. "Did u get it yet," another personality replied. "Send me a link," another editor said.

I can't remember how I got access to it, but of course I got access to it, quickly. The successful distribution of the Google spreadsheet titled "Shitty Media Men" rested not only on traditional modes of gossip—someone who knows someone tells someone else, who tells others, etcetera—but also on new modes that confuse or complicate our understanding of the public/private distinction on which the flourishing of "gossip" rests, namely social media. Someone who knows of someone they have never met, who has heard of someone, who follows two other someones but has probably never met them either, can become aware, quite quickly, that something is afoot, if they are looking at their social media feeds at the right time. Because of the tenuous relationships among all these people, and because of the frantic desperation for drama encouraged by the platform, the initial someone will have few qualms about sending a message to someone else who seems friendly and slightly more knowledgeable. This message will be something along the lines of "Do you know what's going on?" with a link to a tweet suggesting something is going on. Because of the in-turn tenuous relationship the recipient of this query feels to the action, that recipient will feel little conflict about replying, "Yes, here it is." It's all happening in public anyway.

A disclaimer at the top of the "Shitty Media Men" spreadsheet read: "This document is only a collection of misconduct allegations and rumors. Take everything with a grain of salt. If you see a man you're friends with, don't freak out. . . . Please never name an accuser, and never share this document with a man."

"Hey, boyfriend," I said to the boyfriend I was living with at the time, another internet-addicted digital media freelancer. "Look at this."

We watched in fascinated unease as new people entered the document—most but not all anonymized as animal avatars, per the Google system. They began to type names and details into each cell. I got in early—less than twenty names, if I recall correctly, had been entered, and the usual suspects, the stories everyone already knew, were in the first few rows. It quickly began to feel creepy and slightly dangerous to be watching this. If you've ever watched someone edit a shared Google Document or spreadsheet live, you will know what it's like: inferring hesitation in a backspace, seeing momentum in a typo. After a bit of rubbernecking, I left the document but checked it periodically throughout the evening. Within twelve hours, the spreadsheet had grown to seventy entries—which ranged from allegations of rape to banal offenses such as "weird lunch dates"—and then been taken off-line, because Buzzfeed was preparing an article about it that would generate even more attention than it was already getting, which was too much.

A few months later, things were still crazy. Rumors that *Harper's*

Magazine was going to run a story "outing" the creator of the list appeared on Twitter. The creator, the writer Moira Donegan, wrote an essay for The Cut outing herself, thus at least taking control of the narrative. In it, she describes being contacted by a fact-checker for the magazine, which is the first moment she learned she was going to be named in the *Harper's* story. "Katie [Roiphe, the author of the *Harper's* piece] identifies you as a woman widely believed to be one of the creators of the Shitty Men in Media List," Donegan says the fact-checker wrote. "Were you involved in creating the list? If not, how would you respond to this allegation?"

The thing about the tools available to women is that they are usually either weak and ineffective or imprecise and dangerous. They always seem to backfire; they can be wielded against you as easily as you wield them. Donegan writes that she was both "naive" and cynical about the list's potential impacts. "I had become so accustomed to hearing about open secrets, to men whose bad behavior was universally known and perpetually immune from consequence," she writes, "that it seemed like no one in power cared about the women who were most vulnerable to it." Maybe Donegan had believed in the goodness of women, a sisterhood of sorts, which would keep the document only in safe hands—another blunt tool, the idea that women ought to get along because they are women. Sometimes that's true! "Fundamentally, a whisper network consists of private conversations," Donegan writes, "and the document that I created was meant to be private as well."

Let's assume Donegan is not being disingenuous in writing that she believed the list she was building was "private." How could she believe this? It's reasonable to assume she thought she was a private person—she was an assistant editor at the *New Republic*, a low-level employee at a national magazine—so she believed no one was paying

< 38 >

attention to her, even if she was of course doing something in public. What is "naive," and harder to believe, is that she didn't understand that the people she was talking to, and about, would talk; they are professional talkers, and they are in the business of journalism because they like to illuminate social reality, with evidence for their claims. Did she not understand that they would take photos of the list, that it would be available online forever? That a "private" account or "locked" document is only such if everyone who views it agrees? That sex and money are two of the most exciting things to talk about?

Dónegan goes on to say that the list was specifically intended to counteract the institutional mode of journalism, which had, she suggests, caused some of these sexist problems in the first place. "The value of the spreadsheet was that it had no enforcement mechanisms: Without legal authority or professional power, it offered an impartial, rather than adversarial, tool to those who used it." That impartiality comes not from the fact that the creator was anonymous or that the document was crowdsourced. It comes from the fact that every item on the list was unverified: possibly true, possibly partially true, possibly a rumor passed around to the point of unrecognizability, possibly a distorted interpretation, possibly completely made up. There was no way to know what was true or false; the anonymity that gave women protection also discredited them. Every false or vague allegation—"harassment" and "inappropriate" can mean anything—detracted from the credibility of a true or specific one. Possibility goes both ways.

One of the reasons the list was deemed successful was that it initiated several investigations into the behavior of the shitty men named, and several were fired from their high-powered jobs. Now, I think, men are more careful about how they conduct themselves in particular workplaces and industries. Possibly. From a feminist perspective, men who objected that the allegations against them in the document were false were considered collateral damage to a greater mission. This was due, surely, to the sense that the gossip had moved beyond the private sphere and become public; the world was watching, even if the only world watching was the media and publishing industries. It was no longer a whisper network; whisper networks, now, might feel a little more exposed than before.

What is the lesson here? It depends on whom you ask. Either Donegan is a hero who sacrificed herself for the cause of protecting women—she was sued for defamation by one of the men on the list and paid him a six-figure settlement, he told the *New York Times* in 2023—or she is a naive cynic who didn't anticipate that she would be sued for failing to think of the men on the list: how they might react to being falsely accused, how these reactions might accumulate to discredit her project in the long term. Is the takeaway merely that gossip is powerful? Volatile? And maybe the truth is, too? These are clichés, generalities; I wish I could be more specific. "When I first shared the spreadsheet among my women friends and colleagues," Donegan writes, "it took on the intense sincerity of our most intimate conversations." My most intimate conversations do not lack sincerity for being sometimes vicious, speculative, unfair, and misguided; my women friends and colleagues are not angels. That is one of the reasons gossip is so thrilling. It's intimate. It requires trust.

* * *

There has long been a disturbing denial of the reality of social media among its users: it is annoying and upsetting to remember that when one is online, posting or even just "liking" things, one is in public. Watching the boundary between the public sphere and private life evaporate has been disorienting. Is it because of the boring fact that one can be at home and all around the world at once, or is it that one can be out in public, enjoying a nice Negroni at a bar, while at the same time in what feels like one's own little world, alone online? In my personal life I've noticed more and more people making claims that are easily disproved by digital evidence, which has baffled me. An acquaintance emailed me a nice note about an article I'd written and then proceeded to criticize it, for hours, on Twitter; when I replied to her email with a link to an example of her hypocritical behavior, she apologized—not for being blatantly two-faced, but for not liking the article. (Full disclosure: after that, I insulted her.) Another friend told someone that I'd suddenly stopped talking to him, though three unanswered emails in my Sent folder show it was the other way around.

Maybe it's not an issue of the public/private distinction but of memory: the computer remembers details you might prefer to let vanish into the ambiguity of gossip. Conversely, social media produces more and more public figures, insiders to uncountable groups and communities formed outside, in the open air. These public figures use these platforms to produce gossip, fortifying their importance. A lively Twitter feud reveals, to those in the know, a subterranean network of offense and manipulation; regardless of your prior knowledge of the issue, the feud becomes gossip, particularly if one or both parties delete their contributions in shame. Screenshots, or evidence, in recent history known slangily as "receipts," become a kind of commodity; as journalists have become public figures, private people have come to resemble journalists, investigating suggestive posts by accounts both large and small. (Several star Gawker bloggers started their careers as commenters on the site.)

While traditional celebrities act on questionable intentions, and those in the cheap seats like to speculate about PR-orchestrated romances and incidents, I have to believe that at least some of the drama we see online, particularly among the less famous, is genuine, the product of overwhelming emotions acted on rashly. This means that the consequences of publicity—embarrassment, panic, opprobrium, job loss, etcetera, all of which can be quickly summarized as "now everyone knows"—have not been fully thought through. Even the "extremely online"—another dated phrase, but apt—underestimate how online they really are; they seem to think they are online only to their intended audience. In February 2020, at the height of primary season during the presidential election, a young Bernie Sanders staffer, Ben Mora, was fired from the campaign after the Daily Beast found his private Twitter account. He used this account to mock other candidates in a raunchy, internet-inflected rhetorical style favored by what was known then as "the dirtbag left." "Warren is an adult diaper fetishist at her core let's be honest," reads one tweet often cited in news stories about the firing. "Amy Klobuchars face looks like that optical illusion where it's an old lady but also a young woman depending on how you look at it but with her it's just two different old ladies," reads another. The breeziness of his memeified language—the ironically authentic "let's be honest," or the elimination of nonessential punctuation—suggests a confidence that he must have had, because this was ill-considered. Of course an enemy, particularly a political enemy during a high-stakes election, would use whatever methods possible to gain access to potentially damaging information. The methods probably weren't even that sneaky. If someone is in possession of an active private social media account, two things are almost always true: (1) they're using the account to post the sort of things a wider audience might find offensive and thus seek to damagingly amplify, were they exposed to that wider audience, and (2) someone will take screenshots of the offensive material and share them with others. The justification for a private account is the need to let off steam, but one wonders why letting off steam in semipublic social media is so different from letting off steam in a truly private forum, among friends who are less likely to spread it around and who aren't collecting evidence. Probably.

The optics were nightmarish. Political campaigning often feels more like advertising, with the aims of each promoter dully clear, but it is just as much about gossip. The smear campaign, like the whisper campaign, is aimed at inspiring gossip to do its work, albeit with a dangerous, live-by-the-sword risk. At the time, the Sanders campaign was fending off associations with "Bernie Bros," who were caricatured as unsavory internet users who harassed other candidates and their supporters with this same kind of rhetoric; the campaign initially claimed these users could have been the Russian bots that were haunting the election at the time, sowing discord to harm the candidate who, the campaign had to argue, was the only Democrat with a chance of beating the pro-Putin incumbent. Mora lost his job, of course.

* * *

At the end of the Trump administration and the long beginning of the COVID-19 pandemic, commentators expressed a sadness at what they described as the loss of old-school celebrity gossip. "I miss celebrities, I miss celebrity gossip, I miss a good scandal," the culture journalist Anne Helen Petersen said in an interview in December 2020. "When I asked Twitter for their favorite celebrity fuck-ups this year, everyone just named politicians making horrible personal and policy decisions." A combination of legally mandated inside voices and the false urgency of the political moment, which tended to make everyone feel that having a personal life was frivolous, if not insensitive or even unethical, in light of all the tragedies advertised each day, had made everything stressfully boring. Celebrities had retreated to the safety of wealthy privacy; semipublic figures lived in fear, or at least they should have, of being surveilled for violating COVID rules or COVID best practices, among other offenses. Would things never go back to normal?

In the vacuum appeared several gossip-related ventures to reinvigorate the culture of celebrity gossip using the tools of an internet with a bottomless appetite for scoops. At the start of the pandemic in 2020, an anonymous woman employed in the fashion industry resumed using her long-dormant Instagram account, DeuxMoi, by asking the account's forty-five thousand preexisting followers, "You guys have any celeb encounters that you want to share?" It was the beginning of an open-ended quarantine, and they did.

The owner of the account began screenshotting the messages she received and reposting them as Instagram Stories that would disappear after twenty-four hours (okay), with the sender's identifying information censored. Rather than explosive scoops or eye-watering blind items, most of what came through was mundane. Which celebrities tipped well, who was eating at what restaurant, who ordered a sandwich with extra mayonnaise (Chris Evans). Rumors circulating within an industry would make the cut. When information was more scandalous, the account holder told interviewers, she would turn it into a blind item. She would occasionally offer a bombshell: pregnancy rumors, a wedding reported by neighbors. She told *Women's Wear Daily* that an early scoop about the relationship between Olivia Wilde and Harry Styles "turned around the way the account was viewed": she could actually break stories. But the emphasis was always on tame sightings. As DeuxMoi told the *New York Times*, she's no longer interested in things like "so-and-so was caught doing drugs at a party or having a threesome or whatever."

The account grew quickly, with the same approach: post every-

< 45 >

thing, check nothing. A disclaimer at the top denies responsibility for fact-checking: "some statements made on this account have not been independently confirmed. this [*sic*] account does not claim information published is based in fact." While this may seem like a case of trying to have your cake and eat it too, DeuxMoi has mostly remained out of harm's way by documenting her sourcing, paltry though it may be, and offering commentary on whether she thinks any story is to be believed. This gives her credibility. The slight absurdity of the account's otherwise boring scoops does not reveal a pathological obsession with the minutiae of celebrities' lives, as it does when fan accounts collate all publicity of a particular figure. Rather, the ironic distance conveyed in both the pointlessness and huge number of posts makes the account's tips more believable, not less. Chris Evans likes extra mayonnaise on his sandwich. Why would you be telling me this, unless it were true?

The idea was not unprecedented. *US Weekly*'s column Stars—They're Just Like Us! is a pioneer in quotidian celebrity gossip, and predates DeuxMoi by about two decades (it began publishing in 2002). But that column has devolved into curated posts from celebrities' Instagrams, and it cannot be described as a barrage of information. It is not on the cutting edge of celebrity gossip, say. DeuxMoi, by contrast, delivers random tidbits straight to followers' phones and is limited only by the number of tips she receives (a lot) and the time she has to post them (seemingly twenty-four hours a day, seven days a week).

But the real difference between old celebrity gossip and the new wave of maximalist celebrity information is about emphasis. If Stars—They're Just Like Us! highlights the stale irony of Eva Longoria using a cocktail shaker, it also emphasizes that it is Eva Longoria shaking the cocktail. Online forums for celebrity gossip such as Oh No They

Didn't!, which launched in 2004—as well as certain subgroups on Reddit—are often better, or at least more diverting, because they are about "celebrities" as a self-referential category, not about any one person. It doesn't really matter who it is; it's about the narrative arc. "The celebrities are disposable," ONTD!'s tagline reads. "The gossip is priceless."

Truly famous people have always been so famous that they seem, to the rest of us, almost like fictional characters; moralizing about how these are "real people" we're gossiping about has never really stuck because there is no way they can be made to seem like real people, no matter how many times we see photos of them holding venti iced coffees. Real people are not stalked by paparazzi and gossiped about for their condiment preferences; real people are gossiped about only when they do something interesting. And even then, their identities matter only to people who already know them. In 2022, DeuxMoi's identity was exposed by the tech journalist Brian Feldman on his Substack—using only publicly available information, albeit accessed using time-consuming investigative measures on social media—on the grounds that the account holder had been given a book deal and an option for an HBO series: she was a public figure, so her name was newsworthy. But the revelation was not particularly exciting. Few people knew who she was, or really cared. (Her name is Melissa Lovallo.) A few months after her identity was published, DeuxMoi published the autobiographical novel that served as justification for Feldman's outing. Titled after the request many tipsters use as a sign-off, *Anon Pls.* recounts the exhilarating and distressing experience of running the account, from inception to explosion. It begins with a disclaimer: "Guys, just a heads-up . . . While this book definitely draws inspo from events in my actual life, this story is obvi a work of fiction. Any mention of real people

< 47 >

(celebs or normies), events, or establishments are intended only to give the book a sense of authenticity—and FUN. Everything else—characters, dialogue, incidents—I totally made up."

The on-again, off-again relationship between gossip and fiction is on again. Unlike the disclaimer on the DeuxMoi Instagram page or at the top of the "Shitty Media Men" list, this one does not seem obtuse, but just a bit cheeky: designed not to cover the author's legal bases in order to justify the publication of unconfirmed explosive information, but to manufacture harmless intrigue. It marks a shift. At the beginning of 2022, inspired by the same pandemic tedium that spawned DeuxMoi, the journalist Kelsey McKinney launched the podcast *Normal Gossip*. The show, very popular, with more than ten million listens at the end of its third season in 2022, is in some ways the inverse of DeuxMoi's maximalist project: each week, McKinney invites a special guest to discuss a wacky rumor submitted by listeners—"juicy, strange, funny, and utterly banal gossip about people you'll never know and never meet." Everyone is anonymized, and McKinney re-creates the structure of private gossip by relaying the story to her guest in a girlfriendly way, pausing for questions and saucy commentary to create the sense that the listener is eavesdropping on two friends actually sharing stories. The idea is that "gossip is not a sin," as the title of a 2021 op-ed McKinney wrote for the *New York Times* proclaimed.

When gossip is stripped of all identifying and potentially serious details, protected by a barrier of indecipherability so no one gets hurt, so that it might as well be fiction, she's right. But if these defanged crowdsourced public gossip projects are a corrective to, or maybe just a result of, the rampant public-figure production of the 2000s and 2010s, they are also kind of boring. There are now too many people to care about, whose significance must be explained, whose actions can neither be confirmed nor denied; the appeal of anonymity is less about ethics and more about exhaustion. And the stakes of absolute transparency in the social media era are too high: lawsuits, paranoia, uncertainty, more than a few ruined careers and relationships. The old-fashioned way of doing it doesn't seem so bad.

I have always loved gossip, and I probably always will. I heard a crazy story recently, one that truly explained a lot, the perfect, unexpected ending to a minor saga. I wouldn't sacrifice the knowledge for even the highest moral high ground in the world—but I would also never, in a million years, tell you.

< 48 >

MY PERFECT OPINIONS

PART 1: POPULISM

Like many writers, Adam Dalva is friends with other writers. In 2017, one of those writers, Gabe Habash, published a novel, as writer friends are sometimes known to do. Dalva wanted to help him promote it. He told Habash he would review it on Goodreads, the social media website dedicated to reading and books.

Don't bother, Dalva says Habash told him. "That doesn't matter."

"I got angry," Dalva told me during an interview in 2021. He had extended to his friend a well-intentioned offer of online clout, modest though it may have been, and his friend had rejected him. He wanted revenge. As everyone knows, the best revenge is living well. So Dalva decided to become one of the most powerful Goodreads critics in the world. "As a prank," he said. "That was my stated ambition."

Goodreads is a funny social media site to attempt to conquer as a prank, not least because it's one of the only social media sites with widespread name recognition that it's possible to conquer as a prank. Although it's been around since 2007, its significance has remained steadfastly confusing; in 2017, when Dalva devised his revenge plot, it had forty-five million active monthly users. This number is paltry compared to the active user base of, say, Twitter, which, with its 330 million active users in 2017, has always been understood to be the least popular of the major social media sites, the others being Facebook, Instagram, and more recently TikTok. But on Goodreads success is clear-cut: there is a list of the "Best Reviewers" both globally and in individual countries. Getting on this list was Dalva's aim.

At this turning point in his online life, Dalva had been using Goodreads for a few years, but he'd been going about it mostly honestly, without acknowledging the platform's potential for strategy and gamification. The site's stated aim is to "help people find and share books they love"; to the casual user, this means rating (out of five stars) and reviewing books you've read, making lists of books you'd like to read, and getting both algorithmic and human-generated recommendations. There's a "community," should you wish to partake in it by, for example, joining groups that range from Addicted to YA, for young adult literature enthusiasts (60,231 members), to Literary Fiction by People of Color (10,368 members), to What's the Name of That Book??? (98,073 members). There's also a tool for setting yourself annual reading goals, in the hopes that declaring your intention to read one hundred books in a year will hold you to it. Because this is all about books, which have a reputation for being wholesome and edifying, the site inevitably seems like a net positive for the internet, which is usually not wholesome or edifying at all. Goodreads may even be good for literature, which is always thought to be under threat and so can always use nets positive.

In retrospect, Dalva can identify early signs of the trouble that was to come; when he was in graduate school, for example, a professor mentioned, a bit too ambivalently, that he'd noticed Dalva had rated the professor's book four stars, as in not five, years before. I

saw, I remembered, I made a passive aggressive comment about it—
the social media motto. Still, at the time, Dalva thought the site was
mainly a handy place to log his reading, and he had "little sense of
it as a public-facing thing." Maybe because of the site's notoriously
janky UX, or maybe because the audience for books, and especially
for the literary stuff Dalva prefers, is perceived to be so much smaller
than the audience for everything else, it seemed innocent. By 2017,
Twitter could ruin your career, Facebook was responsible for the death
of the truth itself, and Instagram was Instagram. Wasn't Goodreads
more of a forum—the kind of online space that was so niche, or even
nerdy, that the outside world and its consequences didn't bother to
get involved?

* * *

Dalva sought his revenge the only way revenge ever works: systemati-
cally. His first rule was to limit himself to spending no more than five
minutes a day on the site, so that he could pursue his goal "without
destroying my life." His first task was to figure out the site's technical
rules, which are not super intuitive. Rising in the ranks as a top reviewer depends on popularity, which first requires visibility, because,
according to Dalva, the only way you go up in the rankings is to
gather likes on your posts. "That's the only thing that matters, not
comments," he said. Sad, but whatever. To generate visibility, your
posts—your reviews—must show up in other users' feeds. There are
two ways to achieve this. Users are limited to five thousand "friends,"
which works by mutual consent, as on Facebook, but can acquire
an unlimited number of "followers," as on all the other sites (and
Facebook). Adding someone as a friend automatically adds them as a
follower, but there are limits to how many friend requests a user can
send each day, depending on how they otherwise engage with the site;

tricking people into adding you is a "big Goodreads celebrity strategy." (Dalva told me the limit was ten per day; I assume this means
the algorithm was onto him.) "I think you can add more if you also
go to your phone or something like that," he admitted, "but my rule
was no more than five minutes a day."

His "first major breakthrough" was realizing that he could game
the country-specific rankings: "if you are the number-one critic in
Azerbaijan, you [are called the] number-one critic, and if you're the
number-one critic in America, you have number-one critic under
your name. There's no distinction between them," he said. Because
there are very few users in some countries, friending people by searching small country codes in the URL yields fruit. Similarly, "if anyone
in Australia likes one of my posts, my number ranking will go up,"
because there are few users in Australia, so each one has more power
to determine the number-one critic in Australia. As on all social media platforms, popularity begets popularity; it's unlikely many people
will notice you've got a cluster of rare Australians inflating your stats.
They'll just see that you have a lot of followers.

After amassing followers, there is etiquette and game theory to
consider. Editing or adding a comment to a preexisting review will
drive the post to the top of your followers' feeds, but this strategy
must be used sparingly; you might be accused of "churning" reviews
if you do it too frequently. "You don't want that comment," Dalva
said. He would deploy a churn when necessary, during a drive for
more visibility. "If I wanted a post to do numbers, I would churn
it, like, three times," he said. There were also issues of style and context. Multiple short paragraphs, "fractal" reviews, rather than one long
paragraph, tended to perform better; although Dalva didn't mention
this—it contradicts his modus operandi—other Goodreads watchers
have noted that "if you rip a book a new one in an amusing way, you'll

< 53 >

get a golden shower of Likes," as one blogger for the site LitReactor pointed out in a 2021 post.

Finally, Dalva's study of the site had revealed two reliable heavy hitters, likes-wise: political books and classic novels. In 2018, he acquired an advance copy of "one of those Inside-the-Trump-White-House books. I didn't really read it. I just read, like, forty pages, and I gave it a four-star review. I just pulled four quotes from it, because I figured people would want the gossip." For classic novels "that everyone likes," he says he would write something like "I love this book" and generate heaps of approval. (His review of Jane Austen's *Emma* begins, "Oh my goodness, did I love.")

At some point, Dalva got a text from Habash about Dalva's rising status on the site. "I'm getting very frightened," Dalva remembers him saying. "What is happening?"

When Dalva finally got to review *Stephen Florida*, Habash's novel, he "did everything I could. I wrote a long beautiful review at the height of my powers. It's very essential if you want to get revenge on someone." It was the top-ranked review on the novel's page, and for a while, Dalva was ranked among the top five reviewers in the world.

Dalva is no longer ranked as a top critic on Goodreads, nor is he the top reviewer on *Stephen Florida*; that honor belongs to the popular essayist Roxane Gay, whose assessment of the novel was later excerpted as a blurb for the novel's paperback and publicity materials. But first place is a technicality; what's more interesting is how Dalva's life online changed, or didn't, after he amassed "all this power." He had to turn off notifications on his phone, which would overheat when he posted anything on Goodreads. He began receiving "tons" of galleys—the publishing term for advance, not fully edited copies of books that often go out to press and influencers a few months before publication. He received message requests, "weird sexual messages," and offers of free coffee from the publicity departments of New York City publishing houses. "I told a guy at one of those places, a big, big press," Dalva said, "'You know, I review for [the small, respected literary magazine] *Guernica*.' And he said, 'Well, your Goodreads review would matter exponentially more to us, because it is organic.'"

Social media creates the illusion of millions of people spontaneously expressing themselves and their opinions, without the pressures of institutions or editors. While this illusion isn't as cohesive as it once was—a decade of armchair theorizing about social media (guilty) has Adbusted the whole situation, and now we interpret the texts we encounter on social media much more critically—it has taken a while to abandon the idea of the internet as a place of authentic expression, particularly for the slow-moving publishing industry. The pressures of social media are much more variable, and less predictable, than those that shape the writing in, for example, the *New York Times*. Institutions and editors have a mostly stable set of priorities that a media-literate reader will be able to separate from the text eventually published; on Goodreads, or any social media site, each user operates like a writer-editor-institution all their own, even as they exist alongside traditional institutions that must operate profiles on social media, too. One can get to know a particular user over time, understanding her likes and dislikes and biases; one can harbor suspicions that she isn't who she says she is, or learn which of her opinions to treat with skepticism. Nevertheless, what is posted on social media is still seen as more "organic" because of social media's scale: even if I know, and you know, that many users aren't posting in good faith, you and I also assume that there are untold numbers of people who *don't* know this—who are operating under false consciousness when they log in to Goodreads, with its innocently bad site design and wholesome book-focused ethos.

< 54 >

< 55 >

Thus, Habash's assumption that Goodreads doesn't matter is hard to confirm or deny. It certainly matters to one main group: people who use Goodreads. It might also matter to book publicists and other people who work in the publishing industry. Goodreads also matters, begrudgingly, to authors, whose books appear on the site to be rated and reviewed. Authors may also benefit from the editorial side of Goodreads, which publishes newsletters and news of new releases, compiles annual "Best of the Year" lists for various genres (voted by users, not decreed), and creates other content that might get your book in front of potential customers. "I think there's also a power in the fact that writers look at it very hard," Dalva told me. "Constantly."

Dalva's theory is that, due to a combination of dwindling culture budgets at national publications and the difficulty of standing out in a hectic social-media-inflected marketplace, most authors don't get the attention they want and possibly deserve. "They're a little starved for criticism and engagement," he says, "so they're gonna go and look." After he gained status, he started giving five-star reviews almost exclusively; he felt that being more honest in his ratings—setting aside, for a few more sentences, whatever doubts we may have about what kind of honesty is really possible when it comes to a scale of 0 to 5—would have no tangible effect, except to hurt authors' feelings. Dalva described a recent novel that had irritated him. "There's just no reason for me to give a negative review of it," he said. "I think I actually put a review of it up. And I just sort of [say], here's the kind of person who would like to read this. I love negative reviews, but Goodreads [reviews] aren't reviews. They're customer experiences."

* * *

Back to the star rating: we hate it. The thought that Dalva puts into his ratings is common among Goodreads users, though the ratings

usually purport to have fixed meanings that need to be carefully up-
held; a user review of a book on the site, or on any ratings-based
platform, will often include a detailed explanation of how the author
came to rate whatever it is they're rating four stars rather than three,
or why they docked a point. (A recent Goodreads review of Austen's
Emma begins, "3.5 stars rounded up because of the narration.") These
ratings systems, and the pointless strategy they encourage, inspire
tirades: against quantification, oversimplification, and the death of
meaning at the hands of consumerism. How perverse to attempt to
judge works of art, which are multifaceted and complex, on a scale
of 0 to 5! Everyone knows these things are arbitrary, their apparent
precision derived from a set of imprecise factors that, with each added
metric, gets further and further away from the thing itself, the thing
itself being famously hard to approach in the first place. A work of art,
even the worst, most derivative kind, is a unified whole; to rate one as
three out of five stars is to deny that fact.

Yet knowing that objectivity is impossible doesn't prevent us from
striving for it anyway—particularly when there's time and money on the
line. Like most things that seem outrageous because of the way they've
migrated to the computer, the star rating system is not new. The story
begins in 1792, when pretty much everyone in the English writer Mariana Starke's family had tuberculosis. This meant they had to go on an
extended vacation, which was also supposed to save their lives. A popular
treatment for consumption at the time was to make for a temperate climate and breathe better air, so despite the conflicts that had broken out
during the French Revolution, escalating at that very moment to full-
scale war across the Continent, thirty-year-old Mariana and her father,
mother, and sister headed south from their home in England to Nice
and then onward toward Italy. Her sister, Louisa, did not survive beyond
Nice; her father, Richard Starke, a former deputy governor in Madras,

India, died in Pisa in 1794. Mariana and her mother, Mary, continued traveling throughout Italy and Europe until 1798, at which point they returned to England. Mariana herself got sick and then, "encouraged by a hope of being serviceable to those of my Countrymen, who, in consequence of pulmonary complaints, are compelled to exchange their native soil for the renovating sun of Italy," published a comprehensive account of her journey.

Letters from Italy, between the Years 1792 and 1798, Containing a View of the Revolutions in that Country, from the Capture of Nice by the French Republic to the Expulsion of Pius VI. from the Ecclesiastical State: likewise Pointing out the Matchless Works of Art Which Still Embellish Pisa, Florence, Siena, Rome, Naples, Bologna, Venice, &c. With Instructions for the Use of Invalids and Families Who May Not Choose to Incur the Expence Attendant upon Travelling with a Courier appeared in 1800. As was common for the period, the long title is explanatory: Starke's letters first describe in diaristic, sometimes tedious detail the events of the revolution she witnessed and second—here's the interesting part, historically—make recommendations for sights to see and tips for traveling economically through France and Italy with sick relatives. Two years later the book was reprinted and renamed *Travels in Italy: also a Supplement comprising Instructions for Travelling in France,* with most of the tedious revolutionary detail omitted.

These publications marked the beginning of a shift in the mode and meaning of European travel. Since the sixteenth century, the Continent, and especially Italy, had been the site of the Grand Tour, the vaguely questing months- or yearslong journey undertaken by wealthy young men, mostly British, often with a guide or tutor, as a rite of passage. The Grand Tour allowed male members of the nobility and landed gentry to complete their educations by getting cultured: it was an opportunity to see great works of art and hear music they couldn't in England and, in turn, mature as both individuals and future states-men. Nice work if you could get it. But in the years that followed Starke's first travels in Italy, the chaotic Napoleonic Wars and especially the Continental Blockade, Napoleon's embargo on contact between the Continent and the British Empire beginning in 1806, initiated the Grand Tour's decline.

Starke bided her time, writing mediocre poetry. She had already written plays, poetry, translations, and what were known as "imi-tations" of foreign language works, but critics were not always on her side, and she often published anonymously. "I own I have not confidence to stand the public gaze," she wrote in the preface to her play *The Sword of Peace*, "nor vanity enough not to feel embar-rassed as an avowed authoress." But she was confident enough of her expertise in European travel. In 1814, just before the blockade ended and before Britain defeated France, she contacted the pub-lisher John Murray with a prediction and a proposition: once the wars ended, the explosion of emigration and travel to the Conti-nent would create a market for a targeted guidebook in the style of what she'd done before.

Although Murray initially rejected her pitch, sending her else-where, he'd soon come around. The postwar changes to the map of Europe and to the sights, accommodations, and customs travel-ers would encounter there might have been enough reason to up-date her advice, but Starke was also cannily responding to new social conditions that would set the stage for bourgeois tourism—and even middle-class consumerism more broadly—as we have understood it since. The expansion of the British Empire would produce a new civil servant class, of which Starke had always been a part, that would want to see the world; the advent of rail travel at the beginning of the nineteenth century meant people with parameters beyond the yet-

< 59 >

undefined contours of their aristocratic souls would begin to venture out in larger numbers, too.

But where the noble and landed Grand Tourists—who were not tourists as we understand them, obtrusive and annoying, but travelers—might have been abroad for months or years, time and resources were more limited for the bourgeoisie, who also may not have wanted or been able to shell out for a helpful live guide, as the title of Starke's first volume suggests. Although there had been several guidebooks and diaries that focused on the Grand Tour, offering daily accounts of aesthetic cultivation as well as suggestions geared toward the wealthy young male traveler, the new bourgeois tourist with specific leisurely or medical aims had no such resources. So, in 1820, after researching for two years "that I might write from the spot, and trust nothing to memory," Starke—who was, you might have guessed from all her ingenuity and free time, a spinster—published *Travels on the Continent: written for the use and particular information of travellers*, a guide updated for the new map of Europe that had been drawn during the wars. More significantly, in addition to providing tips about what goods and services should cost, hotels and hostels, routes, how to handle fleas and other bugs, and special advice for travelers with consumption, Starke also marked "objects best worth notice in the respective galleries of sculpture and painting . . . with one or more exclamation points (according to their merit) those works which are deemed particularly excellent." It's commonly said that women use exclamation points too often in their correspondence, in order to soften their requests and blunt their declarations; here we see the tendency goes back hundreds of years: "an Egyptian deity, in alabaster!!!," "bust of Venus!!," "the *Madonna della seggiola*, by Raphael!!!!!"

Although Thomas Martyn's 1787 work *The Gentleman's Guide in His Tour through Italy* used exclamation points sparingly to indicate great works, Starke's much more comprehensive and purposeful rating system for the time-pressed traveler was the real innovation, appealing as it did to the needs of a growing class of tourists who could afford only to dabble in the spiritual edification of great works of art and didn't have the time or education to develop a sense of refinement, a taste or illusion of taste, through seeing it all as it came to them. Starke published a few more editions and volumes in this vein, barely distinguishable by title but singular in their new vision; for a while, her books were some of the most famous guides available to English tourists.

As often happens with people who initiate profound cultural changes, Starke came to represent the new class of lesser-monied tourists, and for this she was mocked and lamented by detractors—snobs and scammers, respectively. In Stendhal's 1839 novel *The Charterhouse of Parma*, a redheaded English scholar visiting Parma to research a history of the Middle Ages is ribbed as the ideal customer for Starke's vulgar travelogue, imagining "that at his inn they were asking exaggerated prices for everything, and he never paid for the smallest trifle without first looking up its price in the *Travels* of a certain Mrs. Starke, a book which has gone into its twentieth edition because it indicates to the prudent Englishman the price of a turkey, an apple, a glass of milk, and so forth." The prudence she encouraged in her countrymen was not just distasteful but detrimental, meanwhile, to those hoping to make a quick buck off unsuspecting foreigners. "Another person . . . wrote me a letter . . . protesting that if I persevered in opening the eyes of travellers with respect to expenses on the Continent I might expect to be assassinated," Starke wrote in a letter in 1832.

Naturally, Starke's status as the preeminent people's travel writer didn't last. Her concept was eventually ripped off by her publisher, John Murray, who put out what came to be a better-known and en-

< 60 >

< 61 >

during series called Murray's Handbooks for Travellers starting in 1836, as well as by the German Baedeker guides, which began appearing in the 1830s and are still around today.

If the exclamation mark had stuck, ratings might have kept their whimsical, personal connotation, as well as an optimistic acceptance of art as necessarily enlivening. (Even one exclamation mark indicates a rise in blood pressure!) As time went on, and industrialization continued, though, this began to change: a desire for definitiveness, for completion, for preeminence, and mainly for optimization, took over. In 1900, the Michelin brothers published their first "small guide to improve mobility" on French roads that still saw fewer than three thousand cars per year; the idea was to encourage road trips and sell more tires. Initially, the guides featured practical information: listings for mechanics, gas stations, and hotels as well as other useful tips. The star for fine dining appeared in 1926, followed by the second and third stars; the idea was that there were some restaurants so good, you might travel for them. Like Starke's exclamation points, the Michelin star system rewards merit, however subjective and imprecise a concept that is, without disparaging or even acknowledging the lack of it. The world is full of stuff that is not worth mentioning, and the stuff that is worth mentioning is not uniformly so. If something meritorious falls through the cracks, that's life: a travel guidebook is not a democratic government, purporting to grant the right to be recognized as excellent to every hotel and restaurant. Those who make these valuable judgments about worth are also, very occasionally, fallible.

Recently, that fallibility has become a selling point; travel recommendations today often come in the form of personalized blogs, newsletters, and social media posts that promote the authenticity of both the travel curator and the stuff they recommend instead of attempting to create the illusion of objective excellence. But in the past, you wanted some kind of expertise. The next point in the history of the star rating is the Best American Short Stories anthology, which was first published in 1915 by Edward J. O'Brien and is still published today, with a whole network of other Best American anthologies in its wake (Essays, Food Writing, etc.). O'Brien was driven to publish his guide to the literary landscape because he was skeptical of the popularization of short fiction at the time, lamenting trends such as "a predictable plot tied up neatly with a happy ending" and "folksy" tones. The BASS anthology was intended to ameliorate his "feeling that some of the writers who should be railroad presidents or bank directors are getting in the way of real writers that I ought to be discovering." He took on the task of reading every short story published in an American magazine in a given year, sacrificing himself so that other readers might skip the formulaic efforts of would-be bosses.

To organize and then publicize the results, O'Brien employed a rigorous classification system for short story distinction that is too complicated to be worth reproducing here. Suffice to say he used asterisks to indicate varying degrees of "permanence" in a short story. For example: "Three Asterisks prefixed to a title indicate the more or less permanent literary value of the story." Elsewhere, three asterisks also indicate a story "of somewhat permanent literary value." In his 1921 essay "Say It With Asterisks!," the critic Oliver Herford mocked this "startling invention of comparative Permanence," and what he felt were O'Brien's futile ambitions toward exhaustiveness of rank, by focusing on the typographical indicator that was made to bear the weight of all this culture. Herford jokes about the establishment of a "Federal Licensing Bureau" for the use of star ratings as well as a "Society for the Prevention of Cruelty to Asterisks." Herford was also, naturally, in disagreement with O'Brien about which stories were the best and even about which ones fit O'Brien's lyrical descriptions of what constitutes a good short story. Of one contribution, advertised by O'Brien as "the most permanent contribution to the American Short Story" that year, Herford writes, "It is unmistakably American—the mark of the 'Melting Pot' is all over it—and I suppose it is Short, though it takes a lot of patience to read it, but it is *not* a story in the accepted sense of the word." O'Brien dedicated the next year's BASS "TO OLIVER HERFORD / SUCH IS LIFE" surrounded by a rectangle of asterisks.

As Herford suggests, the cultural rating system is a bit self-aggrandizing for the rater and a bit insulting to the reader. "With a moon and a mariner's compass and a good road map or chart," he writes, "the traveler by land or sea can get along very well without the stars, but in the trackless mazes of literature and art, how would the wandering Philistine fare without Asterisks?" Dorothy Parker implied the same when she reviewed the 1927 edition of the BASS for the *New Yorker*'s Constant Reader column; she joked that whatever O'Brien was earning for his self-appointed task, he should earn more: "More than ever the unsung hero . . . he lists all the short stories of the year, and grades them, unasked." Despite O'Brien's gripes about what is probably best called middlebrow fiction, Parker also found the stories he selected mediocre: "wholly conventional, in this recent conventionality of anguish," with "all the dogged quiet of too-careful writing." If you're going to declare yourself the ultimate arbiter of what is best, both these critics suggest, you must actually have good taste.

Today the BASS anthologies are edited by a different big-name author every year, and they always begin with some hand-wringing introduction about how difficult that year's editor found the somewhat hopeless project of naming the best short stories; any number of others might have been chosen, the editors note, in concert with the moment's preference for authenticity and personal curation over an illusion of ultimate superiority. But O'Brien's project was not just about what is best; it was about identifying measures of objectivity that might transcend the elusive nature of taste. "Permanence" as a quality sought in a work of art was not only about what O'Brien himself thought was good; it was about what he thought other people would continue to think was good. These other people, at the time, were not the masses, but the cultural powers that be: editors, academics, other writers, those who aim the canon. Whether he was ultimately right, he could never know—another useful thing about focusing on permanence. Selling a list of what is "permanent" also suggests that choices about what art someone will or will not engage with are at least in part about making a good investment: What short stories will be relevant in twenty, thirty years? What stories will you want to have read?

* * *

The desire to balance the unquantifiable joys of art and culture with the need to make the most of one's limited time and money remains the implicit justification of not just travel recommendations but most writing published on culture more broadly, and the typographical innovation Mariana Starke used as shorthand for measuring aesthetic or spiritual value under pressurized conditions continues to annoy those of us hawking our priceless wares in the virtual piazzas of public opinion. Maybe even more so. From platforms for expressing one's views on books and restaurants under the guise of aiding your fellow consumer, such as Yelp and Foursquare; to tertiary sites such as Rotten Tomatoes (movies) and Book Marks (books) that collate and quantify professional critics' qualitative assessments of works of art; to the hegemonic omnipresence

< 64 >

< 65 >

of Google and Amazon reviews; to social media websites; to actual publications dedicated to professional, semiprofessional, and amateur criticism, there are manifold opportunities to publish one's views to a potentially large—again, whatever that means to you—audience and to read the views of others, in the ultimate hope of buying something worth it. The idea of rating works of art on a numeric scale is particularly suited to the internet age, when one must wade through an ocean of content to find something that is going to be so good—definition of "good" yours, for now—that it makes up for the unrecoverable minutes (hours) you spent wading through the ocean of content to find it. The internet also makes available tools for ostensibly quantifying or legitimizing this goodness, for outsourcing and streamlining the calculations O'Brien was attempting to perform himself. Amazon's star rating system, for example, is not a simple average of all star reviews; according to the site, the system "considers things like how recent a review is and if the reviewer bought the item on Amazon. It also analyses reviews to verify trustworthiness." The internet is also a great place to buy stuff.

Goodreads is a unique case study for the rise of public opinion sharing because it dabbles in all these areas, and it has this deceptive innocence about it I've already described. While it operates as a social media site, where users "connect" and bicker and develop parasocial relationships as they, consciously or not, try to game the system, it is also, as Dalva noted, a consumer reports platform. In 2013, Amazon purchased the site for $150 million from the husband-and-wife duo who started it; the change did not do much for the interface (still confusing), but it did make the site's possible soft power slightly more powerful: on the Goodreads website, you can find a link to buy whatever book you're looking at very easily, and you can also link your

Goodreads profile to your Kindle, the company's proprietary e-reader that makes up anywhere between 67 percent and 83 percent of e-book market share, depending on who, when, and how you're asking, in part because Kindle books appear in a file format that cannot be read by other e-readers. Trying to read other file formats on Kindle, to be brief, sucks, and if you're not using the actual Kindle device you can read Kindle books on an app for your phone or tablet or computer, which is, I can tell you, nefariously convenient if you are in the admittedly unusual position of suddenly needing to read a specific book quickly, for work, and don't actually have a Kindle device, as I sometimes am. There's also just the fact that Amazon is Amazon and that's the Place to Buy Stuff the vast majority of people know, and most people don't have any qualms about using it and wouldn't really care if they learned they maybe should.

Anyway, when someone is using their Kindle, they can also see Goodreads ratings and recommendations before they make purchases. These are distinct from Amazon ratings. In book publishing, Amazon is the most important factor in a book's commercial success; it accounts for around 50 percent of print book sales from the Big Five publishers and more than 75 percent of e-book sales. Any number of strategies can help or hurt a book on Amazon, but at the end of the day it is on Amazon where the book must sell. Because you have almost certainly purchased something on Amazon at least once in your life, I don't need to tell you that the platform is much more complicated yet nevertheless better designed than Goodreads, but Amazon's platform is also similar to Goodreads', in that a product page features an average star rating, a description offered by the seller, a list of similar products you might want to click on, and a list of customer reviews accompanied by their star ratings. Here books are like any other product, but because Amazon started out as a virtual bookseller, they have a special

< 66 >

< 67 >

status; the star rating for a book on Amazon comes with more baggage than a star rating for a vacuum cleaner, though the latter is far more useful—with vacuum cleaners we are all looking for the same few attributes, and with books we are all looking for slightly-to-very different things. There are also lists of random and often niche rankings on which the product might appear; my first novel was at one point ranked highly in Cooking Humor because, I assume, it contains a joke about pancakes. (My editor notes, "To get more technical, it may be because there are certain keywords in the metadata for the book that cue this, but I don't think you need to mention this here, necessarily.")

When the Goodreads acquisition was announced, the American Authors Guild responded by saying, "Amazon's control of online bookselling approaches the insurmountable." But it's not just online bookselling; by offering books at lower prices, with advertising tailored to algorithmically determined interests as specific as "cooking humor," and then delivering the books evilly fast, Amazon squeezes the entire industry by squeezing brick-and-mortar bookstores, which act as actual community spaces for writers and readers, and by intimidating publishers who have no real choice but to submit to its terms, because it is the single most important factor in whether they will turn a profit. What kind of books sell now determines what kind of books are published in the future, and so the kind of books that are most successful on Amazon are going to take priority over less popular works that may succeed on terms beyond sales (truth, beauty, etc.). The point here is that on some level, Goodreads uses a facade of community and wholesome book-loving to sell stuff, on behalf of an entity that specifically harms actual communities and actually wholesome book lovers. But it is difficult to object, not just because all objections to this kind of hegemonic corporate overlording tend to, at best, generate hearty agreement about which nothing can be done.

Goodreads is also unique in the same way that professional book criticism is unique, in that the criticism takes the same, or similar, form as the object of critique: writing. In professional criticism, this can cause conflicts; a prevailing idea is that those who can't write novels themselves avenge their lost potential by criticizing those who can. At the same time, the most popular explanation for a dearth of negative or even ambivalent criticism is that the writers who review for big outlets such as the *New York Times* are rarely full-time professional critics; they have almost always published or intend to publish books of their own, so they attempt to generate blanket goodwill by being "generous" and positive, holding back their true criticism in hopes of not making any enemies who themselves or whose friends will pan the generous and positive reviewer down the line.

For the pure, innocent consumer, just looking for a good read for her limited summer vacation, this presents a conundrum: How to determine what's best to buy? A solution is to turn to the people—honest booklovers who have nothing to gain from giving a positive review and nothing to lose from giving a negative one. Famously democratic, the internet is where the people live. On Goodreads, this dynamic creates a tension between any individual author (seen to be a public figure, able to get an agent and a book deal and thus objectively privileged) pitted against the democratically righteous normal readers (unagented, in public—but through the force of history that has made us all kind of public, not through any active decision on their part). The readers are doing a kind of public service by offering their opinions, which eventually accumulate into a collective assessment that may help other righteous normal readers make tough decisions about how they'll spend their limited time and money.

For the well-reviewed author, this is a fine setup. For the author who may not benefit from a wide, general readership, it's a psycho-

< 68 >

< 69 >

logical thriller. A common refrain about Goodreads to warn anxious authors away from obsessively checking their stats and developing paranoid fantasies about their haters is that "Goodreads is for readers, not for writers." There is some wisdom in this: writers are also discouraged, strongly, from doing things such as reading reviews of their work and searching their own names on Twitter. While Goodreads advertises many ways for authors to engage with their readers directly—the site's Author Program allows authors to control their author profiles, run giveaways, and participate in Q and As, as well as "show off your taste in literature"—the only way to do so without running afoul of the site's reviewers is to be chipper, conciliatory, and overall nice; it would be difficult, if not impossible, to use Goodreads as an author without at least glancing at reviews. Authors, not famous for their emotional reserve, particularly when it comes to criticism of their work, do themselves no favors by seeking out negative commentary, which is not always entirely fair or factually accurate. In doing so, they expose themselves to the temptation to respond.

In the weeks before her first novel, *No One Else Can Have You*, "about a girl with PTSD teaming up with a veteran to fight crime," was published in 2014, Kathleen Hale was a self-described wreck. "I fidgeted and talked to myself, rewriting passages of a book that had already gone to print," she writes in "Am I Being Catfished?," a 2014 essay about the experience. "I remember when my editor handed me the final copy: I held the book in my hands for a millisecond before grabbing a pen and scribbling edits in the margins." Worse, she began checking Goodreads. "Soon, my daily visits tallied somewhere between 'slightly-more-than-is-attractive-to-admit-here' and 'infinity.'" She was also using Twitter.

One day, roaming the disquieting corridors of the social internet, Hale encountered the Goodreads profile of a woman named Blythe

Harris, who described herself as a tenth-grade teacher with two children. The young, attractive woman had given Hale's book one star, calling it "awfully written and offensive" and "one of the worst books I've read this year." She accused the novel of an insensitive treatment of issues such as PTSD, domestic abuse, mental illness, and rape. Hale thought to herself, *But there isn't rape in my book*, and freaked out.

Such reviews, on their own, need not be too upsetting. Some random person doesn't like your book? Fine. They don't like it because of a misinterpretation that has wormed its way into their field of vision? Oh well. We have all been that random person, disliking books, not reading them closely enough to form a nuanced opinion on them. What's more disturbing is the fanning out, paranoid diagram style, of the implications of that random person's dislike appearing in public. Humans are social creatures, as the saying goes. We like to form groups. "Other commenters joined in to say they'd been thinking of reading my book, but now wouldn't," Hale writes of the one-star review. "Or they'd liked it, but could see where Blythe was coming from, and would reduce their ratings." Already, she writes, it "felt like" everyone hated her.

They didn't, of course, but feelings are like opinions, which is why a common way to express an opinion is to begin with "I feel like." Opinions might be based on logic or illogic, fact or projection, but if they're strong enough they can do some damage. Hale became obsessed. According to a Goodreads veteran Hale spoke to, Athena Parker, who co-founded a (now-defunct) website called stopthegrbullies.com, Harris was known for rallying her followers to harass authors and other users, including, at one point, a fourteen-year-old girl. Hale thought Harris seemed to be baiting her by mocking everything she said on Twitter, which put Hale in the classic bind of the modern image-conscious woman. "Confronting her would mean publicly acknowledging that I searched my name on Twitter," Hale writes, "which is about as socially attractive as setting up a Google alert for your name (which I also did)." At the same time, Harris's commentary on Hale and her book was *also* making Hale look bad.

The climax of the story is that Hale ended up (1) making passive-aggressive comments about the reviewer on Twitter (insinuating that all bloggers are frustrated aspiring authors); (2) internet-stalking her; (3) suspecting she wasn't who she said she was (young, attractive tenth-grade teacher with two children); (4) acquiring the blogger's address through sneaky publicity maneuvering; (5) going to her house in a rental car; (6) not confronting her there; and (7) finally calling her at her office. Posing as a fact-checker, Hale was able to develop her suspicions, but never confirm, that in fact she (Hale) was being negatively reviewed by an older woman pretending to be a made-up character named Blythe Harris, for forever-unclear reasons. While the conversations Hale and possibly-fake-Harris had were illuminating in the way that evocative passages in novels are illuminating of the characters participating, they were not particularly decisive. There would be no definitive answer to the question of whether Blythe Harris wasn't who she says she was, and, if she wasn't, why this woman had allegedly made up a parallel identity to harass authors on the internet by harnessing the power of opinion. Over two phone calls, the woman Hale believed was posing as Harris denied everything. "She said she wasn't Blythe Harris and that she was going to call the police about 'this Blythe Harris person,'" Hale writes. Still, the evidence didn't add up. Hale soon published a self-aware *Guardian* essay about it, later in 2014, that made Goodreads reviewers absolutely livid.

It's hard to see either side of this as being particularly righteous; Hale is, in many ways, the archetypal author Goodreads reviewers see themselves called to judge: she went to Harvard and has the connections (and skills) to write for major publications like the *Guardian*. In 2019 Hale published a book, *Kathleen Hale Is a Crazy Stalker*, that included an updated version of the self-aware *Guardian* essay from which I'm quoting, and it was somewhat predictably excoriated by Goodreads reviewers. (The *New York Times* review was mixed.) The top review on the book's Goodreads page reflects the tone and argument of the book's 427 one-star reviews (63 percent of the total, which average to 2.06 stars): "Who the fuck in publishing decided the woman who stalked a reviewer, paid for a background check on them, took their address from a publishing database & turned up at their house over a one star review should write a book about it??" Most of these reviewers explicitly refused to read the book.

Whether the mob forms organically or is strategically promoted, this tactic has come to be known as "review bombing," and in the years since Hale's crazy stalking incident, it's led to actual extortion and blackmail scams against authors, with anonymous groups sending intimidating emails along the lines of the missive one self-published author received in 2021: "EITHER YOU TAKE CARE OF OUR NEEDS AND REQUIREMENTS WITH YOUR WALLET OR WE'LL RUIN YOUR AUTHOR CAREER." A few hours after the author didn't take care of their needs, one-star reviews started appearing on her books' pages. "It was quite threatening," she told *TIME* magazine.

As a group, Goodreads reviewers can seem as if they are making demands of authors, even if not usually literally blackmailing them. "You are brave," a friend told me when I said I was writing about the site, echoing the advice Kathleen Hale's friends gave her when she became obsessed with her Goodreads reviews: "DO NOT ENGAGE. You'll make yourself look bad, and [Harris will] ruin you." The first demand Goodreads reviewers make is that you do not question, criti-

< 73 >

cize, or acknowledge Goodreads except to promote yourself pleasantly there. If you do not follow this rule, you will at best be accused of bitter motives—narcissism, obtuseness, misguided desire for vengeance—and at worst vulnerable to retaliation. My friend won't let me name her; despite a streak on bestseller lists, as well as an appearance on television, considered a holy grail of book publicity, when her book was published she became a little disgruntled about her Goodreads reviews, sending me semi-ironic expressions of exasperation about them every few days. I could relate. My willingness to write about the site, I told her, was less about bravery than pragmatism, because my first novel is already quite unpopular on Goodreads, with a sub-three-star rating, which is bad, even considering the popular argument that women writing literary fiction about women tend to generate a lower star rating—someone wrote a blog post about this, but there isn't really data on it—so I feel I have little to lose by writing about it. Whatever professional consequences I might face for being unpopular on Good-reads, I have already more or less faced. (While I am not ruling out personal consequences—psychological tolls being taken, disturbing threats being sent—I'm sure it'll be fine in the end.) (Or not!)

The second demand Goodreads reviewers make is about the books themselves. Although there are enough Goodreads users to create diverse groups and subsets of reviewers on the site, and although the same standards ought not be applied to all genres, the point of an average star rating system is not that everything sort of evens out in the end, depending on who's voting: it is supposed to make a statement about value. And the values that help a book succeed on Goodreads are specific: "4.56 stars on Goodreads" does not mean "4.56 stars on Amazon" or "4.56 stars." The issues my debut novel has, for my Goodreads reviewers, are many: the big one is that it was marketed as if it was going to have a lot of plot, in a sort of woman-goes-on-aquest-to-solve-a-romantic-mystery way (got you), but others include the stench of Brooklyn, a snarky narrator that reviewers think is me, and the use of big words. (I was especially called out for using the word "antipodeans" to refer to Australian tourists.) My friend's book has too many jokes. "God forbid that a dog should die accidentally," one top Goodreads reviewer, Elyse Walters, told me while describing themes unpopular with Goodreads users, during an interview in 2022. "They will not read the book." She also mentioned a squeamishness around sex.

As on all "community"-based platforms, the high emotional pitch on Goodreads also causes issues among users, not just tensions between reviewers and authors; one suspects these issues affect users' taste and responses to the books they review on the site. I contacted Walters because Adam Dalva, the top reviewer who rose to his position through scheming and deceit, recommended her to me as an example of someone who uses the site "earnestly." A veteran book club member in her early seventies based in California, Walters joined Goodreads a few months after the site launched in 2007, but she didn't get serious about it until an ankle replacement surgery left her confined to bed for nearly a year. On her iPad she had all the books she could possibly want, and people all around the world to discuss them with. She became pretty good at it. But as her status rose, she began to feel the site had lost some of its magic. The pressure to answer all the messages she received, from authors and editors and other entities hoping she'd check out their novels, was stressing her out, and she wanted to be able to dedicate time to her reviews, which are long and can take, she says, one or two hours if she really loves the book. Like all Goodreads reviewers (officially), she has never been paid for a review, though she receives many free books from publishers, and she has been invited to the Goodreads offices to test some new technology for the app (in

< 74 >

< 75 >

other words to do what sounds to me like more work for free). She did the reviewing because she really enjoyed it; when I called her in 2023 to catch up, she told me she'd stopped using Goodreads for the time being. "I don't even write well," she told me matter-of-factly. "I just love to share. And I love people."

But not all people love people back. As Walters became more well-known on the site, people began to gossip about her; her off-line friends thought it sounded a little catty, like high school, and I am inclined to agree with them. "There was a group of women I really liked—who I still like—but I know they don't like me, and I don't know what I've done wrong," she said. "I guess I'm not guarded." While it could be that Walters's success as a top reviewer will agitate anyone who envies that position—"just impossible to catch," Dalva said, approvingly; "she must read 300 books a year"—the animosity sounded, to me, given certain tendencies among Goodreads reviewers, including what I was told was a kind of prudishness, as if it possibly had something to do with the gossip being spread about her.

"I shared some things," Walters explained. "I shared that there was a time my husband and I had community warm-water soaks in our pool on Friday nights, and we did them clothing optional." Soon enough, someone was going around telling people, "Oh, you should be friends with her, she has orgies," Walters said. It got back to her. Someone sent her an email, letting her know that someone else was going around telling people she hosted orgies. She emphasized that she did not host orgies. "But even if I did, wow," she said. "How would that interfere with your lives?"

* * *

The habitual internet commenter wants to believe that he can interfere with other people's lives, that he has the power to affect something more than a mood (though he also wants to affect your mood). It follows that he feels affronted when someone is hosting weekly clothing-optional warm-water soaks in her pool: Doesn't the clothing-optional warm-water soak host *care* what he thinks about it? Shouldn't she be *ashamed*? Because hasn't she invited his opinion, brought this upon herself, by telling him, everyone, about it?

One should not hold an amateur book blogger to anywhere near the same standards as a professional author, but the act of publication, the way it sort of takes certain things out of your hands, is an experience both can become familiar with. "I had a feeling the motivation behind heckling, or trolling, was similar to why most people do anything—why I write, or why I was starting to treat typing my name into search boxes like it was a job," Kathleen Hale writes in "Am I Being Catfished?" "It occurred to me Blythe and I had this much in common: we were obsessed with being heard." While the generous empath in me wants to assume that it is unknowable pain or hardship that drives people to take up anonymity and harass others online, and that it is a lack of opportunities to be heard that inspires someone to become a forum fixture, the more realistic explanation is not so simple. Plenty of civilians, of all backgrounds, do not take to the internet in an attempt to express their inexpressible pain as pseudonymous characters. Plenty of users who do are not suffering in ways that are demographically significant.

What's funny about all this, why it has this nice aura of absurdity, is that the stakes seem low. People are derailing their lives—in her book, Hale reveals that she checked herself into a psych ward after her experience with Blythe Harris—because of a website that looks like it was designed before the Great Recession. Why? It's hard to say how any of this affects sales or future opportunities. As with many incidents on the internet, most Goodreads melodramas have the po-

< 76 >

< 77 >

tential to flare up briefly and then quickly fade away. Even Hale's status on the site has recovered. Her most recent book, a reported work of nonfiction called *Slenderman: Online Obsession, Mental Illness, and the Violent Crime of Two Midwestern Girls*, was published in 2022, and it has an average Goodreads rating of 3.97 stars. While a few reviews mention Hale's "unmentioned yet easily googlable history of stalking," most praise her meticulous reporting and storytelling. Other evidence suggests that Goodreads is no match for the kind of author whose power they see themselves checking. In 2021, the author Lauren Hough published an essay collection called *Leaving Isn't the Hardest Thing* and soon offended Goodreads for tweeting some harsh insults about a couple of users who'd left her book four-star reviews. (She called them "assholes," specifically.) I wouldn't do it myself, but it seems she was onto something: a review-bombing campaign led to *Leaving*'s star rating dipping quite low. But the book still made it to the *New York Times* bestseller list, and its star rating has since risen to an acceptable 3.30.

Unrepentant, the next year Hough got into trouble defending another writer friend, Sandra Newman, whose book had a premise that was condemned as transphobic by Goodreads users who hadn't read it. Hough mounted this defense on Twitter, in tweets she has since deleted, but screenshots still floating around seem to suggest she was telling these critics that they shouldn't make a habit of commenting on books they haven't read, with some *fuck*s thrown in. Again, I wouldn't do it, but I can't help but admire this other Lauren's willingness to play ball. Her behavior led to the LGBTQ organization Lambda Literary revoking Hough's nomination for its annual prizes, in the lesbian memoir category, for exhibiting "what we believed to be a troubling hostility toward transgender critics and trans-allies and [using] her substantial platform . . . to harmfully engage with readers and critics." Although the latter incident didn't have anything to do with Goodreads, the assumed power dynamic is the same: do not snap at humble commenters, who have it worse than you.

This is not quite true, of course, but it reflects a misapprehension about power in the attention economy: if you make something that is publicizable on one of these platforms, you are seen to be kind of like a famous person, with the material advantages of a pop star and the job security of a politician. My friend Laurel owns and runs a successful bagel shop and café attached to an English-language bookstore in Berlin. Her bagels, to say nothing of her other baked goods, are great, as is her writing on food. She graduated from the Diplôme de Boulangerie program at Le Cordon Bleu Paris and was nominated for a James Beard Award for her first cookbook. For years, she has responded, forcefully, to Google reviews that complain her café's inadequacies, as a kind of rebellion against the fact that these reviews must show up alongside her Google Maps address in order for the café to be listed by the service, which it must be if Laurel wants to do much business at all. (A lack of reviews would also arouse suspicion among the many consumers who like to do their research before committing to a lunch spot.) Her Google reviewers complain about the café's far from unusual anti-laptop policy, about a lack of seating that is entirely projection (one of Laurel's responses is "Dear customers, we have 55 seats. We think that's loads!:-)"), and, above all, about what they consider her surly online attitude. "The person answering to the reviews should grow up and stop acting so miserable," one reviewer writes. "A customer isn't welcome to the café after writing a POSITIVE review except for the fact that she didn't enjoy the latte as much as she did the rest? It's a disgrace and people shouldn't support businesses with ungrateful staff like this. I feel bad for them."

"Ungrateful"—the customer has projected a particular logic of

< 78 >

< 79 >

capitalism onto their relationship with my friend Laurel. In this economy, the logic says, the business owner is always desperate for business and must campaign for it, assuring the picky customer that he is as always right as he's always been told, even though he is often not. The issue is not about decorum, but about the reviewed subject's unwillingness to engage in a fear-based business strategy that lends the consumer dictatorial power.

This is what happens on Goodreads, too. Publishing industry professionals seem to agree that Goodreads is "important" or, as one book editor told *TIME* magazine in 2021, a "necessary evil." It's generally agreed that popularity there can be more consequential for genre fiction and for young adult fiction, which is the category Kathleen Hale's ill-fated first book fell into; the YA community is also famous for its ruthless internet uprisings, which often result in books being removed from publication or radically changed, on often spurious grounds. All this felt somewhat contained within the site's forum mindset until 2023. Shortly after Elizabeth Gilbert, author of the bestselling memoir *Eat, Pray, Love*, announced the publication of her forthcoming novel *The Snow Forest*, more than five hundred Goodreads users, many of whom were Ukrainian, review bombed the book's brand-new Goodreads page because the novel seemed to "romanticize" Russia while the country continued its war against Ukraine. That the novel was set in Russia in the 1930s and, according to its synopsis, concerned a family attempting to resist the Soviet regime by dropping out of society did not seem to matter; shortly after the Goodreads campaign began, Gilbert announced that the concerns of her Ukrainian readers had led her to decide to pull the book from its publication schedule indefinitely.

The literary world was scandalized: Gilbert's decision seemed to be a dramatic, and portentous, overreaction. Heretofore the power of Goodreads had seemed like something you could find irritating but ultimately laugh at; that it could so quickly move a very famous author to pull a book entirely seemed a bad sign for books that might deal with even more fraught themes. The success of this review-bombing campaign would surely inspire more single-issue gangs of readers. How could a publisher, to say nothing of an author, cave to pressures from amateur reviewers who hadn't even read a particular book and who almost certainly wouldn't have purchased it anyway? What consequences could publishers and authors seriously be afraid of? And why doesn't Goodreads prevent this kind of thing? While these commenters have clearly interfered with the lives of the people they're reviewing, the effects they've had are more ambiguous than "AUTHOR CAREER RUINED." Their reviews are powerful only if enough of the right people believe they are.

PART 2: ELITISM

The line about how Goodreads is for readers, not for writers, has always irritated me. Am I not a reader? I wonder, staring at my books. I know, in my heart, that I am not. My problem is not just that I am a writer; it's also the kind of writer I am. A snob, highbrow, and an elitist, I find the concept of plot oppressive, value style over voice, and enjoy an unfamiliar vocabulary word. At the movies, I prefer subtitles; at the museum, I can probably identify a decent percentage of the permanent collection by sight. Unless you count DJ sets, which I don't, the last live music I saw was at the opera; the last theater, an adaptation of Kafka's novel *Amerika*. I hate theater, but I try to go anyway. I like television, but I have not watched a series to completion in years. I feel shame about difficult classics I haven't yet read and pride about those I have. There are few things more satisfying to me than recommending to someone a book or film they've never heard of. I despise a happy ending; a happy ending says, to me, absolutely nothing about life except that humans have a near-universal desire for a happy ending that is basically unfulfillable if you have any critical thinking skills at all. I learned these values at the Ivy League university I attended as an undergraduate; while not everything was spelled out quite so bluntly there, my education introduced me to the resources that I used to develop these tastes and beliefs, the books and magazines and paths of inquiry. I could make use of my dormant Goodreads account to log my reading and bicker with the reviewers there, but I don't want to. I have an outlet, several outlets, to discuss my reading, for pay, for now. I am a professional, and I am in danger.

It has always been this way, but always for slightly different, or evolving, reasons. Critics like me are perennially regretting the deterioration of criticism before noting that critics have long regretted the deterioration of criticism: this is how we get people to care about our criticism, by turning it into an emergency. "The great majority of reviews give an inadequate or misleading account of the book that is dealt with," George Orwell wrote in 1946. He was talking about your standard newspaper book review, but I'd say this about reviews anywhere: newspaper book reviews, "organic" social media posts, consumer reports, and the hybrid form that has emerged on Goodreads. While several publications dedicate space to long, serious reviews that take into account an author's oeuvre and historical or cultural context, these reviews are also often bad—obviously biased, boringly written, full of errors, beholden to some set of values that clash with those of the author or those of a reasonable person. In 1959, Elizabeth Hardwick described "The Decline of Book Reviewing" just as many describe it today: "Simple 'coverage' seems to have won out over the drama of opinion; 'readability,' a cozy little word, has taken the place of the old-fashioned requirement of a good, clear prose style, which is something else." She is often quoted on this in contemporary essays about the topic. A spate of articles around 2010 picked apart a similar "crisis" in film criticism; in the years since Kelefa Sanneh's 2004 essay "The Rap Against Rockism," a landmark corrective against the predilection for rock and roll's faulty authenticity in music criticism, the countervailing principle, poptimism, has come to require a corrective of its own. ("Should gainfully employed adults whose job is to listen to music thoughtfully really agree so regularly with the taste of 13-year-olds?" Saul Austerlitz wrote in the *New York Times Magazine* in 2014.) In 2023, the art magazine *e-flux* hosted a panel titled "Criticism is dead, long live criticism!"

Perhaps the most realistic assessment of all this death and dying is that serious criticism—by which I mean criticism that does not pander to an idea of the average consumer in either taste or execution, that might in this refusal alienate the average consumer, that rejects received wisdom and takes nothing for granted, and that on top of it all is written in Hardwick's good, clear prose style, possibly even counting as literature itself—has always been relatively rare, but not so rare that there isn't at least some space for someone to fret about its rarity, and any sense of history's superiority comes from history's ability to filter out mediocre or worse efforts. What I am going to argue is that while I can't really assess whether criticism is deteriorating per se, as it has always been said to be deteriorating, criticism is certainly threatened, despite an undeniable flourishing of nuanced criticism appearing in publications new and old in recent years.

There are many varieties of professional culture critic, just as there are many varieties of subject, and not all of them are as snobby as I am. Some are more so. I believe my approach is the correct one—I would like to think that most critics believe their approach is the cor-

< 83 >

rect one, but some seem to go about their work pretty cynically—but for the moment I'm going to group us all together: critics who get paid to publish their views on culture on one side and critics who do it for free on the other. Please keep in mind that I have also written a novel, and I read most of the reviews of it without starting a *single* fight, righteous though I would have been in doing so, so I'm allowed to say whatever I want about all sides of this. The book you're reading now will probably also be reviewed, I hope. While I'm defining terms, I'm also going to note that I will use the word "artists" here to refer to anyone who makes creative work, even though in some of these discussions I apply it to figures I would otherwise not want to distinguish as such. (Actors, pop stars, and other entertainers, as well as writers of formulaic fiction in various genres that I'm not going to name specifically because these people I'm sure are already mad at me, if they have encountered this essay, all fall into this unnamed category.) I'm doing this because it's more expedient and because it should be obvious for anyone to understand which groups I'm talking about when; if you would like to take issue with my use of the word "artist," well, that's pedantic. I don't like the word "creator," which would be a more accurate way to refer to this umbrella group of artists, because it has tech-industry connotations, and as an elitist I hate technology.

Just kidding. Sort of.

As with the critics who don't get paid for their reviews, the artists professional critics write about fear and hate us. Unlike the critics who don't get paid, we seem as though we have power as individuals, beyond our ability to continue to get work writing criticism. It is almost impossible to earn a living doing this without losing the plot, as Renata Adler described in her 1980 essay "The Perils of Pauline," but the obnoxious self-image one can develop as a professional critic, with a sought-after mind, is confidence-building, which can translate to other endeavors. A publication, sometimes an old, storied one, approves our message; at least one other person looked at it before it appeared in public. It's likely many more people will read what we have to say than those who will look at any one Goodreads review, or Amazon review, or social media post. We might, from atop our airy vantage, be able to unleash a flood of considerations on these more crowded platforms; this is what we would love to be able to do.

Thin-skinned celebrities also seem to reveal the power we have by occasionally acknowledging our reviews. If no one cared about professional criticism anymore, how would some of the most famous people in the world not only know of, but also get mad at us? "PEOPLE WHO 'REVIEW' ALBUMS AND DON'T MAKE MUSIC THEMSELVES SHOULD BE UNEMPLOYED," the singer and rapper Lizzo tweeted in response to receiving a 6.5 (out of 10) rating by the music website Pitchfork for her 2019 album *Cuz I Love You*. (On Pitchfork, a qualitative assessment written by a single critic is accompanied by a numerical rating, determined by the average rating given by multiple Pitchfork employees. This review called some of the songs on Lizzo's album "burdened with overwrought production, awkward turns of phrase, and ham-handed rapping.") When the singer Halsey received her own 6.5 rating the next year, she tweeted, "can the basement that they run p*tchfork out of just collapse already." She deleted the tweet when she was told she had inadvertently called for the collapse of One World Trade Center, the location of the Pitchfork offices; apologized and explained that she "Just figured I could poke at them back with the same aloof passive aggression they poke at artists with!"; and then deleted that, too. In 2022, a critic for the *New York Times* panned the ironic slasher flick *Bodies Bodies Bodies*, calling it "a 95-minute advertisement for cleavage and Charli XCX's latest single"; one of the film's actresses, Amandla Stenberg, interpreted the cleavage comment as a

< 84 >

< 85 >

personal slight and sent the critic a private message on Instagram that read "ur review was great, maybe if you had gotten ur eyes off my tits you could've watched the movie!" A few months prior, Charli XCX herself was photographed leaving the London restaurant Sexy Fish wearing a crop top with the phrase "They don't build statues of critics" printed on it; the dig is an updated version of a quotation that has served as words of encouragement for artists since the 1930s, when it was attributed to the Finnish composer Jean Sibelius in a book about his life. (This book was reviewed by Adorno, a terrifying critic who described sequences in Sibelius compositions as being "like a baby who falls off a table and injures its spine." Although he's more frequently called a theorist or philosopher, Adorno also doesn't have a statue, as far as I could find, but he does have a monument in Frankfurt. It's a desk inside a glass cube.) In 2023, Seth Rogen took a different tack when he appeared on the podcast *Diary of a CEO*: pathos. "I think if most critics knew how much it hurts the people that made the things that they are writing about, they would second guess the way they write these things," he said. "It's devastating. I know people who have never recovered from it honestly . . . that's something that people carry with them, literally, their entire lives and I get why. It fucking sucks." Other celebrities who have gotten mad about this issue include Ariana Grande, Justin Bieber, and Olivia Munn.

Although I am a critic myself, I resent the idea that artists should never respond to reviews, which extends beyond Goodreads and consumer reports platforms and is considered a best practice. I resent it because I would like to believe in the possibility of actual intellectual debate about culture between critics and artists that would not immediately turn to artists accusing critics of snarky jealousy and creative failure and everyone else accusing artists of being blind and sensitive about their work; I would like, basically, a return to the incensed letter to the editor, but on a larger scale. I think this could be kind of fun. There's a disturbing, self-defeating, and borderline self-hating idea among some critics that artists ought to be a little stupid, so that the creative spirit may have fewer obstacles to expression, which is wrong. (A great artist *may* be a little stupid in some ways, but it is not a requirement.) Unfortunately, none of the examples I've just cited are even close to this utopic dialogue that I'm envisioning would help create the culture sphere I want. These celebrities are not driven to respond to critics out of a passion for art and their beliefs about it. They make no substantive commentary about the content of the reviews to which they object. They are merely sensitive and using that sensitivity strategically. Against a critic, high-earning entertainers morph into struggling artists, putting their heart and soul on the line only to be rejected by an ungrateful, misunderstanding intellectual; to debate the critic would be to accept the critic's terms, which would mean a bad review could ever be legitimate. The implication of these outbursts is that there shouldn't be bad reviews at all, which would mean there wouldn't be any reviews at all; reviews would quickly come to be recognized as meaningless exercises in publicity, as many already are.

It's hard not to see these celebrities as completely lacking in perspective, but at least this dynamic offers more evidence of how power is understood in the attention economy. While critics, as a group, may be living rent-free in celebrities' heads, they still have to pay rent. Sort of. The chattering classes tend to come from backgrounds that range from middle-class to very wealthy; this is also true of celebrities. For the sake of not getting too charts-and-graphs about it, let's say the average percentage of former rich kids in each group—celebrities and professional cultural critics—is roughly equivalent, meaning they are working from the same point of economic advantage in early life, but with different influences. Again, generally speaking. In terms of

< 86 >

cultural capital, actual capital, potential earnings, actual earnings, and manpower (as in number of possible defenders in an internet feud), the celebrities are winning handily. Most professional critics—especially those who write for Pitchfork, who tend to be young freelancers—do not have full-time jobs or stable incomes, and this is only getting worse. The slow eradication of outlets that actually publish professional criticism means that there is barely anywhere that is capable of elevating a critic from the lowly status of social media poster to the ambiguous status of byline; on top of the well-documented deaths of alt weeklies, culture desks at national newspapers, and more recently smaller publications like the short-lived *Astra Magazine* that published serious if not super-well-paid reviews and critical essays, digital media outlets have also shrunk operations dramatically. Any publication that puts out criticism is always simultaneously tap-dancing for an audience increasingly skeptical of the enterprise—audiences have also been known to come out against negative reviews—and looking over its shoulder to see if its own masthead is next. On the other side, we have these celebrities, who make just, like, tons of fucking money, albeit sometimes in ignoble ways. Out of some combination of a thirst for drama; easy access to drama production; an ignorance of the media landscape except for the knowledge that drama production usually translates to visibility, which translates to sales; the oversensitivity of the (generally) spoiled middle-class-to-very-wealthy child; and maybe somewhere in there the mournful recognition that they have alienated themselves from the masses in order to provide those masses with entertainment, these celebrities cannot bear the power dynamic whereby some *writer* might get a little attention by leeching off *the celebrity's* hard, soulful work, because it seems it is never enough to have just, like, tons of fucking money. So the celebrities expose themselves as completely lacking in perspective.

NO JUDGMENT

This is my opinion, as a professional critic; lucky for celebrities lacking in perspective, it doesn't mean much. Seth Rogen must suggest a negative review is not dissimilar from emotional abuse—people *who have never recovered*—because he is rich, and he cannot really claim any other harm done. He is rich in part because the professional critic has little influence on the market. A string of bad reviews doesn't often tank a novel destined for the bestseller list; a couple of great write-ups is probably not enough to help an independent film achieve the sort of sales that would render it a commercial success. En masse, reviews *can* have some effect, reminding potential audiences over and over that a work exists and, slowly, shaping the discourse that informs artists and producers, who might read what we write and, *maybe*, incorporate it, not even particularly consciously, into a future work. But as an individual critic, the only real power I have against a subject is psychological.

It's the same psychological power that anyone on the internet has, and its strength and effects depend on any number of factors, ranging from what other reviews the artist being reviewed has received, to whether the artist being reviewed ate enough that day, to good old-fashioned mental health. But when backed by an institutional imprimatur, conveyed in a cultivated, considered way, the professional review is more capable of activating the subject's defenses. Not only does a negative professional review make the reviewed artist feel that paranoid sense of possibility that everyone will see and agree with the negative review, but it also says, "I do not care how much money you have; to me, you are small." Hence the potential for the professional critic to develop an obnoxious self-image and for the reviewed artist to imagine, briefly, that the critic has some power over him. The torment the reviewed artist experiences is not nothing: although they hate us, they also know they would miss us if we were gone, as Adam

< 88 >

Dalva suggested when explaining why he gives only five-star reviews on Goodreads. To put a work of art into the world and get nothing but Instagram likes as feedback is not the same as having it described carefully in a newspaper or magazine, approved by an editor. The Instagram like is a volatile currency, and a *New York Times* review is more stable. A Goodreads review is Monopoly money in a game you're betting $50 on. Maybe in twenty years the critical profession will fade even more than it has; it was only recently that there arose workable means of widely publicizing creative work besides traditional media coverage. But for now we have a tension between the old school and the new, which is that artists can be wildly successful in every material way and still feel as though they have failed because a twenty-seven-year-old at Pitchfork deemed their efforts middling, and the artists can speak from the narrow perspective of that momentary upset to the twenty-seven-year-old at Pitchfork pretty much immediately.

What's most upsetting to the artist being reviewed is the recognition that, despite their power and their PR teams and their hair and makeup, they cannot actually control what others think of them; they cannot manipulate every twenty-seven-year-old at Pitchfork into singing their praises. Even a positive review, when celebrating not quite the right things, can be disorienting: *that is not what I meant.* Whatever I say, positive or negative or ambivalent, I might permanently alter, or at least "complicate," as we might say in a review, the image an audience member has in their mind of a previously beloved artist. I might even ruin it. This is to say nothing about whether I have made some good points that might aggravate the artist's insecurities or whether I am truly an idiot with no understanding of the art form that I am discussing. Both possibilities are distressing to the artist being reviewed, of course.

But all that is character development. The plot is straightforward.

The most recent and frequently cited example of the limits of professional criticism, broadly construed, is what happened to Jeanine Cummins's 2020 novel *American Dirt*. Paid a seven-figure advance, hyped all around via the publisher's marketing department, and selected for Oprah's Book Club, the book was pilloried on publication, first by Myriam Gurba, in a widely circulated pan for the website Tropics of Meta. Parul Sehgal, then working as a staff book critic for the *New York Times*, wrote that the novel "flounders and fails," with "tortured sentences," thin characters, a too-excited "fascination" with "the gradients of brown skin," and a shallow lack of politics, despite its superficially political premise. (It is about a Mexican bookseller who is forced to migrate undocumented to the US with her young son after the rest of her family is murdered by a drug cartel at a birthday party.) Within the insular literary world, the novel's publication was widely understood to be a huge mistake; few people who take themselves seriously as writers would have been caught dead reading it, except to write a negative review. Eighty-two writers, among them "many prominent, bestselling, prizewinning writers," published an open letter on the website Lit Hub asking Winfrey to "remove the influential imprimatur of Oprah's Book Club, as you have in the past upon learning that a book you'd championed wasn't what it first seemed to be." Cummins's publisher, Flatiron Books, canceled her book tour because booksellers and the author herself were receiving "threats of physical violence." In a statement, Flatiron sort of admitted it had fucked up, saying the furor exposed "deep inadequacies" on the publisher's part. On Goodreads, the novel has 504,332 ratings, with an average star rating of 4.37. It was a number-one *New York Times* bestseller and has sold more than two million copies. I am sure the controversy led more than a few people to pick up the book and see for themselves. This is elitism at work: the elitists make a lot of valid points, refusing to, as

< 91 >

the meme goes, "let people enjoy things," and the people will enjoy them regardless.

* * *

What I've just described isn't really what comes to mind when we hear screeching about "elitism" and "elites," even if some of the reviewers mentioned are specifically looking down their noses at the pop culture they're criticizing. In recent years, the terms have been most closely associated with conservatives' critique of liberals as whiny babies insulated from the real world by wealth and education; "elite" is now often modified with the adjective "coastal," because that's where such people tend to live. That critique, which implies not only that liberals are out of touch with reality but also that education is ironically what makes them that way, naturally infects debates about culture. Culture has long been discussed in terms of how rarefied it is—usually according to versions of the highbrow/lowbrow classification—and of course the link between the ability to appreciate high culture and wealth and education has been historically strong. Remember the young aristocrats on the Grand Tour.

Yet as the figurehead of this conservative moment shows, the relationship between class as in money and class as in sophistication is not exactly straightforward today. Commentators often pointed out the hypocrisy of Donald Trump's rage against coastal elites, arguing that of course he is one, too, but his elitism is very touchy: the classless rich protect themselves from feelings of inadequacy by differentiating themselves from the intellectuals who made them feel dumb when they were all attending Ivy League universities together. There are many easier ways to signal wealth now than reciting poetry or sitting through an opera, both of which can be boring and mentally and emotionally taxing, and besides, today high culture is accessible to anyone with an internet connection. Even if you can't travel to Italy, though that's also much more accessible than it was at the turn of the nineteenth century, you can easily learn whatever you want about the Renaissance for free. Knowing a lot about the Renaissance no longer means you're rich; it means you're interested in the Renaissance. You have a better chance of being interested in the Renaissance if you have some money, but it isn't necessary.

The status benefits of knowing and understanding high culture, even just in order to talk about it at parties, have dwindled. No one is scandalized by an otherwise successful person saying they haven't read a novel in years. An app, Blinkist, offers bullet-point summaries of nonfiction books so that people can "get the key insights" in "just 15 minutes"; the idea is that it's important to be aware of at least some books and that within those books are contained at least some ideas you might want to know, but the books available on the app are almost entirely self-help, in one way or another. At a time when nearly everyone, of all classes, believes they have limited time for culture, the principle of Mariana Starke's travel guidebook stands: if a reader is concerned about making an investment of limited time and energy to read one book, she could do worse than picking a novel that, as a conservative estimate, more than a million people liked and that, even if she doesn't like it, will be something she can discuss with other people because of its high profile. She will get some longevity out of what might otherwise be her wasted time.

Although there is no real pressure to be "cultured," there is a disdain for people who do not like pop culture—who eschew Rihanna, Marvel movies, and genre fiction. This disdain, again, does not really correspond to class; it is entirely defensive and personal, though it seems to have roots in a political point: the outdated, classist idea that highbrow equals rich and lowbrow equals poor, so that to disparage

< 92 >

Marvel movies is to disparage the masses who just want to relax after a hard day of underpaid work. While this may tend to be true—my ascent into elite education and subsequent class mobility is what made me aware of and interested in, say, modernism—again, it is not *necessarily* so. Long-held ideas about culture have become distorted by social media and its influence on opinion.

During the Trump administration, culture was held to a particularly strict but not particularly rigorous set of standards, whereby all art was expected to do something politically in accordance with the values of the coastal elites assumed to be its main if not exclusive audience. Everything was reviewed in terms of the light it could shed on political injustice. The concept of representation—of diverse races, genders, identities, and experiences—was considered a baseline criterion for all works and was often the quality on which a work was considered to have succeeded or failed. At the same time, awareness of "privilege" meant critics and commentators were constantly both acknowledging their own advantages and tasked with imagining millions of Americans suffering more than they. Combined with the (again) outdated, classist idea that privileged people are cultured and underprivileged people are not, there arose a seductive fallacy: people without privilege like bad art, and it is the privileged class's responsibility to represent that view.

Meanwhile, what we like had become so enmeshed with our identities that an attack on our preferences came to feel like an attack on ourselves. This manifested in a couple of different ways. One was to suggest a meaningful relationship between fans' identities and critics' takes (i.e., if you don't like a certain singer, you might be homophobic or, at the very least, misunderstand the singer's significance to gay men). Another was mob-like attacks on both professional critics and on civilians just opining on Twitter; the "Swifties" are famous for these. When defended, weak opinions become stronger, and an opinion arrived at by whim or gut feeling becomes something a person *really believes*. A Swiftie is not just a fan of Taylor Swift but someone who identifies as a Taylor Swift fan, who dedicates significant time and energy to her love of Taylor Swift—it follows that she would feel that an insult against Taylor Swift is an insult against herself.

All the while, remember, criticism was dying. It seemed a good solution for critics to indulge their guilty pleasures and avoid more difficult fare by devilishly advocating for pop culture. Because of web traffic metrics and the simple validation that comes from being able to very approximately quantify readers through social media response, a professional critic's greatest achievement, in terms of career advancement, is to publish a review a lot of people read, which is much more likely if you're talking about Taylor Swift. Untold numbers of people are sitting around looking up stuff about Taylor Swift every minute. That's another way we're not so different from amateur reviewers on Goodreads or really from anyone who posts what they think online. If we didn't want people to read what we had to say, why would we publish it?

* * *

In 2023, Charli XCX posted a series of tweets elaborating on her notorious T-shirt in response to a short piece in the *Guardian* by the established music critic Laura Snapes. In 2016, Snapes gave Charli XCX's EP *Vroom Vroom* a bad review on Pitchfork, accompanied by a 4.5 rating, calling it "pointedly uncommercial and abrasive" and "ferociously trite." In this 2023 mini-essay, Snapes regretted the review, saying she had come to change her mind about the artist after seeing her perform live and after "the general collapse of society," which made an album "that sounds like a pep rally at the edge of a black hole" more appeal-

< 95 >

ing. "This is why reviews are kind of silly in my opinion . . . ," Charli (if I may) tweeted, "like if the sway of culture and popular opinion is the thing that's forcing a journalist to reconsider their review with hindsight then what's the point of even reviewing in the first place?" She went on: "i think sometimes reviews are more about the culture or scene that surrounds an artist or the genre of music someone makes rather than the work itself - & it sort of produces this nervousness to be on the wrong side of culture or a fear to not be delivering the known 'cool' take."

She's right: the only way critics can truly sustain their practice is by fearlessly facing Hardwick's "drama of opinion" and attempting, as much as possible, to ignore the increasing pressures of popularity. (Internet.) This may mean sometimes contradicting the inexorable forces of history; this may also mean taking a page out of Goodreads's book and standing by what they think, though ideally on a foundation of expertise and consideration rather than unstable gut feelings. Charli is wrong about Snapes's initial "take," though; the abrasiveness and uncommerciality Snapes criticized in 2016 will always be cool, and it is Charli XCX's more recent mass success, decidedly un-, that has probably led the critic to reconsider.

That elite opining on art often teeters on the brink of meaninglessness is well documented, but it's strange to see it serve the masses rather than the elites we have come to hate. Adam Dalva's manipulation of the Goodreads system is the inverse of a more familiar story about class and high culture; traditionally, it's the lower- or middle-class striver who infiltrates the elite through cunning and mimicry. In Whit Stillman's 1990 film *Metropolitan*, the middle-class interloper Tom Townsend makes explicit the structure of this narrative while flirting with the young socialite Audrey Rouget at a black-tie party on the Upper East Side. The pair are discussing Jane Austen, about whom Tom has expounded rather confidently before revealing he hasn't read any of her work. When Audrey expresses genteel surprise at his audacity, Tom maintains his boastful poise. "You don't have to read a book to have an opinion on it," he replies. "I prefer good literary criticism. That way you get both the novelists' ideas as well as the critics' thinking."

Like Stendhal's Starke-reading scholar in Parma, Tom is a red-head: a unique and uniquely sensitive soul. So attuned to the reality of how aesthetic judgments are made—so influenced by other people that an encounter with a primary source is kind of irrelevant and done in service of making jaunty party conversation—Tom devised a policy that matter-of-factly revealed the lack of consideration that often goes into so-called highbrow assessments of literature. The system allows him to participate in the elite culture that seems closed to him without investing nearly as much time or energy as reading an entire novel requires. While the film gently mocks him, operating in what will become Stillman's specific brand of lightly deadpan irony—Tom displays little pathos in this moment, not ashamed that he's been exposed as a fraud, nor aggressive in his defense of his blatantly middle-class priorities—it also offers him some redemption, in the form of aesthetic development: he eventually reads some Jane Austen, and he likes it.

Dalva's easy manipulation of the Goodreads algorithm is a perversion of this class logic because Dalva comes from the world of the elite. Not only is he an editor at *Guernica* magazine, as he mentioned a long time ago, but he also writes for magazines like the *New Yorker*, has an MFA from NYU, is on the board of the National Book Critics Circle, and works as an assistant professor of creative writing. Although his foray into Goodreads success came slightly before some of these accomplishments, the fact is that he is dipping his toe into mass culture—only because, as far as I can tell, the water there is so warm.

< 96 >

< 97 >

This is also not new. (Nothing is!) Elites have always produced most culture, low- and high- and somehow especially middle-; in the academy, in the Academy, in writers' rooms, in newsrooms, on set, on the bestseller lists, at publishing houses, in the studio, you will find stacks of prestigious degrees, more often than not supported by white-collar parents. The exceptions are pop stars and actors—they have to start too early—but you will often find an encouragingly similar profession in their bloodline. Any suggestion to the contrary is a lie. The possibility of having it both ways, to enjoy the privileges of being an elite while shirking the responsibility of difficulty, seems to seduce many of us. Like the masses, like pretty much everyone, we also want money. "Most of the American novelists in our day are university men," Van Wyck Brooks writes in his 1915 book *America's Coming-of-Age*:

> It is in a spirit of real humility that they set themselves to the composition of richly rewarded trash. . . . it is modesty that lies behind the best-seller . . . And the worst of it is that precisely these writers of immitigable trash are often the bright, vigorous, intuitive souls who *could* make literature out of American life.

* * *

I don't really know why I write criticism. It's difficult and time-consuming to write a book review—much more difficult and time-consuming, per word, than any other kind of writing I do. (Rhyming poetry is the easiest.) It's not the best-paid gig, nor is it the best way to get attention from readers. The audience for book reviews is small. Sometimes I become energized by a feeling that I need to right some discursive wrong being committed by my colleagues when they praise bad books or misunderstand good ones, though I know my reviews change little in terms of sales or popular opinion. Sometimes I feel that I love an author so much that it is an injustice to their work that more people do not read them; I would like to steer even a few readers in their direction, and in order to honor their work I feel it is essential that I do so through careful consideration of its qualities rather than yelling about how it's soooo good. It's probably a bit too much about an illusion of justice for me, really. There's certainly the added benefit of shoring up my sense of myself as someone who cares about such things; no doubt I obnoxiously like being able to say I am a literary critic, even though or because very few people know what that means. Surely there's some relationship between enjoying obscure books and enjoying having an obscure status in the already relatively obscure literary world.

The "drama of opinion" plays a role in the construction of this self-image. When I express an opinion in criticism, I tend not to think of it as "just an opinion"; I think of it as a reasonable conclusion drawn from varieties of evidence. I think it is correct. I think I can see things clearly and anyone who disagrees with me is missing some part of the picture; I think that whatever I may be missing from my interpretation is a matter of articulation, not misunderstanding; I think descriptions of criticism that highlight its subjective nature are defensive maneuvers that allow critics to avoid the consequences of being wrong. (Ultimately, private embarrassment.) I think "Why I'm Right" should be the subtext of any piece of critical writing, balancing as it does subjectivity with objectivity.

I would like to say that dedicating any time or energy to criticism comes from a belief in the importance of art. I fear making this claim would be a bit too valiant for me, so I will cite some other people doing so. In 2019, Martin Scorsese got in trouble when he told *Empire*

< 98 >

magazine that Marvel movies are "not cinema." Here he was operating as a critic, I'd argue; he is undeniably an expert on cinema, and he was critiquing it in this commentary. He went on: "Honestly, the closest I can think of them, as well-made as they are, with actors doing the best they can under the circumstances, is theme parks. It isn't the cinema of human beings trying to convey emotional, psychological experiences to another human being."

Marvel fans and, more important, Marvel employees and independent contractors, were upset. While Francis Ford Coppola echoed Scorsese's sentiments, calling the movies "despicable," Marvel actors and directors and associated business people defended their franchise without acknowledging that the large sums of money these movies pay them and generate were clouding their perspective. They cited the great emotional experiences millions of people enjoyed together while watching the movies, as if to suggest that critics of Marvel are cruelly insulting these millions of people and denying them the legitimacy of their feelings—their *collective* feelings! The Marvel defenders allowed that Martin Scorsese is "entitled" to have an "opinion," being Martin Scorsese, being one of "everyone," but they felt this opinion was "old-fashioned," "sad," and unfair. "I think original content inspires creative content," Captain America said. "I think new stuff is what keeps the creative wheel rolling. I just believe there's room at the table for all of it. It's like saying a certain type of music isn't music. Who are you to say that?"

This dumb question gets to the heart of today's crisis in culture criticism. Who is the director of *Taxi Driver* to say what is and isn't cinema? Who is the director of *Taxi Driver* to say that *millions of people* are wrong?

It is of course true that not all books are literature, not all movies are cinema, and not everything we hang on the wall is art. All music is music, I think—not my area of expertise—but the principle holds: not all music is worth spending any time thinking or talking about. What am I missing? Not all television is *Twin Peaks*. (I'm leaving out forms that can't be widely distributed, which, in this age, don't tend to suffer from or enjoy mass popularity, for some reason.) While it's true that popular forms of entertainment often inspire intense emotional experiences—the swell of ecstasy in the chorus of a pop song, the anticipation at the climax of an action movie, the twinge of romantic recognition in a chick-lit novel—they inspire these intense emotional experiences because they are designed to do so for as many people as possible; they serve the lowest common denominator, emotionally and intellectually, so that they can generate more profit. This is how they trick you: the emotional experience they produce is so intense that it distracts from stilted dialogue, bizarre plotting, a clichéd message. Many people like these things because they are made easy to like.

* * *

The drama around Scorsese's comments was so generative that Scorsese wrote an op-ed about it for the *New York Times*. Unfortunately, he began by walking back his claims. "The fact that the films themselves don't interest me is a matter of personal taste and temperament," he writes. "I know that if I were younger, if I'd come of age at a later time, I might have been excited by these pictures and maybe even wanted to make one myself. But I grew up when I did and I developed a sense of movies—of what they were and what they could be—that was as far from the Marvel universe as we on Earth are from Alpha Centauri." Although he went on to clarify his point that Marvel movies, and the potential for blockbuster success they represent, crowd out independent and arthouse films at theaters—meaning there isn't actually

< 100 >

"room at the table for all of it"—his accommodation to the people with a vested interest in never hearing a bad word about Marvel movies was disappointing, particularly because the bad words do not affect their bottom line.

The bigger concession he makes, though, is to the idea of subjectivity (double meaning): I like what I like, he suggests, because of who I am. He submits to his critics' idea that his expertise is just "an opinion," like an asshole. Because he can't now emphasize that his opinion derives from a particular set of ideas about cinema and art that are based on something outside and beyond himself, he must also submit to the conflation of his opinions with his identity, perfect and complete, essential and thus unassailable. It's about the journey, not the destination. It doesn't matter if some irrefutable piece of evidence counters our gut feeling or an expert in the field reveals the nauseating extent of our narrow-mindedness. An opinion is objectively subjective. It can't be wrong, but it can also never be right.

To reduce appeal to a matter of taste and temperament is the most boring way to be irrefutably correct. Taste and temperament are contingent, of course, but they are also mutable; the same class or cultural background or historical moment will produce radically different people with radically different tastes and temperaments, or could, and people can change their taste and temperament, if they want to. That taste is determined largely by what is available is what's old-fashioned, sad, and unfair. "If people are given only one kind of thing and endlessly sold only one kind of thing," Scorsese writes, "of course they're going to want more of that one kind of thing." Masquerading as egalitarianism and as social justice, popularity constrains and limits, restricts and holds back. It makes people spend thousands of dollars on concert tickets and waste countless hours on stupid websites. It disguises an entitlement—to think—as entitlement. For my money, there are few things more fulfilling than encountering a difficult text, film, or work of art and then spending some time thinking about it, discussing it, and uncovering the meaning in it. I pity people who resist this difficulty and who argue that it is not for everyone. It is, or rather could be. There are lifetimes' worth of wonderful, difficult, strange, and unclassifiable books, essays, films, recordings, performances, and images online, available for free or very cheap. One can go down the ladder, making excuses: Some people don't have reliable internet connections. People who work all day are tired and just want to relax in front of unimaginably dumb movies. They're not wrong to do so. But still: I'm right.

< 102 >

WHY DO YOU LIVE HERE?

n 2013, an astronaut on the International Space Station tweeted a striking image of contemporary Berlin, which is encircled by a train line called the Ringbahn and divided down its approximate, shaky middle by what used to be the Berlin Wall. Though the Wall came down in 1989, the astronaut's photograph shows an enduring contrast between West Berlin's bright white fluorescent streetlights and East Berlin's yellow sodium-vapor streetlights; it's striking because, well, lights. At night on a top-floor balcony along the Maybachufer in Kreuzberg, near the former border, one can see a similar difference—not just because of the streetlights but also because of density and urbanization, which are not unhistorical but which are nevertheless less dazzling to contemplate. Regardless: look west and it's bright; look east and it's dark. It is hard to accept that this is the present moment you're looking at—the present moment in the West being, in my mind, so homogenized, so easy, so organized by unfortunate design. Thus, when you can, it's nice to pretend that you are not seeing long-term effects or political consequences or the ways history tends to live on materially but that you are actually, somehow, looking at the authentic past. You can see history, walk through it, if not—once you

< 103 >

go back inside to your laptop that is also your workspace, to stream music and television algorithmically served to you—actually live it. Berlin is a great place to do this.

That image of Berlin recurs and makes the rounds periodically, the way images on the internet do. Someone will save the image and post it themselves, not acknowledging the original source; someone will save the image from that person and post it, not acknowledging the secondary source, not knowing the original source; et cetera, et cetera; the crowd oohs and ahs. Demographically illustrative maps and aerial photographs do well on social media; they are how I tell myself I have effectively severed my linguistic ties to the American state where I'm from and how I know the most popular genre of porn watched there in 2021 was "BBW." Like most things on social media, these maps and photographs are not exactly the last word. On the ground, walking through the city, the most obvious difference between former East and West Berlin is not in streetlights but in public transportation: in the former East—or *The Recent East*, as the title of a 2021 novel had it—they kept the tram system that West Berlin eliminated in favor of buses, subways, and, as the German car lobby anticipated, cars. The practical result of the divide is that when biking in former East Berlin—which extends all the way to the now hip part of the city center, where you can buy overpriced Scandinavian pastries and reasonably priced Scandinavian fast fashion—one must be aware of getting stuck in tram tracks, which are slightly wider than a bicycle tire.

If you are, like me, an American, you might never have lived in a city with a tram or a city hospitable to cyclists, so the experience of getting your bicycle stuck in tram tracks might be totally unfamiliar and thus not robustly convey the metaphor that I'm about to use

< 105 >

it to convey.* So I will first say that it's terrifying, both because you will probably immediately fall and because once you are falling you are in danger of being hit by a car or a quaintly historical tram. The experience of falling because you are suddenly stationary is also an atypical one; the initial moment of confusion gives way to a kind of cartoonish realization that lends itself to humiliated revisits in the mind (if you survive). Okay, so here's the metaphor. The clichés of Anglophone writing about Berlin are like this: you might be thinking nonstop about maneuvering at a strong enough angle to avoid getting stuck, and then somehow you find yourself explaining that the place "has always been a city of exiles." There's just not a lot of space available for you to ride freely. Berlin not having the international reputation of, say, Paris—toward which I don't even need to gesture with a couple of nicely chosen details in order for any reader to understand what I mean when I say "Paris"—the German capital requires a little background. (The clichés would have me refer to it at least once as *die Hauptstadt*, and soon.) One feels compelled to repeat the basic political and cultural tidbits so that everyone can get a sense for the place despite either having never been there or having once had a middling time in the wrong part of town, eating sausage near the Reichstag and looking quietly at the Holocaust memorial, making a quick stop on the way to Amsterdam or Munich or Prague.

Per the two-days-here, three-days-there whirlwind European tourist's estimation, Berlin is an acquired taste, a city you either love or hate, "ugly" compared to other cities in Europe, or a place that "you really need to know someone who lives there" to enjoy. An essay for this tourist begins like this: Did you know the city is built on

---

* An Irish friend once insisted that Boston was known as the Europe of the United States. "They have a tram!" she exclaimed over our laughter. Anyone who has been to Boston will know why this is funny. What's disturbing is that *she has been there, too.*

sand? That there exists here a world-famous techno club, Berghain, that is so revered it might be thought of as a cathedral or religious temple, so that waiting in the famously long line to be scrutinized by famously difficult and inscrutable bouncers is a kind of holy ritual? That dancing might also be thought of as a ritual (and is, obviously, ecstatic), and so might be taking drugs (Ecstatic)? That in 1919 Rosa Luxemburg was drowned in the Landwehr Canal, and in 1939 Christopher Isherwood published *Goodbye to Berlin*? That they sell this dish called currywurst, which no one eats, and operate in the German language, which no one speaks? That the city is full of "ghosts"? That the rents are cheap and the culture, long attractive to artists and indeed exiles, is one of freedom and experimentation?

Have I crashed yet? No, I'm still going. Beneath this googleable surface is another layer—the elusive expertise one gets from a month-long stay, from return visits during the high highs of summer; the fact that people, a certain kind of people, want to come back, to fuel the clichéd narrative that Berlin once was going and now is, following this steady stream of dabbling arrivals, "over." Still, we have smoking indoors, drinking outdoors, *Ostalgie*, Club-Mate. No one jaywalks, though the WALK signals are way too short. There is a fundamental difference between Berghain and Panorama Bar, which is upstairs, and "lab," which is where the gay sex parties take place. A rented bike; a friend who lives in Neukölln; a friend who DJs at . . . is it called Renate? "One of the few remaining squats in the city." The moody, lyrical vocabulary words that seem to come most easily to those who can't otherwise order a beer in the local language: *Fernweh, Heimweh, Fremdschämen*. No one works. Everyone is queer. Sudanese falafel, which comes with peanut sauce. High ceilings and hardwood floors, with a balcony, sublet from an academic on a fellowship or sabbatical. It is a place that welcomes part-timers, undecideds, com-

< 107 >

mitment phobes, and, yes, artists. You can get a good idea of its reputation from the slogans these kinds of people include in their "Why I Came to / Left Berlin" essays, published by the *Guardian*: "poor but sexy," coined in 2003 by the former mayor Klaus Wowereit; "if you can't make it here you can't make it anywhere," which I saw printed on a drawstring backpack in the gift shop of an art gallery sponsored by Deutsche Bank. Inevitably, in the past few years a new one has crept into the conclusions of the trend pieces and overwrought op-eds: "But all that is changing."

*　*　*

Like many people who live here, I moved to Berlin for no good reason, and I have no good excuse to stay. I mean "good" according to the terms of ostensible necessity, according to principles that eliminate a wide range of life options and narrow them down to what must be done, painfully or not. I came for no job, no love I imagined would last especially long, no family, no academic program or dubious arts residency, no arbitrary yet burning desire to learn the language or understand the culture developed in some would-be forgettable moment in childhood that in retrospect can be seen as consequential. I did not happen to have a best friend with German parents who instilled in me a fascination with spaetzle; I did not study German in college and find myself unexpectedly good at it and increasingly attracted to the silly culture. In expats' answers to the question "Why do you live here?" there's often a watery and confusing moment of revelation in the past, a random visit that became a turning point: "I just really liked it," they often say, "and I wanted to come back." But I didn't even have that. I had a bunch of people telling me how good it was. I can't remember whether I believed them. They all rolled their own cigarettes. None of them spoke German.

**NO
JUDGMENT**

The following story is necessary, but I warn you its conclusion will be dissatisfying; you will finish it probably still not understanding why I live here. The first time I moved to Berlin was for a reason that is neither bad nor good but interesting: I came here for a few days while studying abroad in London, at age twenty, and fell in love with my pub crawl tour guide. (If you can believe it: I didn't want to go on the pub crawl, which was as uncool as I imagined it would be, but my friends made me.) An aspiring writer, in possession of a thrilling British accent, the guide taught me that Berlin was very cheap, that it was very fun, and that it would be a good place to work on one's writing without having to get a full-time job. I was shown around enthusiastically, to bars and very cheap restaurants and abandoned places that in other, richer cities would have been turned into banks or expensive apartments long before. ("Berlin is so abandoned," my boyfriend guide would repeat. Explaining why would fall into the cliché category, but basically because a lot of it was destroyed during World War II and then because it was divided into two cities until 1989.) I went back to the US with a long-distance, hilariously employed British boyfriend; a plan developed that I would finish school and then move to Berlin, taking advantage of the city's cheap rent and Germany's unique "artist visa" scheme, which genuinely does feel like a scheme, as in something naughty, when you apply.[†] When I arrived to live there, at twenty-two, I had been to the city twice, for a total of about fourteen days; my only other experience in Germany was a disastrous trip to Munich during which I drank four liters of

---

† After two months of interviews, I finally got a room in an apartment with two German girls who wanted to practice their English; it cost 242 euros per month, all bills included. My boyfriend and I found the extra two euros "sweet," even though at the time I also mentally measured prices by the average cost of a falafel sandwich, which was €2.50.

< 109 >

beer and came to in a bottom bunk belonging to a shiny-faced guy who went on, per Facebook, to become a management consultant. What did I even know about World War II? I have no idea what I knew about it, much less the one before that. What did I know about the Berlin Wall?

I also didn't know that I was part of another kind of cultural tradition associated with the city: to be young, to come here, to go to raves, to take drugs, to hang out. Before my arrival I had taken Ecstasy once, and I had reacted with what I now know is a classic response, in that I purported not to feel anything as I expressed my deep and special appreciation for the people around me; you could say I didn't even know I'd taken it. If I'd known that I was doing what many people had also unknowingly done, I probably wouldn't have gone. In his 2013 essay "City of Rumor: The Compulsion to Write About Berlin," Gideon Lewis-Kraus writes that Berlin "had come to represent a place where nobody got up in the morning, and when they did get up it was with some reservations about the prospect of the day." Robert Walser had a more generous reading in 1910, and it's a relief to feel that it still rings true: "A city like Berlin is an ill-mannered, impertinent, intelligent scoundrel, constantly affirming the things that suit him and tossing aside everything he tires of. . . . An artist here has no choice but to pay attention . . . he must constantly pull himself together as a human being, and this compulsion encircling him redounds to his advantage."

Regardless of the emphasis—to be honest, both interpretations sound right to me—again, I had no idea. I also had no idea that in unsuspectingly participating in this tradition, speaking English to my English-speaking friends while walking around the streets of my cool, affordable, and thus gentrifying neighborhood, I would become the representation of everything that threatened to put a stop to it. Here's what I knew about "expats": the summer before I moved to

Berlin, a man told my friend, who told me, that until you figure out what you're doing with your life and where you want to live, "expatriate communities tend to be better educated, and more interesting, than what you will find in your home country." I knew about Paris in the 1920s, vaguely, but I didn't particularly aspire to that, because, as you might have guessed, I found any kind of too-specific lifestyle aspiration embarrassing. Besides, there was no real way to twist what I was doing into live intellectual history. Without the presence of an overwhelming number of—key word here—*working* intellectuals and artists, cliqued, I could not imagine that my life was remotely similar to that of Hemingway et al., though there was a short-lived writing group that became slightly incestuous and then disbanded. (My boyfriend was in it, too.) I organized a reading series and had emotional moments in the street, once throwing a beer bottle in tearful frustration. But this did not a romantic existence make.

I have since learned what's been going on and what I've been doing here for all these years. The expatriate lifestyle is understood as an extended visit that either ends in a penniless, tail-between-legs retreat or becomes legitimized by any number of "real" pursuits, including but not limited to the purchase of property, the acquisition of a native lover, and the learning of the local language, which as a native English speaker with a freelance income sourced from elsewhere or from an international company that operates in English, you do not have to learn but should if you want to feel like you "really live" here. Until at least one of these conditions is met, life is conditional; though not all expats who live this way are young, there's a sense that they will someday have to grow up: figure out what they're doing with their lives and where they want to live. They are hesitant to acquire furniture or books, worried about having to sell them off if and when they leave, even if that won't happen for years. They are hesitant to make friends,

< 111 >

real friends, because all the friends they might and want to make, like-minded people in similar life stages, are like-minded people in similar life stages, wondering if they're just in a phase, looking at the door (the Google flight tracker).

I left suddenly after about two years, because I was miserable. I was irrationally terrified of running out of money and having no recourse due to the work restrictions on my visa. I found the poetry readings unbearable and learning German torturously boring. It was often very dark and cold. I needed to seek my fortune in the country of my birth, where fortune-seeking is not seen as suspicious but rather part of the point. I probably said I hated it here, and meant it.

But almost as soon as I got back to the US—New York—I tried to legitimize a return to Germany. I applied for a popular fellowship to study for one of these English-language master's degrees at Berlin universities that people will do primarily in order to get a visa, and I got the feedback that I had received an 8.7 on the committee's assessment of my application when I needed an 8.9 to win the fellowship. Every few emails to my ex, now a best friend, would have some line about wanting to move back to Berlin. ("I feel so insanely EMOTIONAL about Berlin!!!!" I wrote in the summer of 2018.) I kept getting New York–based boyfriends, and I wanted to see how things would go with them. Meanwhile, we or I would go back to visit Berlin for weeks or months at a time, and I would run into acquaintances from my past who would express confusion about whether I lived there or not.‡

---

‡ "Berlin is a village" is another cliché, though I've mainly heard it applied to my neighborhood, Neukölln. Recently I received a string of texts at 1:30 in the morning: at a spot along the strip of cool bars that at least one newspaper article has (ironically) called Neukölln's "Riviera," a friend had spotted the man with whom I was fighting or possibly breaking up. My friend dutifully reported the details of their conversation: boring, boring, boring. Then he came back with a gem: "Oh . . . he dyed half his hair black? Don't know if you knew about that." I did not.

How is such a casual lifestyle possible? Am I secretly rich? Since 2016 I haven't had a "real job," meaning I work freelance and almost exclusively online; when I came to Berlin for extended periods, I would sublet my apartment in Brooklyn and save money on the trade-off, even including the cost of a plane ticket. I can, like many members of my milieu, live anywhere, or become a "digital nomad," flitting around from international tech hub to international tech hub, taking my Instagram photos, patronizing Australian cafés. Logistics are the gateway to freedom, and freedom is impossible to waste. Finally, at the end of 2021, I shipped all my stuff here.

I'm telling you all this just so you know whom you're talking to: someone who is part of a group. I was born a citizen of the country where, legendarily, huddled masses and wretched refuse immigrated to seek better lives for themselves and their families; I have, as a citizen of that historical best place, easy access to countries where, now, life is much better. I will never tire of seeing the uncomprehending European blink when I explain that in the US a ride in an ambulance costs, on average, $1,200, often with insurance. (In Houston, 100 percent of ambulance rides are out-of-network.) Sometimes they will send a fire truck with the ambulance, just because; that costs money, too. I could probably have made it work in the US, but I didn't want to. It is nice to go to the dentist and not worry the expense will require the sacrifice of future vacations. It is nice to live in a culture in which taking multiple vacations per year isn't considered suspect. It is nice to walk around the village, to drink a beer in the middle of the day. It is nice that no one works, or that everyone works in bizarre, unfollowable patterns and is available to meet you for beers in the middle of the day. That none of these are seen as good enough reasons is what defines the group I'm in. "We're

< 113 >

not teenagers who left in search of frontier gold, and even if we grow sick with loneliness, as happened to Old West pioneers, no one's going to point out the distance we came," writes Claudia Durastanti, an Italian-American writer who moved to the UK, in her 2022 book *Strangers I Know*.

> No one's going to point out that my friends and I moved to England and died two thousand kilometers from where we grew up, and why might that be? Perhaps because we weren't driven by pioneer winds, didn't conquer any wastelands . . . because we settled down in already overcrowded cities and worked near the dwellings where we slept in the humidity and incomprehension of the owners, these western outposts marked on a map in search of our kind . . . because, for many of us, our leaving wasn't really necessary or all that hard.

Durastanti is right: the vestigial sense that relocation should be "necessary," and therefore difficult, still inspires inappropriate compare-contrasts between free-roaming "expats" (or "digital nomads") and immigrants. But then she gets caught in the tracks, falls over. "After Brexit, expats became immigrants like all the rest; some consider themselves stateless, others, exiles," she continues. "To feel more elegant, we define ourselves as strangers."

It's tempting for anyone writing about expatriation and migration in the twenty-first century to conflate the various groups who engage in it, to make a political point. I once had a conversation with an American who insisted on calling herself a "migrant" to Germany; she was here on a postdoctoral fellowship, which she got using her PhD from an Ivy League university. A popular rhetorical question to ask in these circles is, "Why are some people called expats and others immigrants?"[§] The question is supposed to expose the racist lie at the center of the distinction; the idea is that brown people are called immigrants and white people, expats, and that by calling everyone the same thing we can build solidarity and highlight the injustice of a legal system that allows some people to enter while others are violently turned away. As if denying the radical difference in situation would help change it whatsoever; as if the pro forma paperwork I had to fill out to get a visa as an American freelance "artist" links me to someone who almost died getting here and must follow strict rules in order to stay. (To say nothing of the postdocs, who have administrators to help them fill out the paperwork.) Really, the semantic distinction exposes the truth of the world; it is rich people—and here I mean rich in options, rich in ways to be stable, if you want to take advantage of them—who are called expats and poor people who are called immigrants. Expats can choose, immigrants must choose; expats can leave, immigrants intend to stay. Generally, this corresponds to race, but not necessarily: think of all the delivery trucks

---

§ "Refugee" is a legal distinction; according to the 1951 Refugee Convention, a refugee is "someone who is unable or unwilling to return to their country of origin owing to a well-founded fear of being persecuted for reasons of race, religion, nationality, membership of a particular social group, or political opinion." An "asylum-seeker" is someone seeking refugee status or asylum (another legal term). "Migrant" is not a legal category but rather an umbrella term that can refer to anyone who moves, domestically or internationally, temporarily or permanently. My irritation with the postdoc's insistence on describing herself as a "migrant" is technically incorrect but spiritually, I think (obviously), right. In common parlance, "migrant" suggests struggle and urgency, as in the European "migration crisis," precisely because people who apply for legal refugee status and are not granted it are often forced to leave the countries to which have attempted to migrate. The word implies this struggle: the struggle to become legal, to find a place. The term "lifestyle migrant," which according to the 2009 academic paper "Migration and the Search for a Better Way of Life: A Critical Exploration of Lifestyle Migration" by Michaela Benson and Karen O'Reilly covers figures such as the "residential tourist," the "rural idyll seeker," and the bourgeois bohemian and is more appropriate for people like me and my postdoc enemy.

< 115 >

that went undriven in the UK because the Eastern Europeans who drove them had bureaucratic problems after Brexit. (Many European liberals experienced *schadenfreude* when learning of the empty shelves in British grocery stores.) We are here because we want to be, in other words, and might not even miss where we came from. Just because we could have it better doesn't mean we have it bad.

* * *

The traditional insult to lob at an expat being obnoxious—by speaking English loudly or German poorly, by wearing clothes that look too clean or too put together, by expressing uncool wonderment at some obvious phenomenon or landmark that one should really know about already, by being in some way entitled—is not that he is a migrant but that he is a "tourist." In the May 2022 issue of the "multi-lingual street journal" *Arts of the Working Class*, which is distributed internationally and based in Berlin, a short essay on Venice and the art world was called "If It's Called the Tourist Season, Why Can't We Hunt Them?" A footnote establishes that the title of the piece is an "appropriation" of an iconic piece of Barcelona graffiti: "Why call it the tourist season if we can't shoot them?" After Venice, the Catalan city has become an epicenter of the tension between tourism and local life. During the pandemic, the absence of tourism revenue hurt economies—more than two hundred businesses in the center of Barcelona closed between March and September 2020—but refreshed locals (provided they didn't lose their jobs). "Tourism had eaten up all of the public space and relegated us locals to a role of extras on a set," one resident of Barcelona's Gothic Quarter told *TIME* in 2021, echoing Elizabeth Bishop's 1965 poem "Questions of Travel": "Should we have stayed at home and thought of here? / Where should we be today? / Is it right to be watching strangers in a play / in this strangest of theatres?" The Gothic Quarter resident had lived in the neighborhood his entire life, but he no longer enjoyed hanging out there. Tourists don't patronize the kinds of venues locals enjoy in town—often because tourists don't know about them, and locals don't want tourists to know about them, because their annoying presence would ruin their spots—and tourists also drive up rents by insisting on staying in expensive Airbnbs, which, absent strict regulation, are more profitable to operate than renting the same apartment to locals at market rates, no matter how soaring. What's more, tourists harsh the vibe. They stand, obnoxiously, in the middle of the sidewalk, it used to be looking up at the tall buildings, now looking at their horrible cell phones, in a way that is somehow different from the way that locals stand in the middle of the sidewalk looking at their horrible cell phones. Tourists are free, briefly, from responsibility, both in their lives and to others. "These Tourists!" represent "that moping Son of Idleness," as Wordsworth writes in his 1800 poem "The Brothers," "some glance along / Rapid and gay, as if the earth were air / And they were butterflies to wheel about / Long as the summer lasted."

What most people want in life is to be able to do what they want, and the groups who can accomplish this are naturally resented and treated with suspicion. As a creative young professional in a changing city, with no job and few local ties, with incomes from other countries, I am not so different from a tourist. While I like to think I'm unobtrusive, savvy, and cosmopolitan—while I know where the cool bars are and have many friends and acquaintances in town—I also remain unburdened by necessity. The desire to seek out "our kind" looks ridiculous compared to war or the need to provide for a family.

But Durastanti's examples aren't about wars or famines; they're about colonization. The historical pioneers with whom she contrasts

< 116 >

< 117 >

herself and her friends are nothing like the migrants in Europe today. Two interpretations beckon: (1) (more generous) Because today's millennial "migrants" are not charting new territory and thus
making something they at least believe will be new and better for the
world, they are frivolous. (2) (less generous) There is a way expats are
colonizing our new homes, shaping them in the image of what the
writer Vincenzo Latronico calls, in his 2024 novel *Perfection*, a generation's "identical struggle for a different life." The cafés that cater to
freelancers, the identical meaningless job titles at identical pointless
start-ups, the midcentury furniture, the monstera plants, the "Yoga
in English" advertisements. Despite our infamous economic precariousness, we do go to bars and restaurants, a lot. The bars and restaurants we like tend to look a certain way and cost a certain amount.

But—and this is a genuine question, not rhetorical—is it really
our fault? Because of our visibility, expats and "residential tourists"
are said to be responsible for things for which we simply cannot be
responsible due to the smallness of our cohort, at least half of which
includes graduate students (and postdocs) who can barely decide what
to wear each day, much less destroy an otherwise flourishing European
metropolis. Nevertheless, it is often said to be our fault: rising rents
(expats will pay way above market rates to be done with the whole
charade of the global housing crisis, since the rent here is so much
cheaper than back home); the proliferation of annoying cafés, deco-
rated in a bland, possibly Scandinavian style;⁵ the hearing of English

---

⁵ In 2016, the writer Kyle Chayka termed this "strange geography created by technology" "AirSpace": "the realm of coffee shops, bars, startup offices, and co-live / work
spaces that share the same hallmarks everywhere you go: a profusion of symbols of
comfort and quality, at least to a certain connoisseurial mindset. Minimalist furniture.
Craft beer and avocado toast. Reclaimed wood. Industrial lighting. Cortados. Fast
internet. The homogeneity of these spaces means that traveling between them is fric-
tionless."

everywhere and consequent dilution of the local language; eventually, the strollers blocking the sidewalk.** To combat this bad reputation as an English-speaking expat, you must graciously make small talk with any stranger who approaches you outside a convenience store or bakery, even if they are so drunk that they keep telling you about their son who lives in Kansas but doesn't like it. You must do so in the language they expect of you: bad English if they want to practice, functional German if they don't. You must not open a café, a bar, a natural wine store, or combination café / bar / natural wine store. Though it is understood that Germans barely tip, an American accent makes a promise: the service staff know you come from the land of tipping, and they probably have at least once been there and had to tip waiters themselves, so you have to tip them relatively generously, because your presence there is contributing to the slow Americanization of their culture, meaning that your presence means that one day everyone will have to tip them.

A sticker I've been seeing around Berlin recently reads, "TOURISTS GO HOME EXCEPT ME." The ironic hypocrisy of this mantra points a finger at any number of targets—most of whom probably don't pay local taxes—but also implies the truism driving the conflict between tourist and resident: travel is nice and, when done well, promotes all those warm liberal values that counteract racism, nationalism, and xenophobia. Residents of one place are (almost always) tourists elsewhere; it is a core tenet of social democratic politics that working people need vacations. While we may encourage, for environmental reasons, the taking of trains and the exploration of our "own

---

** In Germany, parents are entitled to a government allowance for up to twelve months after a child is born—*Elterngeld*, or parent money—and are offered guaranteed childcare and parental leave. Americans who want to have children say it would be foolish to move back to the States before taking advantage of that.

< 118 >

< 119 >

backyard," we also live in a globalized, mediated society in which people are constantly looking at pictures of Thailand, and it makes them want to go to Thailand, for not entirely impure reasons. (Another German compound word that English speakers like is *Flugscham*, which comes from the Swedish *flygskam*, meaning "flight shame.") While there are many ways to be a good tourist—responsible, unobtrusive, positively impacting, possibly even participating in some kind of fruitful cultural exchange—most people are not. In Barcelona, a 2021 ad campaign attempted to attract "high-quality" tourists—those who patronize what we might call "authentic" businesses; who participate in the "local lifestyle," whatever that is; who are not interested in merely taking their pictures and saying they were there.

I will admit, shamefully, that, like a dating app user, I love to travel, and that part of the reason I like living in Berlin is that it's in the middle of Europe and therefore very easy to temporarily leave. I do not love to travel because I like seeing sights; I love it because I like (the illusion of) really *being* somewhere new. When I arrive in a new place, the rituals are well established: buy a cultural pastry; take it to the top of the local hill, from which you can imagine you've experienced the entire place; consider and then reject the idea of visiting another cathedral; get a drink instead; think, *I could live here.*

Berlin seems to convert that thought to action more than most cities—because of its flexibility, its amenability, its adaptability, its ease—and this encourages the lifestyle migrants. Why? It's boring to say it's the cheap rents, but it's mostly the cheap rents. Although they are famously rising, living in Berlin remains much more affordable than in Paris, London, New York, etcetera. The groceries are cheaper, a meal in a restaurant is cheaper, a drink at a bar is cheaper. There is a robust culture of vintage, reselling, and thrifting. Health insurance is expensive, but you don't have to pay much if you don't earn much, and unlike American health insurance, it actually covers things. The wealthy are around but not ostentatious. The arts are publicly supported.

The ease is not actually just about cost and policy, though that's a big part of it; it's also about language and culture. Another thing people often say about Berlin is that it's "not really Germany." They mean that any grand ideas you have about *Germany* as a concept do not really apply. "What is the reason for your visit to Germany, and how long do you plan to stay?" Walter Abish writes, quoting a common question asked at customs, at the beginning of his 1980 novel *How German Is It*.

> To admire Germany's remaining castles, churches, cathedrals . . . a day or two attending one of a number of Wagner or Beethoven music festivals, and once there, with the Bavarian mountains providing a scenic backdrop, several hours reclining on the sweet-smelling grass while listening to the heavenly music. Then there are the Dürers, Cranachs, and the works of Holbein the Younger. . . . They also come to visit the grave of Goethe and to walk in a German forest and absorb that spiritual attachment to nature that underlies all things German.

This is emphatically not why people come to Berlin. I've tossed around the "not really Germany" line when I need to quickly explain to someone that, if they want to visit me, they shouldn't expect castles or forests or fine arts, and that if we spend several hours reclining on the sweet-smelling grass while listening to heavenly music, it will be at an open-air rave, and we will be on drugs. What I gain in expediency, I lose in depth. The American analog, a political strategy deployed by both the right and far left, is the rubric by which New York

< 120 >

< 121 >

City is not the "real America," despite being home to more Americans than anywhere else in the country; rather, the "real America" is Cleveland, or better yet Akron, or better still my home state, West Virginia. The logic goes: only the shittiest parts of the country, with the most stereotypical people, are the real thing. Thus, the only "real" part of Germany is a satellite Oktoberfest celebration in the Ruhrgebiet. Similarly, Munich is as German as Los Angeles is American—that is, aberrantly so, yet very. But why anyone would want to see, or "experience," the "real America" is as confusing to me as why anyone would want to experience the "real Germany"; the way outsiders affect and influence a place is much more "real" than isolation.

* * *

There is an ostensibly clear way to distinguish between a tourist and a resident or between a tourist and a legitimate visitor. Conventional wisdom says that you should of course learn the language of the country where you live, in order to participate in its culture and politics. In practice, this isn't a good enough reason. As Xiaolu Guo writes in her 2020 novel *A Lover's Discourse*, English is "always in the atmosphere like pollen from the plants permeating the air, whereas German was like a specific mountain in the landscape which you had to have a particular ambition to climb." The point of learning a language is to appreciate the beauty of a foreign literature, film, or the language itself—to enjoy the surplus pleasure of language learning, in other words. Or you learn it to get around. But in Berlin, as in many European capitals (even Paris), "everyone speaks English." There is no pressure to learn the local language, particularly if you are secure in yourself, or entitled, or not easily humiliated by mishaps that take place in quotidian interactions with people you will never see again. Lydia Davis expresses the entwined senses of responsibility and pointlessness that torment the German language learner in her short 2020 poem "Improving My German":

> All my life I have been trying to improve my German.
> At last my German is better
> —but now I am old and ill and don't have long to live.
> Soon I will be dead,
> with better German.

The poem's humor is driven home by the fact that this is it, in its entirety: the result of improving your German is that you will speak better German. Whether this is worth the pain it causes is unclear. "I heard a Californian student in Heidelberg say, in one of his calmest moods, that he would rather decline two drinks than one German adjective," writes Mark Twain in his 1880 essay "The Awful German Language." He laments the words "so long that they have a perspective" as well as "the similarities of look and sound between words which have no similarity in meaning." In group German classes, participants will express a frustration so deep it is as if they do not understand why they are there, at a round table under fluorescent lights, being asked, they're not totally sure, what their hobbies are. It seems everyone resists learning German by reverting to their own nationalistic stereotypes, attempting to differentiate themselves from the language by any means possible. I once took an intermediate intensive German course, which met for four hours a day, five days a week. My fellow classmates included an Italian couple who had moved to Berlin to open a pizza restaurant; a Bulgarian graduate student in philosophy who multiple times attempted to insert conjugations of the word *ficken* (to fuck) into his responses to our oral (ha ha) exercises; an Egyptian who worked at a cell phone store and was constantly trying to sell us plans and data;

< 123 >

and an extremely competent Canadian woman who had moved to Berlin with her musician boyfriend and often offered to share her snacks with me. The Italian husband frequently interrupted his Italian wife to correct her, regret her lack of skills, or speak on her behalf; I spoke out of turn, made it worse by falsely and overenthusiastically attempting to help the Italian wife find her words in a nicer and brighter way than her harsh husband, and sounded, surely, like a character on a television show all these people shouldn't feel compelled to watch but do. I thought private lessons might better accommodate my unique learning style—irritable—so for about a year during the pandemic I took private German lessons over Zoom with a cheerful socialist named Bernd. I felt I was constantly disappointing him. I never had anything to talk about. At some point I asked him how to say "to make a friend." "We don't really do that," he replied.

Death and murder pervade Twain's essay; Twain often proposes that the inventor of various unthinkable patterns or rules or exceptions to rules in German should be killed. I'm not so extreme, but I understand the existential quandaries that arise. If I find myself overwhelmed by the impossibility of lining up all the little grammatical endings the language requires and doubting that all the young savvy Germans I see every day really speak with such pointless precision, I cycle through some emotions: first doubt, then anger, then despair. The meaninglessness of suffering! Though my German is adequate, I still find myself in a shop or bar and totally perplexed by a recurring crisis: Is it possible that there is an infinite variety of ways to order a coffee in English? Yes, of course. In your native language you often mutter, misspeak, attempt a joke, fail. In English, I once asked a barista if we could "discuss the sandwiches." My pronunciation, challenged by the varieties of English I hear every day, slides into Britishisms or into an awkward pretentious overenunciating compensation for my native Appalachian drawl. If I say the name of my profession, *writer*, naturally, I sound like a redneck if my interlocutor knows what rednecks sound like. More often, I sound as if I am someone who rides.

But okay: How is my German? You want to know this for some reason; maybe because you want to imagine moving here yourself but can't imagine yourself performing the accent. At various points over the past six months I have described my German skills as "not bad," "okay," "decent," "decent and getting better all the time," "fine," "terrible," "bad," "B2/C1," "B2ish," "B2," "C1," B1," "good!," "nicht perfekt," "fucked up," "on pause," and "lamentable."†† Also, just now, "adequate." I have responded to the question "Do you speak German?" with "Yes," "Sort of," "Not well," "Not well but not bad either," "More or less," "As well as I need to," and "I don't know." If I were a graduate student, I could follow the advice I've heard: "if you can read a menu in the language then you can put it on your CV." But I'm not a graduate student, and I have no CV. My ability to speak hangs on my mood, my level of inebriation, and the extent to which I have been speaking the language already. My confidence has an inverse relationship to the attractiveness of my interlocutor; I am worst at speaking German with fellow Anglophones who are fluent, whom I also can't seem to stop going out with. "Get a German lover," everyone says, as if German men aren't notorious for never moving in to kiss women they have been dating for months. A boyfriend, a native Polish speaker, explained that he improved his German by going on Tinder dates with natives and pretending not to speak English. He said his dates found him very annoying. Unfortunately, although I don't know why I came here, I know it wasn't to be annoying.

---

†† The letter-number combinations refer to the Common European Framework of Reference for Languages, the European standard for determining language proficiency.

< 125 >

I also did not come here to be stupid, but speaking German, I am. While the literal translation of words and phrases from the German can illuminate the logic of the language or help you remember vocabulary words, it doesn't really help you manage moments of communication breakdown. You cannot figure out how to say "turtle" in German by free-associating until you arrive at "shield-toad" unless you are a creative genius. (And even then, you'd have to know the German words for "shield" and "toad.") You can, sometimes, arrive at the German word for something by pronouncing the English word in a German accent. (I really need, for example, *eine Routine.*) My success rate on this is about 50 percent. In quick moments of incomprehension involving slurred speech, mumbling, or a strangely breathy delivery, it is impossible to tell whether someone is not speaking clearly or you don't know the words they're saying; speak with an accent, and they assume it's the latter. Why does it matter if they know you know the words they're saying?

The humiliation of being corrected on a misused word or strange pronunciation is more instructive than any flashcard could be, but I refuse to risk such missteps, though when the tables are turned, as they often are, speaking to Germans in English turns up delight after delight. My enjoyment of English as a second language, or ESL, is not, I think and hope, patronizing, but rather an appreciation of a relationship to English that I could not as a native speaker mimic. "My brain functions like a pierced sponge bag," says Malka, the French-speaking subject of Alice Gregory's 2016 essay "In the Shadow of Geneva Eating Dry Bread." She is describing pregnancy. "I look left when cars are coming from right, put my toothpastes in the fridge, forget lunches scheduled with friends." Even technically correct English sentences take on a cheering verve when we know they're spoken by this totally fluent, non-native, presumably accented character: "The last witch was burned about one second ago in Switzerland," Malka says. "I should look it up. It is such a primitive country. Fondue? That is the most complex dish we have." When speaking English, Germans will often use the present progressive tense incorrectly, as in "since five years I am living here," because they don't have a present progressive tense and like to try it out. That usage of "since" is a direct translation of the way they convey the continuous past: "seit fünf Jahren wohne ich hier." (In speech, they use what we call the present perfect—I have lived here—to convey the past tense.) It's all very, and I mean this is the most respectful way, cute. But I, the hegemon, will never seem cute speaking incorrectly the languages I have in some way forced into minority status. The best I can do is keep quiet and occasionally demonstrate surprising capability due to lowered expectations.

The ambiguity and distance literal speechlessness allows can be seductive, as Ben Lerner makes clear in his 2011 novel *Leaving the Atocha Station*. The narrator, Adam Gordon, is an American living in Madrid on a Fulbright fellowship conducting a possibly romantic relationship with a woman named Isabel. He tells the reader in many different and funny ways—though he's not a reliable narrator on this topic—that he's not great at Spanish. While this creates supreme anxiety for him, he also makes it work. "Isabel assigned profound meaning, assigned a plurality of possible profound meanings, to my fragmentary speech, intuiting from those fragments depths of insight and latent eloquence, and because she projected what she thought she discovered, she experienced, I liked to think, an intense affinity for the workings of my mind." Their "most intense and ostensibly intimate interactions were the effect of her imbuing my silences, the gaps out of which my Spanish was primarily composed, with tremendous intellectual and aesthetic force."

In other words, the best part of their relationship was the way

< 126 >

they imagined they might be communicating, and the projections go both ways. Adam's inability to understand a seemingly tragic story Isabel tells him in Spanish renders it all the more poignant: "I formed several possible stories out of her speech, formed them at once, so it was less like I failed to understand than that I understood in chords, understood in a plurality of worlds." But he is also, naturally, alienated by these dynamics; imagination does not a life make, and a sense of unreality hovers over everything the expat does. In Madrid, he is a smoker; he promises himself he will stop smoking as soon as he leaves. But will he leave? Or will he become a smoker? Can he "live away from my family and language permanently, even if I could work out the logistics"? His anxieties—about not working, yes, but also about having no "profound" connection to his work and life, which then leads to anxieties about the weird lies he tells about his life and the work he's not "really" doing—are fears about becoming something new, maybe, but also about needing to "renew contact with the reality of my life." His anxiety about not experiencing poetry or art "profoundly" echoes his anxiety about not experiencing the "authentic Spain," which he "only defined negatively as an American-free space." "I tended to find lines of poetry beautiful only when I encountered them quoted in prose, in the essays my professors had assigned in college, where the line breaks were replaced with slashes, so that what was communicated was less a particular poem than the echo of poetic possibility." His experiences throughout the novel, while intense, all have this quality of having been once removed, whether because they take place in a language he doesn't fully speak or because they are mediated by a distance from both his "real" home and his temporary home. One cannot live on an echo of poetic possibility forever; disappointment follows just as often, if not more, as fulfillment.

Berlin is also a famously difficult place to learn German. The authentic Berlin, extant merely in idea or not, is not an American-free space, just as German is not an English-free language. If you come to Berlin and never notice the omnipresence of Denglish, or overhear someone who sounds like they're from California, you're probably not doing it right. We've been occupying Berlin for a long time. What's more, Germans here are not like the stereotypical French; overt national pride is not something they will risk, and in Berlin, they don't usually publicly humiliate you when you try and fail to speak to them. One free German course designed to ease expats into the language has the urgently selling title: "German—Why Not?" It's often said that Germans "like speaking English," because within a certain class and age group, speaking English allows them to practice something they are good at, and it's fun to be good at things. On the flip side, having to parse all the prepositions the intermediate German speaker crashes together while trying to discuss *Enteignung*—or "expropriation," a word you might not even know in English, so rare is the concept in Anglophone nations—would require from them a level of patience they do not have for their own children, who are permitted to freely harass strangers at cafés and restaurants. (German dogs, usually found sitting patient and off leash outside the grocery store, are by contrast well trained.) Germans compound the issue by saying things like "Eh, English is better anyway" when you lament your laziness and stupidity, and because they have this matter-of-fact wisdom about them—and because, as an American, you maintain unshakable hegemonic tendencies and enjoy being flattered—you believe them. It's hard to imagine a younger German advocating for his country's good qualities. "I hated Berlin the first time I moved here, in 2005," a German friend, from Hamburg, tells me. He's about forty, if that's useful to know. "It was too German. When I came back in 2011 it was better, more international." The second time around he started a music blog and met his friends online. To paraphrase the old AOL tagline, online is America, and it's there where the way English has permeated other languages is most obvious (and fun). "Das ist schon irgendwie next level falsch," a German I follow on Twitter says, meaning "That's kind of next-level wrong." "Just the absolute worst. Hatte ich ganz vergessen," says another, complaining about the Deutsche Bahn—he'd totally forgotten how bad it was. In a 2022 interview about social media criticisms of the company's continued business relationship with Russia, the CEO of Ritter Sport, the German chocolate company, complained that "das Land der Dichter und Denker ist heute eines der Poster und Hater" (the land of poets and thinkers is today one of posters and haters). It is hilarious to hear one's beloved spin instructor apologize for being "ein bißchen sweaty" (a little sweaty).

Like all the instructors at this exercise studio, she teaches her courses in English. Such policies are often explicitly aimed at "inclusivity," but the use of English also serves an elevating function: English is considered worldly, though the people who speak it natively are famously not. (We did, however, popularize the concept of spin class—you're welcome.) Visiting a friend at her job at a hospital in Milan, Claudia Durastanti notices an area marked, in English, "Cancer Center." Her friend tells her "that English was used to evoke a sense of efficiency, to reassure visitors and to increase the hospital's standing in the best-practices world ranking system." If you don't speak Italian and you need to go to the hospital in Milan, no matter whether you are the hegemon or a humble visitor from Korea or Romania, you will find communicating in ESL somewhat convenient. There is also a wholesome progressive justification for speaking English, the lingua franca for a constantly cycling population of educated people from all over the world (even some Germans); it's cool to be at a party where you can talk to a Russian, a Swede, and a Peruvian at the same time, and also kind of beautiful. After the war in Ukraine began in 2022, the pervasiveness of English in Berlin is also the reason some Ukrainian refugees were able to take up service jobs there on arrival, despite speaking (and why should they?) no German whatsoever. (Migrants from Africa and the Middle East are of course not granted the same allowances.)

Beyond the fact that your interlocutor will almost certainly switch to English for mutual ease—unless, I find, you are at a doctor's office or government appointment, the places you most need to understand what someone is saying to you—there is likely no city in the world with more bad German speakers than Berlin. This means there will always be someone around who's worse at it than you are, making you feel okay and thus not proactive about your own bad German, and it means you may accidentally pick up incorrect pronunciations or usages that then tail you for years, like calling someone who is too polite to correct you the wrong nickname forever. A common experience is approaching the counter at a bar or café and confidently requesting what you want, only to be met with a similarly uncomfortable accent and a mutual embarrassment that neither of you wants this interaction to continue in the language you must nevertheless keep speaking in order to compete in the game expats have been playing and losing forever: Who deserves to be here? "Each member of this shadowy network resented the others," Lerner writes of Adam Gordon's fellow expatriates in Madrid, "who were irritating reminders that nothing was more American, whatever that means, than fleeing the American, whatever that is, and that their soft version of self-imposed exile was just another of late empire's packaged tours."

Do I ever pretend I'm not American? No. But I like to dilute the country's influence. A few years ago, I read an article in a fashion magazine about the enduring quality of German underwear. The next time I was in town, I bought a pair. They were ideal in the sense that there was nothing wrong with them—soft; breathable; no panty lines; don't ride up; look good in the way you want German underwear to look, namely sleek but normal. But what I liked more was the idea that I could be a person who, though I lived in the US at the time, wore only German underwear. I quickly became, through force of will and very mild logistic planning, such a person. What did I think this meant about me? That I was subtly worldly, with specific and honed tastes, and slightly quirky. That I was not like other Americans living in the US. Moving to Germany rendered that quick identity marker moot; if in the US I was able to avoid other Americans who'd lived in Berlin—they hadn't done it right—now I am put in constant contact with Americans who live here, forced to confront our identical struggle for a different life. Most of them probably wear German underwear, too, and I bet they don't go around bragging about it.

* * *

The question of where, or what, is "here" is more open than a demographically illustrative map suggests. For all its particularities and the enduring quality of German underwear design, Berlin is beholden to the same homogenizing forces that other major cities are: the internet makes everyone want the same things—to be able to use "next-level" as a modifier regardless of your native language—and the tech industry makes those things a reality. I love to hear anecdotes about the good old days, the times when the cities I've lived in were better and cheaper, because like most people of my generation I'm a masochist, and in general I hate my life. I like to have my sense that the life I hate would have been better if I had just been born fifteen to one hundred years earlier confirmed.

On a trip to Paris at the end of 2021, I visited the Pinault Collection at the Bourse de Commerce—a fantastic private contemporary art collection located in the former stock exchange. I didn't research what exhibitions were showing for my visit, so I didn't know an untitled set of wax sculptures by the Swiss artist Urs Fischer would be installed in the grand rotunda, beneath the spectacular marouflage dome. In the center was a full-scale replica of the sixteenth-century Giambologna sculpture *The Rape of the Sabine Women*, surrounded by seven chairs—a Mandé seat from Mali, an Ethiopian Oromo chair, a Ghanaian Ashanti chair, a Bwa seat from Burkina Faso, a set of two airplane seats, a wheeled office chair, and a Monobloc white plastic garden chair (you know the one). Next to the central sculpture was a male figure dressed in contemporary clothing, a blazer and khakis, his glasses resting on his forehead as he looked on. All these things—wax, remember—had multiple wicks and were on fire; the sculptures had been melting since the exhibition began about six months before I arrived. When I saw them, they were maybe 50 percent disintegrated.

I was stunned: over the past ten years, the trend for "Instagram art" has spawned countless experiential, set-designed, multicolored, and vaguely clever art installations apparently conceived to be shared on the app. They usually don't reward standing and thinking; they're appealing to the child and childlike adult, and they reflect internet culture more than they reflect the culture of whatever city they're located in. Yet here was a work of art that was wittily eye-catching and deliciously photographable but also, impossibly, good. The Instagram-worthy aspect is that this guy made a full-scale replica of a Mannerist sculpture—as a *candle*! The "real," or original, sculpture is in the Piazza della Signoria in Florence. I skipped around the gallery, euphoric,

< 132 >

< 133 >

taking my pictures. A sculpted wax face—emptily spherical eyes, Roman nose, shocked open mouth—lay amazingly on the ground; a fragment of curls was detached and lying about a foot away. There was an entire forearm plus elbow, extending to a hand, index finger separated and lying next to it, like a double-jointed teenager showing off in class. Dried wax drippings hung from the remains of the sculptures and dotted the floor. All of it was extensively photographed. The work is about time, which of course photography is also about. The male figure, modeled on the artist Rudolf Stingel, watches it pass, thoughtfully or critically; a postcard of his half-melted body made a great fortieth birthday card.

The setting of the show is not insignificant, though the sculpture was originally displayed as part of the 2011 Venice Biennale, in a slightly different form. (There was originally just one chair, a replica of the one in Fischer's studio. In her 2020 article on the work, art historian Cristina Baldacci calls this a kind of "self-portrait.") The paintings around the Bourse de Commerce rotunda's dome, installed in 1889, depict scenes of travel and France's trade networks; Fischer selected chairs he modeled out of wax based on his own travels, too—hence the airplane seats. It's exactly the sort of exhibition one might take a low-cost flight, skimping on luggage to avoid fees, just to see. These low-cost flights make me feel even less like I live in Germany and more like I live in Europe, and they make Europe feel like it's not quite Europe anymore, but a replica of itself.

Then there is the building, the Bourse de Commerce. A superficially anti-capitalist argument about the trend for buffing formerly functional grand old buildings into commercial spaces beckons, but I'm writing this paragraph in Tallinn, in a hotel that used to be a train depot, and a few weeks ago I was in a hotel in Maastricht that used to be a monastery; in Berlin there's a new hotel that used to be a women's prison. "Probably the decline of the hotel dates back to the dissolution of the ancient unity of inn and brothel," writes Adorno in *Minima Moralia*. "It used to be a brothel!" a 2013 Tripadvisor review of the Ghent Marriott notes (four stars). The culmination of this tendency is the market hall that used to be a market hall, like New York City's Essex Market (sadly relocated to a slick glassy new building across the street) or Berlin's Markthalle Neun. The market hall is no longer an essential space in Western culture; the places where people used to go to buy meat, produce, and bread from independent vendors have been replaced by supermarkets—cheaper, more convenient, and requiring less of that stressful face-to-face interaction we have come to hate so much. But the buildings are still there, ideally protected by architectural heritage ordinances, and they're just so cool, so they've been repopulated with food vendors, usually upscale, and have become activities or experiences, rather than errands. High rents and thin margins mean many small businesses can't afford to start up; the market hall that used to be a market hall is a good space for potential professional chefs or small-batch (local!) manufacturers to determine whether they can generate enough business to sustain themselves on their own. Or they are, increasingly, outposts of small local chains, there to generate more brand awareness.

It sometimes feels as if the world's formerly great cities are melting like overpriced candles, threatening to vanish and leave behind only the stylish containers they came in. I feel a little dirty visiting a private contemporary art collection, or staying in a slick hotel, or spending a Thursday night trying to decide which of twenty-seven struggling street food vendors to patronize; I feel a little better if there is some veneer of "authenticity" to what I'm doing, or if authenticity or historicity is a vector through which I can engage in this utterly contemporary practice. I gaze up into the neoclassical rotunda as the

< 135 >

effects of globalization are reflected ingeniously around me and feel that I'm finally *experiencing* something. It's unavoidably uncomfortable that the rotunda is being looked at by slightly too many other people crowding the room, speaking their languages, thinking about whether the exhibition catalog will fit in their carry-on. Everyone in that room knew that our predecessors were not loafing around trying to decide between kimchi burritos and tandoori empanadas; they probably would have found the garishly pastel color palette that predominates in such spaces alarming. Still, unlike when I was in New York or Berlin, I experienced only a brief urge to have seen an earlier, more intact version of the Fischer sculpture. I think I was there at exactly the right time, about halfway into its collapse.

* * *

I live in a city that used to be two cities, in a country that used to be a different country; this is another one of those clichés. It's a cliché because it presents an unavoidable fact about living in Berlin that helps create the sense that we are not living in the right time, that we have missed something: venues that used to be other venues abound. An art opening in the East German Communist Party's Central Committee hub for the Department of Transportation; an event complex in a former GDR radio station; a bar that used to be a bar; a cinema that used to be a cinema. It's especially exciting, at least at first, when the function remains the same: people used to go to this cinema, just as we are going to this cinema now. Tradition? No, but maybe continuity. The movies now are different from the way movies used to be. The cocktails strive hopelessly for contemporaneity. Time goes on. Soon enough we see how the symbolic contours melt and slowly harden into something else, and we become sad. I try to remember, when I hear the stories of the good old days and how little everything cost,

that I don't actually want to live in an apartment that was last reno-
vated in 1993, where I'd have to shit in a toilet in the kitchen and cut
my feet on the rotting floorboards. But I can't deny that it would have
been nice to pay less rent, and to have no idea what an iPhone is.

How else might we allow history to remain present while the present becomes the future? One summer, a boyfriend and I stayed in an
apartment building that used to be the site of a factory that produced
gas mantles for the city's street lamps. It was transformed into apartments and commercial spaces in 1912. Decades later, in the 1980s,
commercial spaces in West Berlin were going empty, so a state-owned
real estate company rented some of these spaces cheaply to artists.
From our beautiful, historical balcony we could observe the alienated
residents of a sterile, ugly student apartment building across the street.
Despite the violinist who could be heard practicing Brahms every af-
ternoon, we imagined life was truly dismal over there. A guy often sat
naked playing video games while his girlfriend, we thought, cleaned
his apartment. Sometimes she sat in the bed and watched. We looked
up the rents and found them egregious. We could not help but worry
Berlin was finally "over."

We would also walk around the neighborhood, known as a
"working-class neighborhood," remembering but not exactly sure that
the beloved club that used to be a city pool, ultimately shut down in
2015 due to its absolutely treacherous fire safety setup, was around
there. Where was it? We hypothesized its past existence in several
buildings in the vicinity. Finally we looked it up. Yes. Yes, it was.

This isn't the authenticity we wanted, but the yearning for an authentic experience is also not what we think it is. Throughout Europe,
the curvaceous font of a Bolt taxi; the suddenly quickening pace of
a Wolt food delivery worker; the drug-friendly raves promoted on
Instagram; the white space; the vending machines in airports that, for

< 136 >

< 137 >

some reason, have hashtags like #FoodFastItalia advertised on them—major bummers, all. But the omnipresent branding of international start-ups is as authentic as a restaurant that's been serving the same pork recipe since the 1500s. What's sad about it is that recognition—that what we're doing *is* authentic, as authentic as a farm with no running water in the middle of Romania or a French restaurant that serves only the organs of baby animals. This is how we live, how we eat, how we get around, now. What we are seeking is not something authentic but something different, new, or even actually foreign, something that produces the gaps in understanding that allow us to imagine possibility there.

Germany, and Berlin in particular, makes a good case study for the new culture globalization has created, because while the city resists the homogenizing effects of capital admirably, it has also long been malleable. What outsiders tend to think of as "authentic" German culture is either kitsch or fascist or both; what insiders tend to think of as authentic culture bleeds too much into value judgments.‡‡ The irony dripping from the first lines of *How German Is It* flows directly to the Third Reich, and it is hard to think of a quality that someone might describe as "so German" that is unequivocally positive. The stereotypes about Germans—about their sense of humor, somehow both overliteral and inscrutable; their food, white and heavy; their entitlement, evident in everything from the way they (do not) discipline their children to the sense that they would try to conquer Europe again if they could (and, by some measures, they are)—do not usually belie a sentimental fondness that foreigners have for them, but rather what Abish calls "a mixture of envy and a certain disdain."

---

‡‡ Another way of putting this is that I couldn't tell you what authentic American culture is like—reality TV surely makes the list—but I could show you a good time in New York City or a bleak time in West Virginia.

In Berlin, many expats express a grudging acceptance of what one must put up with to live in Not Really Germany (which, remember, is great); in other German cities, I assume there is the presence of one of those precedence-taking factors, a job or lover or lifelong Germanophilia, to calm the irritation. For the expat, the frustrations of life in a new country do not feel necessary; their unfamiliarity gives them an unreal cast. No matter how many people tell you that Germans "love rules"—and yes, the way they calculate energy bills is completely nonsensical—it's still hard to believe they really live life like this.

Yet what seems like authentic Berlin is not something many people would pay for a flight to see. I find myself swooning in a predeparture area when I see the telltale signs I'm in the right spot: several elaborate goths who look like they'll disembark for a taxi directly to Berghain, wearing their heaviest black platform boots and a scowl under neon-dyed hair; sets of parents with distinct accents, speaking languages that are jockeying for prime position in their annoying children's developing minds; pairs of backpacking hippies, white, with anachronistically questionable dreadlocks.§§ Once I'm in Berlin, I like the graffiti, not the "street art"; I like that you can still smoke inside some bars and clubs, that it is "ugly," that everything has been destroyed, rebuilt, broken again, smashed together. This is the setting where everyone, everywhere, seems to be having a long lunch date with a dear friend. On every third block, you run into someone you know and may or may not want to see; on every fourth, you see someone wearing one of those modified mullets, tasteful mullets,

---

§§ After a white woman with dreadlocks won the Nobel Prize in Literature in 2018, it seems those who campaign against such things in the United States have softened on the question of the particular combination's inappropriateness. In Germany, which adopts issues in American identity politics a few years too late, and with a misplaced fervor, a singer was disinvited from a climate protest in March 2022 because she sported the same style.

< 139 >

with short or almost nonexistent bangs and a little quip of curls on the nape. The judder of a bike on the cobblestones, through which you must brace yourself. The clinking of several bottles of beer in a backpack. The smell of sulfur in the kitchen, the hair-flattening water in the shower. "The daytime impresses him with its empty hours and its fibrous texture, like glass wool," writes Maylis de Kerangal in her 2016 novella "The Cook," and I know just what she's talking about—the sudden plunge from delirious summer into inarguable fall, the dread of winter, when daytime is only fibrous for a few hours. It remains remarkable how many people smoke; it almost seems that more people smoke now than they did five years ago. Or maybe I, now an actual smoker, just notice it more.

In 1925, Nabokov wrote "A Guide to Berlin," a short set of observations about seemingly banal features of Berlin life: the large black pipe on the sidewalk outside his apartment; people (construction workers, a baker, the postman) going about their workdays; the Berlin Zoo; and the streetcar, which the author believed would "vanish in twenty years or so, just as the horse-drawn tram has vanished."

"That's a very poor guide," his "usual drinking companion" tells him when they meet at a pub. "Who cares about how you took a streetcar and went to the Berlin Zoo?" While his friend is haranguing him about his choice of subject matter—overall, Berlin itself is "a boring, foreign city, and expensive to live in, too"—the narrator notices yet another banal occurrence: a child, the son of the pub's proprietor, examining a magazine and then looking out at the room, "the picture he saw every day of his childhood." When the narrator's friend remarks again that he doesn't understand the narrator's interest in such trivialities, the narrator thinks, *How can I demonstrate to him that I have glimpsed somebody's future reflection?*

The twenty-six-year-old Nabokov explains the value of relaying these images as a literary project: the point is "to portray ordinary objects as they will be reflected in the kindly mirrors of future times; to find in the objects around us the fragrant tenderness that only posterity will discern and appreciate." But he's not making just any old observations. The structure of the story, or guide, suggests that being a foreigner is like being a child: as newness transitions into familiarity, memories are made when the difference between newness and familiarity crystallizes—when you realize what has happened. Though no one living in New York or London today can claim that Berlin is "expensive to live in" (but all that is changing), I set out in part to explain what I like, or love, about Berlin because I wanted to demonstrate its value in some way to those who, like Nabokov's drinking companion, don't get it—because I am now, somehow, attached to images and routines that may seem to others insignificant or even cliché. Today I occasionally find myself walking down streets I first saw eleven years ago and experiencing an almost nauseating nostalgia. The feeling is not "I used to walk here, when I was younger," or even that I miss being younger (I do not). I often think during these moments the same thing I've always thought during these moments: that I wished I lived here. Absurd, because I do. Not absurd, because what I'm experiencing is the urge to be in a moment before I knew what walking here would mean, when someone else could glimpse me saving images for future recollection—when I had no idea what I was doing. This is our condescending idea about the past, the place we wish we could authentically experience. We imagine, because we have the privilege of living in the present, that everyone back then was a little less aware.

Like everyone in any major city, I fear the dissolution of my favorite places, the sacrifice of bars and clubs and restaurants to rising costs and time. As every year goes by, the stakes become higher; it's one more year that I've been walking on this street, going to this bar.

< 140 >

I see a photograph, even a bad, sentimental one, of my neighborhood and feel warm inside, badly sentimental. Worse, the photograph is hanging on the wall of my favorite café. I've been going to this café for eleven years, though they still don't give me preferential treatment. Eleven years is not that long, but it's long enough to know their Wi-Fi password has never changed. I couldn't have known, back then, that I would find this touching.

I AM THE ONE WHO IS SITTING HERE, FOR HOURS AND HOURS AND HOURS

For writers too lazy to keep a diary, too neurotic to report the news, too self-centered to review others' work, and too prosaic to compose a poem, writing fiction is, really, the only option. Happily, writing fiction does not come with the disappointment of settling for the last resort; it is also the best option. There might be functions served better by other forms—education, information, advocacy, argument, gossip, prurience—but there is nothing better to write or to read than fiction, broadly construed. Fiction can contain any percentage of truth and retain its status as fictional; it can expand to fill a huge space or contract to fit in a dark, cramped one. To write it, one might conduct research, as in reportage; or make use of memory and personal experience, as in memoir; or comment at length on other works of art, or art in general, as in criticism; or use form and language provocatively and idiosyncratically, as in poetry. One might also insert, wholesale, a work in one of these forms into a work of fiction. "The only obligation to which in advance we may hold a novel without incurring the accusation of being arbitrary, is that it be interesting," Henry James wrote in 1884. "The ways in

< 143 >

which it is at liberty to accomplish this result . . . are as various as the temperament of man, and they are successful in proportion as they reveal a particular mind, different from others. A novel is in its broadest definition a personal impression of life; that, to begin with, constitutes its value, which is greater or less according to the intensity of the impression."

Isn't this nice? Isn't this wonderful? Yes. Yes. But lately—this has always been a problem, but I'm concerning myself with it as of lately—readers have become skeptical of fiction and particularly of its possibilities. Over the past fifteen years or so, the "personal impression" part began to really upset people. It was overshadowing everything else, they said. It was gentrifying the novel form with its little observations about the internet and identity politics, with its unwillingness to build a world of its own. Why were novelists now always just talking about themselves? No one knew what to make of it, or even why it was so annoying to them. This led to all sorts of irritating things being said and written about the phenomenon, which, despite having a name coined decades ago, many people couldn't really believe was actually a thing.

The personal, I felt, had done nothing wrong. It had done, actually, many things right. Its popularity in fiction at this particular moment made a lot of sense. Maybe everyone was mad about the historical moment we were trapped in—the past fifteen or so years? Not unlikely. The past fifteen or so years have seemed uniquely unglamorous, uniquely unworthy of being preserved in prose fiction, the best of all literary forms.

I became so irritated by all the unfair attacks on this phenomenon that I began to develop a deep appreciation of it. I liked it so much that I was even able to excuse crimes committed in its name, and I vowed to one day defend it. "My autofiction essay," I would say to everyone I met. "I'm writing an essay about autofiction." They screamed. They cried. They begged me not to. They asked for it.

WHAT IT ISN'T

A piece of fiction that merely draws on an author's life. A selfie. Social media. Reality television. Fiction about cars.

I'm not saying that autofiction isn't like any of these things; in fact, autofiction is like all of them. However, two things may share similarities without completely transforming into one another. This is an important lesson for romantic relationships as well as for literary criticism.

WHAT IT IS

Critics do shy away from referring to it directly. Sometimes it will appear in scare quotes or as something "so-called"; it is often referred to as "what is often referred to as autofiction." A 2018 review of Michael Leiris's 1934 novel *Phantom Africa* in the *New York Review of Books* referred to "the celebrated 'autofictions' of Karl Ove Knausgaard," who two years prior gave an interview to Denmark's Louisiana Museum in which he bragged, "I think less about autofiction than anyone else." In the words of Dale Peck, it's a form an author might "indulge in"; he wrote that in 1997. In 2023, it had a "slow, self-driving hum," which an author under review managed to "escap[e]." It is simultaneously both "voguish" or "trendy" or "popular among writers who live in Brooklyn," the worst place in the world, and also actually something with a history so long and international it's tiresome to even mention: look, say critics with perspective, at the I-novels of early twentieth-century Japan, at what Russian formalists said about genre, at gay literature of the 1980s and 1990s, at anything happening in France in the past 120 years. "*The Pillow Book*? Hello?" Sighs are heard. "What about Coetzee?" a man in the back cries out. "Why isn't Coetzee part of this conversation?" The absence of Coetzee seems to prove the flimsiness of the discussion. If Coetzee were involved, there would be some gravitas, some sense of stakes.

An idea without stakes is hard to take seriously. In 2021, the website Lit Hub published a funny article called "10 Definitions of Autofiction," which included principles such as: "3. When you write about something bad you've done, that's autofiction. When you write about something bad done to you, that's memoir." And "7. If you follow the author on Twitter, that's autofiction." The same year, Joyce Carol Oates lamented on Twitter that it was "strange to have come of age reading great novels of ambition, substance, & imagination (Dostoyevsky, Woolf, Joyce, Faulkner) & now find yourself praised & acclaimed for wan little husks of 'auto fiction' with space between paragraphs to make the book seem longer . . ."

Does it exist at all? One might look at all these scare quotes, and at the perhaps too-wide variety of texts critics claim are autofictional, and conclude that it doesn't. In 2021, Ange Mlinko wrote in the *London Review of Books* that the term has "something miasmic about it"; her evidence was that critics hadn't affixed the description to the work of Yiyun Li, whose recent books include a memoir, a novel in the form of a woman's imagined dialogue with her son, who died by suicide, and a novel whose protagonist is an eighty-one-year-old woman living in a retirement home. Only one of these is autofiction (the imagined dialogue). Even if they were all autofiction, though, critics' shortcomings are not exactly objective evidence of conceptual bleed; the argument for adopting common usage as official definition—as in the lost battle of "literally" with the definition of "figuratively"—need not apply to vocabularies of expertise. The point of the concept is that it's bloody confusing.

A man tweeted: my students say "novel" when they mean "long book." This generated discussion for days. Is it wrong to be attached to the meaning of words, like "novel"? Is it in fact elitist, counter to the nature of language, which is alive and constantly changing, to care that a novel is not just any long book, and an autofictional novel not just any novel with a character based on the author? Part of the issue is that books are commodities—their commodification often transcends their transcendent qualities—and confusion is not a selling proposition. In a 2021 article for the trade magazine *Publishers Weekly*, a publisher and writing coach explained that autofiction "is one of those labels that ultimately doesn't matter to the industry." There are Amazon book categories for Dentistry and Clean & Wholesome Romance, but not autofiction, which is kind of insulting. "If an author has written a work of autofiction, the book can only be labeled as a novel," the coach decreed, not incorrectly. A book-length work of autofiction is always a novel because the nature of fiction is that it can contain some unacknowledged fact; a work advertised as "nonfiction" makes truth claims about everything in it, while a work advertised as fiction does not. "If you're calling something fiction," Elif Batuman said on the *Longform* podcast in 2018, discussing her autobiographical novel *The Idiot*, "you're saying whether or not it happened is not really important." Some reckless hedonists believe that in a just world the American publishing industry would abandon formal classifications altogether, because the way a reader interacts with a book before they open it colors their experience of the text—this is why people fear "spoilers" and why some refuse to read plot summaries or listen to their friends' opinions about movies and books before watching or reading them. Without labels, the reckless hedonists believe the reading experience could be more pure. Ironic, for hedonists. They also believe this is how it's done "in Europe." I disagree. First, because I live in Europe, and they call books "novels" all the time, and second, because I occasionally like to repeat factoids that I learn from reading nonfiction, and I want to be sure I'm not saying something the author just made up.

That's not to say the factoids in fiction are false—just that you have to google them to be sure. This googleability is part of what, I'd argue, led to the rise of autofiction, which I will now finally define. Autofiction is a form more than a genre. The terms "form" and "genre" are sometimes used interchangeably, and there are many, *many* academic theories of genre, but because this discussion deals with literature in the general and popular sense, and genre has a particular definition in this context—"genre" fiction refers to romance, fantasy, etcetera—I think it's useful to distinguish them. A literary form is a structure, or even a guiding principle; a genre, content. Autofiction is sometimes called a genre because it is first and foremost fiction—that's its structure—and because autofictional novels could be said to follow certain conventions, such as the inclusion of references to the writer's career, critical digressions about external works of art the author-narrator encounters, and a moodily naturalistic style. But I'm arguing it's better to call it a form. In nonfiction, "what really happened" is the form; in fiction, the form is possibility, again broadly construed—what might happen, what might have happened, what might happen if. This possibility may or may not involve an authorial avatar. In autofiction, the form is the author himself—not what really happened to the author or what the author really thinks, but what the author figure, the person we imagine when we read the name on the cover of the book, might do or think in contexts that may or may not hew to what really happened to the author—what might happen, or have happened, if the author himself were, or had been, in certain situations. At the beginning of Ben Lerner's 2014 novel *10:04*, the narrator summarizes it succinctly. When his agent asks how he'll expand a (real) story he's published in the *New Yorker* into a novel, he writes that he should have replied, "I'll project myself into several futures simultaneously . . ."

The autofictional form is created by the interplay of two projections (imagine a light show): (1) the kind of projections the author always engages in while writing fiction (what might happen, etc.), and (2) crucially, the reader's idea of the author, with the acknowledgment that the reader's idea of the author is being simultaneously constructed by the author's public image (or lack thereof) as well as by the text in which the autofictional narrator appears, which the reader is theoretically reading right at the very moment its form is being, ha ha, formed. It's created, in other words, through the relationship between the author and the reader.

As in fiction, it doesn't matter whether anything written in an autofictional novel is "true" or not; what matters is that, in the text, it's a version of the actual author doing or thinking or watching it. Can we incorporate the automobile pun? Yes, though the review I quoted earlier already did it: a work of autofiction must also be *driven* by the author figure. (A cheeky cameo doesn't count.) It doesn't actually matter whether that figure shares any biographical details with the author of the book; what matters is the effect, created by the actual author, passively or actively, that the text you are reading concerns the life and/or thoughts of the person whose name is on the cover. The term's original definition, proposed by Serge Doubrovsky in notes to his novel *Fils* in 1977, is a work of fiction in which the author uses his own name for the narrator or protagonist; the novel was advertised as "fiction, of strictly real events and facts." Both

< 148 >

< 149 >

strategies—naming and labeling—are now some ways to suggest the connection. Others include calling your book "autofiction" in interviews; making the narrator or protagonist a writer, with writerly travails that might map onto your own; and utilizing other googleable elements in a text to create a link.

But it's not enough to have the link; the link must be live. The autofictional text must seem as if it's happening somewhat spontaneously; it must take place in a contemporary-ish moment, not an alternate reality or the 1990s. It must seem as if it's really you. This effect is not only created by the book's content, its narrative, but also, crucially, by its voice, which, while sort of natural, isn't stream-of-consciousness or messy. Because the natural voice of a writer should be a bit more literary, a bit more refined, than your average person's, shouldn't it?

REALITY EFFECT

You could call it that, but it's taken. Autofiction tends to dispense with Barthes's old-fashioned reality effects: the detailed description of a sitting room—say, for the purpose of accumulating evidence of realism—is seen, in the context of the otherwise verifiable autofictional narrator's voice, as pointless.

You might also be tempted to say the autofictional voice is mimetically representing something. But what? If you've read any of the paradigmatic examples of twenty-first-century autofiction—Knausgaard's *My Struggle*, Teju Cole's *Open City*, Lerner's novels, Sheila Heti's *How Should a Person Be?* and *Motherhood*, Tao Lin's *Taipei*, or Rachel Cusk's *Outline* trilogy—you can't really say they're doing that. They don't seem, in toto, to resemble extemporaneous speech, or monologues, or diaries, or essays, or memoirs, or novels. The autofictional voice that creates the illusion of a thinner boundary between the author and the reader is most similar to the effect created by social media. Which, to be clear, the form predates. But they did both become popular in the Anglophone world at the same time.

TRUTH EFFECT

In a 2021 essay on W. G. Sebald, Lerner refers to the author's "truth effects," which include his famous use of photographs in the text, his use of "techniques and tonalities [that] are more often associated with nonfictional genres (the essay, the travelogue, reportage)," and his use of a narrator that "so closely resembles him." In psychology, the tendency to believe false information because it's often repeated is known as the illusory truth effect. One way to create a truth effect, then, is to expose a reader to the same information multiple times, in different contexts, and thus imply that it's been independently verified by multiple sources. On the internet there are so, so many of these.

SCENE INSPIRED BY A POPULAR MISREADING
OF ANOTHER ESSAY BY ROLAND BARTHES

Clutching a late-model iPhone, a hand bursts through the earth, followed by weird moaning. The weird moans are saying, ". . . first thing in the morning." What was that? "I try to write," the moans are saying, "first thing in the morning." Dirty, beleaguered, having lost a recent manuscript in a hard-drive crash that could not be reconstituted, mutteringly reminding itself of something it read somewhere that claimed both Hemingway and David Foster Wallace lost manuscripts at crucial points in their careers, the hand digs itself out. "I

< 151 >

need new author photos," the author rasps. "Do you know anyone who takes good author photos?"

FAKE ACCOUNTS

For the entirety of this long essay, I could pretend, modestly, that I haven't published a novel myself—that my interest in this issue is purely theoretical. However, as a critic and reader I know that people who have read both *Fake Accounts* and this essay—any of my essays— will necessarily, consciously or not, be reading them in some way "together": that the essay will shed light on the novel and vice versa.

This has always been the case. Now, however, there's a lot more text for the reader to work with. My tweets, my tweets. If I could have once scoffed at the audience's nosiness, suggesting that the reader interested in the unstable relationship between myself and my characters must have an unsophisticated view of literature, today I must regret giving that reader enough rope to identify me as a person who's into bondage. The preponderance of evidence for the author and her particular existence is probably part of what led Rachel Cusk to conclude in 2014 that fiction was "fake and embarrassing." Even for writers who eschew social media, like Cusk, the proliferation of literary journalism in the internet age—or "books coverage"—has made it more difficult for authors to deflect speculations about the relationship between their personal lives and their fiction while giving them many opportunities to talk about the places where the two overlap. It's a truism in the world of book publicity that if you can come up with some personal story related to your book—if you can narrativize its making—you should. The *Romansbildung* is excellent fodder for author interviews; readers want a story, and they want to see growth and change, even if the actual experience of writing a book is full of stops, starts, and influences that might seem utterly random. For a writer, the happy ending to any hardship, interpersonal or merely writer's block, is the book being promoted today. That autofictional novels often perform that same narrativizing is one of their conventions and one of the ways they seem more "real" than other novels—they acknowledge that the author is a writer, with the priorities of a writer: the author wants to write a book.

This is not to say everyone should or will have read my novel, or my tweets, or whatever else I publish and draw conclusions from it all together. But the fact is that they could. The big, open question for the future is, How?

WHO CARES?

In his 2019 book *Character as Form*, Aaron Kunin writes that "literary characters allow you to hold something that seems bigger than your hand, in your hand." An autofictional narrator is a character who doesn't allow you to hold her in your hand; she emphasizes that life cannot be held in your hand. The autofictional narrator is like a real person in that she is live, not fixed; she could go on forever, as Knausgaard demonstrates, or at least for a couple of posthumous publications after she dies. Readers like to praise the lifelikeness of characters; they like to imagine how they might act off the page. But most characters do not actually walk around contending with the reader's fantasies. The autofictional narrator, by contrast, does exist, in a different form, beyond the book.

People fucking hate that. They want to hold hands! Actually, they want to arm wrestle. They want to beat the author, emerge victorious over her. When readers express the commonplace idea that they enjoyed a book because the characters "seemed like real people," because

< 153 >

the book was so lifelike that the readers were able to forget where they were and spend time in "that world," what those readers are expressing is an appreciation not just of the book's ability to make them forget their troubles, their daily grind, whatever. They're also expressing an appreciation of the book's ability to make them forget that they were reading at all. A book that constantly reminds the reader that someone not dissimilar from them wrote it and published it and produced it as a book is not going to do that.

Haters tend to claim two main reasons for their dislike of autofiction. The first is that it's cheating. "As a memoirist, if I'm honest, I have sometimes just thought of [autofiction] as a name for writers who aren't brave enough to call their books memoirs, a kind of veil that allows for the option of saying, 'Well, it's fiction!' to avoid the discomforts of being asked personal questions, or questions that might make them vulnerable in the ways that memoirists are vulnerable," Melissa Febos told the *New York Review of Books* in 2022. "But I know that's a rude and simplistic view." At a time when little seems "real" and everyone's lying, the author who calls her book a fiction must be lying, too.

The second reason given for a hatred of autofiction is that it's navel-gazing—that the mundane details of an author's life told in a meandering tone could be interesting only to the author. If something interesting had happened to the author, and if they weren't such a coward, they would write a memoir (and memoirs often tend to sell better). Since the author of autofiction is a boring wimp, she just records whatever old thoughts and anecdotes she has lying around and calls it a novel. Readers find the implicit request for their time being made by this boring self-obsessed memoirist-masquerading-as-novelist infuriating.

Infuriating, too, is that people will read it—they'll spend the time. "It doesn't matter how boring you think you are," one start-up founder told the *New York Times* in 2021, "there's someone out there who would find your life interesting to the point that they're willing to pay." She runs a company that allows TikTok "creators" to monetize every aspect of their lives by conducting polls in which fans can vote on their day-to-day decisions: examples of such decisions featured in the article include "which sweater they should wear today, or who they should hang out with and where they should go." As if to counter the nefarious turn this service could obviously take, the big example given is laughably innocent: a fifteen-year-old influencer surveys his 3.3 million followers about whether to play dodgeball or catch with his friends. This is not so different from what autofiction, at its worst, is like: you can see the boring cowardly author trying to determine what people on social media might want to read. But at least with TikTok you have some visuals, and they last, like, what, two minutes max?

A CELEBRITY

The great trick of autofiction, what makes it so appealing to the contemporary writer, is that it allows the author to access the benefits of memoir—chiefly that memoir is less fake and embarrassing than fiction and, bonus, more similar to gossip and so manufacturing of intrigue—without the author having to "own" or answer for any of the information being revealed or not revealed the way she would if she were writing nonfiction. Unfortunately, in this celebrity-obsessed time we live in, readers might be distracted by the gossipy mentality the explicitly unstable combination of fiction and nonfiction tends to inspire. *Is it true?* even the most open-hearted of readers can't help but wonder. In order to justify their fixation on the details of the author's

< 155 >

life they might be able to glean from the text, the reader becomes unable to resist the temptation to think of an author as an actual celebrity. The reader then becomes resentful, maybe even jealous, that this author has just recorded any old thoughts and feelings they had lying around and *become* a celebrity. The reader falls prey to the dad-at-the-Rothko-exhibition fallacy: *I* could do *that*.

For the past two decades plus, the possibility of any one individual gaining wider significance than average seemed tantalizingly near and especially desirable, maybe even more so than it did before. This happened for a variety of reasons, including most obviously the popularity of reality television and the rise of the social internet. There is a disconnect between what we know the individual to be in the world (insignificant) and what we feel ourselves, personally, to be (not just significant but the most significant). Fame promises a way to release this tension: to stop being an individual whose particular existence is basically irrelevant to the functioning of the collective and become a known character whose self-regard is justifiable because he represents something—he can be held in the hand.

"How should a person be?" Sheila Heti asked in her 2010 novel of the same name, starring a narrator with her same name. "For years and years I asked it of everyone I met. I was always watching to see what they were going to do in any situation, so I could do it too. I was always listening to their answers, so if I liked them, I could make them my answers too. I noticed the way people dressed, the way they treated their lovers—in everyone, there was something to envy." This earnest investigation into the development of a soul the old-fashioned way leads her nowhere. Finally, she hits on an answer: "How should a person be? I sometimes wonder about it, and I can't help answering like this: a celebrity."

She goes on: she wants to be the only celebrity around (there should be only one example of everything, like an asexual Noah's Ark). She wants "a life of undying fame that I don't have to participate in. I don't want anything to change, except to be as famous as one can be, but without that changing anything. Everyone would know in their heart that *I* am the most famous person alive—but not talk about it too much." The ironic joke here is that many people actually do want this, in some hidden or not-that-hidden part of themselves, and the fact that they have no chance of quietly becoming the most and only famous person alive prevents them from really considering the drawbacks of realizing the fantasy. Here Heti presages the critical response to that novel and her next one, *Motherhood*. Because both feature narrators who seem "all but indistinguishable from Heti herself," as one critic had it, attacks on the narrators' irritating self-obsession (I'm paraphrasing) often became attacks on what critics perceived to be Heti's own character, double meaning intentional. ("Grow up, Sheila Heti!" was the subheading to the *Slate* review of *How Should a Person Be?*) To be fair, the narrator of *How Should a Person Be?* was named Sheila, and the subtitle is a "novel from life." She seemed to make it worse for herself by declaring in its early pages that "character exists from the outside alone." Traditionally, literature is said to be like life. But autofiction also makes life like literature, by seeming to invite the reader to criticize a real person, a real life, as if she is merely the narrator of a novel.

Of course, we do this kind of thing to each other all the time. Our minds insert clear solutions to foggy problems; we take our friends' repeated romantic failures and explain them in terms of their relationships to their fathers and what's been going on in politics. But public figures bear the brunt of our little ideas about character.

The quote "In the future everyone will be world-famous for fifteen minutes" is often attributed to Andy Warhol, but it's very possible he

< 157 >

never said this. The world-historical potential inaccuracy was born when two Swedish curators were working on the book to accompany a 1968 exhibition of Warhol's work at the Moderna Musset. They were using as source material a box containing "everything written by and about Andy Warhol." One curator told the other that he'd missed a famous quote in compiling the book: the "fifteen minutes" one. The second curator objected that if this quote had been in the box, he would have seen it. The first curator replied: "If he didn't say it, he could very well have said it. Let's put it in."

The Andy Warhol character seems likely to have said this both because of what we know about his work, which concerns the reproducibility of popular images, and what we know about other things he's actually written or said. It also doesn't seem like he'd mind having these words put in his mouth. Not literally everybody is famous in the future that is now, particularly when we get granular about what "famous" is. But everybody can be known to an audience wider than the people one has met live, in the flesh; everybody can amass a readership of at least some complete strangers. These complete strangers naturally construct identities for us based on what we tell them.

HOW DO YOU KNOW I'M MARRIED?

Is this a violation? Is it offensive? Or is it only fair? In a 2021 essay for the *New York Times* called "Our Autofiction Fixation," the novelist Jessica Winter described an "audacious" interaction she had at a party with a woman who assumed Winter had undergone in vitro fertilization because the protagonist of her first novel did. Winter was disoriented, but did not "begrudge" the woman her assumption: "The expectation that fiction is autobiographical is understandable for the simple reason that so much of it is."

When a critic or cultural journalist notes that the protagonist or narrator of a novel "shares certain biographical details with [*author*]," or "bears (more than) a striking resemblance to [*author*]," or "who, like [*author*]," the critic is not necessarily flagging a work of autofiction. Are they being coy? Yes, probably. The critic who does this is trying to trick you into being very interested in the piece of criticism or cultural journalism they are writing by suggesting that you can extrapolate from the author's novel the author's *true* beliefs and *real* biography. The critic is suggesting that it is the author, not the critic, who is being coy about the nature of the relationship between the text and the author's life. A reader's knee-jerk reaction to accusations of coyness is usually, What are you trying to hide?

The critic or culture journalist making these cutesy little gestures is not merely trying to get your attention, however. They are also clarifying the conditions that have led to the renewed popularity of autofiction over the past fifteen or so years. The resources to confirm or deny any one detail as autobiographical have expanded; one can access most interviews a living writer has ever done, and the number of outlets that will publish such interviews—which, along with listicles, engines of recommendation, and other noncritical articles about books published on the internet (again, "books coverage")—has grown. This is because of the drive for web traffic, which equals advertising revenue, in digital media; thus it is also due to social media.

The author concerned with privacy must be careful in this environment, when any one utterance can be multiplied via these same channels. "How do you know I'm married?" Sally Rooney asked a *Guardian* interviewer while discussing the publication of her novel *Beautiful World, Where Are You* in 2021. The interviewer pointed out that Rooney thanks her husband in the book's acknowledgments. Without a paranoia about information flows, easily developed by re-

< 159 >

flecting for just one horrified moment on the overwhelming interconnectedness of the internet, one might forget that if one says something in public, it will be heard. Particularly if you're as famous as Sally Rooney.

Rooney's apparent guilelessness about her own self-revelations was "amusing" to the *Guardian* interviewer; to me, Rooney's resentment that celebrity "happens without meaningful consent—the famous person never even wanted to become famous" is surprising, if not suspicious. *BWWAY*, the novel they were discussing, is her third, published after she became a literary celebrity with the crazy success of 2018's *Normal People*, and one of its two main characters is a young Irish author who is so famous she can buy a tower, albeit also resentfully. There is only one such person in the world, and given the nature of the character—she is very famous—we can eliminate the usual doubt that creeps in when we try, pathetically, to attribute elements of an allegedly fictional text to a nonfictional being: namely, that usually when one reads about romantic turmoil or a terrible parent in a novel, one must say to oneself, "Ah, yes, this *could* be based on the author's 'real' experiences, but there are many people in the world like this." In the case of *BWWAY*, we know there is only one person in the world like this, and her name is on the cover of the novel. Because the character is very famous—or, rather, about as famous as an author can be—we can reasonably assume that we would know anyone else who was like that.

This is not to say that the author character in *BWWAY*, Alice Kelleher, *is* Sally Rooney; nor does it mean that *BWWAY* is autofiction. "Autobiographical" is a usefully vague word; it just means that some portion of a work, unknowable but definitive, derives from the author's life. How does it derive? Again, usefully vague. One hopes that undergoing a unique experience like becoming one of the most famous authors in the world at the age of twenty-nine would allow the author to shed light on that experience in some meaningful way. The famous author in *BWWAY* expresses many obnoxious and annoying ideas that an ungenerous—or realistic—reader might want to pin on Sally Rooney herself, given that it's unlikely she's cavorting around with many other young female Irish novelists whose millions of dollars (euros) disrupt their lives. But at the same time, Rooney's ability to represent these ideas at a distance suggests she understands her own ambivalence about it and how it might be received. At the beginning of *BWWAY*, Alice meets a Tinder date, a working-class local named Felix, and when he asks her about her job, she becomes "slightly nervous, which expressed itself in a shortness of breath and a kind of self-mocking expression." Felix "watched this performance impassively." The scene continues. It's clear Felix doesn't know who she is. But you do.

SELF-AWARENESS

There's almost no way to read this scene, the first in the novel, without thinking about the person who wrote it, and I don't think much is gained by trying. The rare reader who arrives at *BWWAY* without the baggage of Sally Rooney Awareness will have a fine time interpreting the scene, in an innocent, classical way; the average reader, however, will have a more layered reading experience.

For her part, Alice is visibly uncomfortable because she knows how this is going to look. Sally Rooney's characters were some of the subjects of a 2020 *New Yorker* article by Katy Waldman called "Has Self-Awareness Gone Too Far in Fiction?" Part review of Naoise Dolan's novel *Exciting Times*, part broader diagnosis of a trend in contemporary fiction, the piece describes what Waldman calls the "re-

< 161 >

flexivity trap": the desire to perform "authenticity" by acknowledging one's flaws, sometimes through "self-protective irony," other times just by stating them and then moving on. The issue, Waldman argues, is that this acknowledgment "rarely resolves the anxieties that seem to prompt it." Fictional characters in recent novels are constantly doing this—fretting about being "good" people, with "good" politics, while actually doing little to be good—just as real people are.

That Waldman's targets are all fictional characters behaving annoyingly reflexively doesn't matter; the issue, according to her, is that it is not enough to merely represent hypocrisies of belief and action, no matter how realistic they are, if the novels in which they feature do not offer some sense of change but instead merely depict a boring, circular anxiety. She argues that because these characters reflect the stated politics of their authors—whose mystery is foiled once again by having given interviews—the authors have a responsibility not to "capitulate[e] to the very values" their novels aim to critique. The *Künstlerroman* today is thus "stunted"; where a coming-of-age story ought to involve growth, contemporary novels "halt the journey midway through, leaving their characters tuned to problems but unable to solve them."

Waldman implicitly incorporates autofictional narrators in her critique by listing Heti, Lerner, and Kate Zambreno as other offenders; her assumption that these authors share the values of their self-reflexive avatars is less of a leap than a skip. But self-awareness has a different function in autofiction. As a form, autofiction is *about* self-awareness; it represents self-awareness formally. Why would such a thing be popular now, in what Waldman calls "these self-conscious times," when what have been called "privilege disclaimers" increasingly preface any piece of personal writing, and casual surveillance of one's peers is a favored pastime? The relationship between Alice

Kelleher and Sally Rooney provides a clue: it's difficult to write about one's life without at least someone acknowledging it. The acknowledgment is self-evident, baked in.

Now, you might argue that Rooney has done it the honorable way—without making too much of a fuss about it, without wringing her hands, without making the reader fed up because this is all really about her. But I'm fairly confident that Rooney's actual experience of fame, her actual thoughts and feelings about it, are more interesting than what she grants to Alice in this novel; Alice is two-dimensional, pseudo-intellectual, and unenlightening. In distancing Alice from herself, Rooney writes like someone who is imagining the life of a uniquely famous author rather than living it; she writes, in other words, what anyone could. The book might have been better if she had explicitly acknowledged herself. And anyway, anyone with a passing understanding of psychoanalysis might say that it's impossible for self-awareness to go too far. It can only make wrong turns.

MY SECRET THOUGHTS

To be respectful, critics and interviewers refer to "the narrator" or "the protagonist" and apologize when they slip and refer to the same as "you." Others forthrightly ask, How much of your novel is auto-biographical? The answer, for me, is 72 percent. This is absolutely not how you're supposed to read a novel, and indeed when people make inferences about me based on the narrator of my book I become annoyed and sometimes actually angry. Seventy-two percent might be autobiographical, but you can't presume to know *which* 72 percent! The implication is that what I've published in my novel are my secret thoughts. Sometimes this implication is considered sexist—no one doubts a man when he says that he has made things up, but women

< 163 >

are seen to be overwhelmed by the confessional impulse and thus unable to imagine, unable to stop expressing our secret thoughts for even a moment.

My response to this is that, first of all, they're not my secret thoughts; I published them. But what's confused here is less the notion of "secret" than the notion of "thought": we are treating thoughts, in this formula that, yes, I did make up, as if they are beliefs, or convictions. The novel allows the writer to present thoughts or ideas without having to subscribe to them. The thoughts I put in a novel, that I grant to a character or even to my autofictional narrator, need not have the same consideration or weight as the thoughts I put my name on in, say, this essay. Yet it is sometimes assumed that if an author is capable of thinking something, they must on some level believe it. (Readers with a passing knowledge of psychoanalysis are once again looking hopeful, ready to strike.)

The issue is in using character profiles and content, rather than a holistic interpretation of the work, to learn something about the author. For example, I've run into difficulty with a line from the middle of *Fake Accounts*: "Did I ever cheat on Felix? Yes. Of course. I cheat on everyone." No relation to Sally Rooney's Felix; mine is named after one of the hosts of the leftist podcast *Chapo Trap House*, as a joke. When a new boyfriend said to me, laughing, that he didn't trust me because I cheated on all my boyfriends, it took me a moment to remember (and angrily respond) that in fact I had not cheated on all my boyfriends. My understanding of myself is apparently so malleable that I was surprised when I tallied up the score and found that I hadn't cheated on a single one, really. (The breakups follow a pattern: slow painful death, one night I kiss someone else, and we break up next day. Sometimes I'm in an open relationship and the kissing is even legal. The point is that the kissing follows, and does not

precede, the true end of the relationship, which must then be made
explicit through the act of breaking up. Anyway—) When I realized
I had somehow gaslit myself this way, I remembered the moment I
wrote the line, when I felt that I truly knew what this mildly reckless
brand of selfishness, communicated with false bravado to avoid any
uncomfortable realizations, would be like, even if I in fact had never
really cheated on a boyfriend. After this upsetting conversation with
the new boyfriend, in which I was able to courageously accuse him
of being a bad reader and domineeringly, possibly sexily, insist on a
reframing of his literary approach, I recalled, painfully, a couple of
instances when I'd had the chance to sleep with not just any external
source but extremely good-looking ones, and I had turned it down.
Talk about righteous!

But I get it. As a novelist, I make the opposite mistake; I think
that anyone who has read my novel knows everything they need to
know about me, and anyone who has not is missing out on some
essential aspect of my personality that they cannot achieve true intimacy with me without. In order to know everything they need
to know about me, a person must be capable of performing and
willing to perform a sustained, deep, and close reading of the novel.
What they would learn are my preoccupations and the unanswer-
able questions that fuel the churning of my soul; they would not
learn much about the trajectory of my life or what I think about it,
because even when I do include stories or memories directly from
my life, they're not flagged as such; they're mixed in with completely
fictional stories, partially fictional stories, stories I've taken from
other people, and stories from other sources that I've then edited
using the power of my imagination, which, despite being a woman,
I *do* have. What you can learn from the line "I cheat on everyone"
is maybe something about my selfishness, my perverse desire to be

< 164 >

< 165 >

the kind of person who cheats on everyone and declares it falsely shamelessly, my overblown guilt about how I conduct myself in relationships such that I could easily imagine having cheated on everyone. A secret thought: maybe sometimes I feel I may as well have cheated on everyone; falling out of love, or never feeling it in the first place, can feel like a betrayal. The point is, you can't learn anything about what I've actually done, about what has happened in my life that has led me to (possibly, probably) feel this way. And of course I'm someone who believes that actions, what we do with our secret thoughts, are very important, too.

WHAT DOES LOLITA HAVE TO DO WITH THIS?

If one were stupid and/or evil, one could make an argument that all explicitly autobiographical fiction gaslights the reader by obfuscating what is true and what is false, or by, in the case of my adulterous impulses, making the false seem so true that it can even fool the person who came up with the fiction. Nabokov dramatizes this argument in *Lolita*. A third of the way through the novel, Humbert Humbert has married Lolita's mother, Charlotte Haze, in order to be closer to the light of his life, fire of his loins. He comes home one day to find Charlotte writing a letter "in a scorching scrawl"; she has gone to moderate effort to snoop through his desk and find the diary where he has been recording his secret thoughts—his negative impressions of her and his pedophiliac fantasies of her daughter. She is naturally livid and horrified, and says she's leaving the house and barring him from ever seeing "that miserable brat" again. He tells her that she is hallucinating and crazy—classic gaslighting, *mon gars*—and explains in the most direct possible terms that "the notes you found were fragments of a novel. Your name and hers were put in by mere chance. Just because they came handy."

Plausible. This is how naming characters in novels often works. However, we know HH is lying, at least on the level of the action of the novel, because we have been told we have been reading a version of the text that Charlotte snooped through—Humbert's diary—so we're able to understand immediately the grave scrape he's gotten himself into. He considers fabricating new entries in the diary or making changes to what's there and using that to prove she's hallucinating and crazy.

If he had managed to do this, the story would move forward in the same way it has so far: "Have written more than a hundred pages and not got anywhere yet," Humbert notes a bit later. The novel is, until this point, one about fantasy, about creating and deepening the sense that something might happen one day. But when? What enables the plot to move forward, and the fantasies to be realized, is an action by the author, a device that refers to the novel's fictionality through its obviousness: the deus ex machina. Charlotte Haze goes through the ironically termed "raped little table" just after HH has been entertaining highly specific fantasies about drowning or at least heavily sedating her and just before she is incredibly hit by a glossy black Packard off-screen.

On one level, this scene depicts the relationship between one's "real" thoughts and the hypothetical autobiographical novel in which one might hide them: the real thoughts might easily be called a novel and assumed to be fictional, at which point the extent to which the writer has hyperbolized, narrativized, or otherwise distorted his memories becomes totally irrelevant. The narrative has been edited, padded out, and stylized on the level of the text (Humbert Humbert is doing the editing, etc.). In terms of metafictional dramatic irony, however, we also know he's telling the truth. The novel we are reading is not the real (imagined) transcription of the diary Charlotte finds, but a sup-

< 166 >

< 167 >

posedly new version of the diary, which HH purports to have memorized photographically in order to tell this story from the psych ward and his jail cell.

Not to shift blame, but Humbert Humbert is a fictional character: he could not realize his fantasies without the novelist creating the conditions and making him do it. This is not the same thing as the novelist carrying out the acts himself. Despite overlaps between the author and narrator—by the time HH refers to his desk as "raped," we understand that he's self-aware enough to be deploying irony, or rather that Nabokov has lent him his own sense of irony—Nabokov repeatedly asserts the fictionality of *Lolita* in the text. Author of "no fewer than six" fictions that "wholly or partly concern themselves with the sexuality of prepubescent girls," according to an essay by Martin Amis, Nabokov is of course invested in this fictionality—in emphasizing that while writing a novel is an act, it is not the acts that take place within that novel. "Imagine me," HH says a bit later, hoping to generate sympathy in the reader when his attempt to molest Lolita in the deep sleep of a sleeping pill fails. "I shall not exist if you do not imagine me; try to discern the doe in me, trembling in the forest of my own iniquity; let's even smile a little. After all, there is no harm in smiling." The character Humbert Humbert exists only through being imagined; there is no harm in enjoying the prose. The fact that he is fictional is what allows us to enjoy what some critics have decried as an overly seductive style.

FOR THE STORY

In *Lolita*, the writing of a novel is a possible disguise for Humbert Humbert's secret thoughts, which themselves are the betrayal. Today, it is the writing of a novel based on one's secret thoughts that constitutes the betrayal: the power to make public a sensitive issue or an uncharitable interpretation—at a time when it is relatively easy to snoop around and figure out who's based on whom, and when fiction is presumed autobiographical unless proven otherwise—is not nothing, ethically speaking.

The extent to which one fictionalizes is always dangerous: you take some detail, some important details, and then see where they lead. You can change whatever you want—you can make the story better, the contours brighter, the characters less identifiable—but the people involved in the details are onto you. They read the book and say, "But it didn't happen that way." The real fear is not only that they might get mad about the disjunction between what really happened and how you've depicted "it" ("it" becoming, in your telling, a new it entirely, maybe) but also the possibility that they might think you're delusional or rightly clock the unstable relationship between your fantasies and your work. They might see how the alternate path you took in your fiction ends up in the same place, the place you couldn't admit you were trying to go when it was actually happening. They might come out of it thinking they look worse as fictionalized versions of themselves than they look in reality, or they might come out of it thinking you should have told them that this was what you thought when it was actually happening, instead of now, years later, in this frankly lazily camouflaged form.

The thing is that what really happened is often a better story. The desire to disguise reality or keep details to yourself, to save yourself or others the embarrassment, can harm the work. For example, I was recently involved in an interesting romantic situation. Most of my friends and confidants respond to my exciting tales assuming that I would one day write about it; after they'd heard a couple of anecdotes, they wouldn't even ask whether I intended to write about it, just declare that when I did, I needed to keep such-and-such in mind. Once

< 169 >

you start thinking this way you have a problem: you start playing out, to conclusions both logical and not, novelistic fantasies about this interesting romantic situation. You always create psychological profiles of people you know well; that's not an issue. But the fantasies, the narrative possibilities that are constantly occurring to you: once they become possible scenes, everything gets a bit four-dimensional. There is a professional justification for the fantasies to have a high level of detail—to be based on personal experience, ideally.

This affects not only the eventual work in which the situation appears but also the situation as it's being lived. You start to get asked whether you are doing things "for the story," as if that's a bad reason to do things. But of course you're not doing things for the story; if you can think of the story, you don't need it to actually happen to write about it. It is not hard to imagine how you'd feel if something happened to you that didn't actually happen to you. (This is the source of the idea that fiction teaches empathy: writing fiction requires it.) If you are doing things in life that make for good stories, it's because you want to live an interesting life. Maybe the inspiration for the kind of life you want to live comes from stories or from the sense of wondrous possibility that reading stories has always provided, but as long as you avoid arsenic and buying luxuries on credit from the manipulative local merchant, that's not so bad.

Point is, what's embarrassing about representing the fantasies you don't eventually live out is precisely that they *don't* originate in a desire to write a good novel; they originate in a desire to live out the fantasies. The good novel is a by-product, a consolation prize. If the people with whom I was interestingly involved were to one day read what they'd inspired, they might not just get angry at a perceived invasion of privacy or use of their intimate details for professional gain, but feel appalled that I am even capable of imagining it having gone in that fantastical way. If I depict a tension between two characters that in life I may have only imagined, or desires that may or may not be reciprocated, the danger is not just that strangers will be walking around thinking all this crazy stuff might have really happened; it is that the (possibly) unreciprocating parties might think I wanted it to happen—that my true feelings are contained in the plot of the novel I based on the relationship and discernible to anyone, if they know where to look. Return to the desire to live an interesting life, for the story: if you manage to make crazy stuff actually happen, there's no need to worry about exposing your fantasies as such.

But then you run into another problem. When something interesting or provocative or unique or unbelievable happens to me, I cannot help but feel that if I do not put it in a novel, not just in a magazine or an essay like this one but a novel, it will go to waste. In an essay, the interesting event's profound and multifaceted meaning will be fixed in fact-checkable reality—whereas when you turn an event into art, it is allowed to "take on a life of its own." The issue is that the interaction in which the turn of phrase or salient idea originally occurred might have once felt special, both to you (you the individual, not you the author) and to your interlocutor (who, as you might guess, may be a lover), and to recycle it for professional purposes, even if those professional purposes do double duty as art and thus transcend the petty earthly concerns of status and money, would tarnish if not heartlessly destroy the special moment you shared. If my life is contiguous with the art, it might constitute self-plagiarism to make a joke to a lover and then put that joke in a novel, to say nothing of lifting a lover's joke for my own glory, even if I put it in the mouth of a character who resembles in more than one way the lover in question. When you start thinking like this it encourages miserliness and conservatism, which is not the kind of mindset you want to have going into the creation of art.

< 171 >

MY CHARACTERS

At a London party, two friends of mine were in the upstairs bathroom doing cocaine when, according to them, a man burst through the unlockable door, "Kramer-like," with his girlfriend trailing behind him. "Are you guys doing cocaine?" he asked ironically nicely, and my friends couldn't deny it. But first they wanted to know: "Who are you?"

"Have you read Lauren Oyler's novel?" the man replied. This was not such a strange question; I was also at the party, which could be classified as "literary," being thrown by another literary critic. If we're being honest, I had also been the one to advise the man, when he asked where he might find cocaine, to "go to the bathroom and see if the people there are doing it." I was somewhat irritated, because I always have to do everything.

"Yes, of course we've read Lauren's novel," the friends replied, though I don't know if it's true.

"I'm Felix," the man said, and then he did their cocaine.

I recalled that he was less enthusiastic about the few connections he shared with Felix when another friend wrote to him and commented after reading it, "She made you fat." I had also "made him" American, a painter, a disgruntled social media manager, an anonymous internet conspiracy theorist, and a slippery, uncertain figure who could not be pinned down in terms of character traits or biographical details. The structural similarity between this ex-boyfriend and the Felix in my novel can be reduced to the setting and plot of our meet-cute. Which is a great story, not discounting it, but in terms of character I would say this ex and Felix have close to nothing in common. This ex is a wonderful, open, and honest person, and he is British.

Why would a wonderful, open, and honest British person want

to align himself with the complicated American villain of a novel? Cocaine is one answer, but it's not the only one. It could be the quick high of proximity to publicity. More likely, though, is that this fantastic ex is ever so slightly guileless, not gullible or doofus-like or even lacking in irony, but ignoring briefly the fact that he was being read in that moment, just as my two friends may have read Felix in the novel.

Weirdly, many of my ex-boyfriends, who do feature in the novel as a collective Greek chorus, have willingly accepted the idea that Felix "is" them. A man I dated for three months—and whose involvement in the writing of *Fake Accounts* boils down to the fact that I came up with a joke, told it to him, and then reproduced it in the book— was lamenting our breakup to someone or other; when they asked him what my novel was about, he wailed melodramatically, "It's about me!" "This character sounds like me? Is this me?" another friend wrote to me, of a man the narrator of *Fake Accounts* goes out with once. No, I told him, that passage is based on our mutual friend, who himself had alighted on a different detail about Felix that came from our relationship. Not coincidentally, it was only the guy who *did* work as a social media manager who demurred when he was asked how it felt to be fictionalized. But again, he's great—no complaints.

When advance review copies of *Fake Accounts* were released, a prominent novelist, older than I am, contacted our mutual British publisher: the novelist had been alerted to the existence of a minor character in my book who shared their name. This novelist, apparently more of a writer than a reader, was told that the character in my novel "seems to be based on [them] and . . . [would] like the character's name to be changed." After momentarily panicking, I read the passages my editor attached for reference and confirmed what I knew to be true: except for the name, the novelist and this minor character had nothing in common. I did not change the name, but this behavior all but guarantees the novelist's likeness will appear in a future work, though of course called Alex or something. As I told my friend Jeremy, who felt weird that I'd also included a character named Jeremy, I'd always thought that the name of a character was a reliable indicator that the character was *not* based on someone with that name, unless you're in a very particular kind of novel. "Still," Jeremy said.

Do my friends and this random novelist fear, or perversely assume, their identification with these characters because the narrator of *Fake Accounts* is autofictional, winkingly so, and they worry that if one part of the novel is understood to be "real," the rest will be too? Or do they see a mirror where none exists because they "want to be seen"? In contemporary therapy lingo, to be seen is not simply to be viewed; the phrase implies a desire to be acknowledged in all one's beautiful complexity and to be sympathized with. If I see you as a manipulative whiner or an entitled neurotic, that doesn't count; if my friends and new enemy actually recognized themselves in these characters, they would feel differently about the book. "The truth seems to be that no one likes to see himself described as he is, or cares to see exactly set down what he said and did," Truman Capote told George Plimpton in 1966. I imagine it's worse if the descriptions and settings-down are accompanied by even less flattering augmentations. The woman who actually inspired the character not based on the prominent novelist stopped talking to me the year before my novel was published, after I sent her a draft of the manuscript, and assured her, mendaciously, that she and this unflattering character shared certain superficial similarities, but the character was not based on her. In fact, I had reproduced a conversation we'd had more or less nonfictionally.

Sounds pretty bad—but I did this weighing the risks. This friend was never very nice to me, quite self-important, and ultimately only inspired this character without possessing her most noxious qualities.

More important, I stand by the critique that the somewhat unbelievably stupid reproduced conversation implies, so I didn't particularly regret it. Actually, I would do it again. The conversation was so unbelievably stupid that I felt betrayed by it—more betrayed than when this friend blew me off, or whatever.

THE MEANING OF LIFE

I do not know how I would go on if I couldn't justify all bad or even inconvenient things that happen to me as possible future material, in whatever form it may take. This is insensitive, I know, but readers of my work will be able to discern that I endure great suffering at the hands of my own mind, so they should give me a pass to say things like this. If I were not a writer, I would surely come up with other coping strategies for my suffering beyond translating it into structured prose. It's very possible my suffering would be diminished if I did not write; I would certainly think less about the meaning of my suffering if I did not have to convey it, covertly, to others, and if I did not believe that in doing so I am contributing to a project bigger than myself (truth, beauty, human connection, whatever you want to call it).

REVENGE

"Writing, I'm convinced, is often nothing *but* revenge," Terry Castle writes in her memoiristic essay "The Professor," "a way of twirling one's mustache, donning buckler and sword and feathery hat, shaking one's gauntleted fist at the gods. You get to be Puss-in-Boots-on-a-Tear. And why shouldn't you? What other feeling is one supposed to have after one gets clobbered."

Having been wronged renders many of the ethical considerations about representing real people in writing moot. Betrayal is a contract: commit one, and you sign away your rights to the story, not that you ever had any in the first place.

PRIVATE PROPERTY

"As everyone knows who has ever heard a piece of gossip, we do not 'own' the facts of our lives at all," Janet Malcolm writes in *The Silent Woman: Sylvia Plath and Ted Hughes*. "This ownership passes out of our hands at birth, at the moment we are first observed." The exchange that ought to right this injustice is that everyone has the power to observe others; we are all engaged in a reciprocal project of living and watching others live.

Still, it doesn't work that way. We all may be observers, but we don't all write it down and publish it, and even this presumes entirely good faith on behalf of the observer, which most observers frankly just don't have. Is this unfair? Or rather, is it unfair in a way that is somehow adjudicable—in a way that can ever really be rectified? In Europe, where autofiction has been a dominant mode for decades, several court cases and controversies in recent years have focused on writers of texts that fuzz the line between truth and fiction, and in so doing seem to implicate real people. In 2016, the Norwegian author Vigdis Hjorth published *Will and Testament*, a novel about a drama critic named Bergljot whose family has fractured in the more than twenty years since her revelation that her father molested her as a child: one sibling sides with Bergljot, the two other sisters side with the father and mother, and all this comes to a head when the father announces that when he dies he'll split up his estate equally among the four children—except for two sentimental holiday cabins, which he intends to leave to the sisters who have taken his side. Then he actually does suddenly die. In the novel, Hjorth, already a prominent author in Norway when the book was published, seemed to suggest, using the clarifying vagueness of autofiction, that the story was based on her own life; a Norwegian reporter found, among other things, that Hjorth had reproduced certain documents in the novel verbatim or almost verbatim and, according to her furious sister, Helga, did the same with conversations, text messages, and emails. We know this latter detail because Helga said so, and because she wrote a novel called *Free Will* in response; it's about a woman whose sister, a writer, destroys their family through false allegations of incest.

In 2020, the French journalist Hélène Devynck accused her ex-husband, the author Emmanuel Carrère, of violating an unusual legal agreement: during their divorce, he had promised not to write about her without her consent and to get her approval on all passages in which she appears. When a new book, *Yoga*, referred to material from an older work in which she appeared, she claimed Carrère had reneged on their contract. Some thought Devynck's expectation that, in Carrère's words, she could "forbid" him from not only writing but from "having written" something, was ridiculous; others, according to the *New York Times*, thought it an example of "how women are finding new ways to wrest back control of their own narratives, especially after fractious divorces."

This model of narrative misunderstands the definition of the word: one can produce one's own narrative at any time. In reality, Devynck was wresting control of *Carrère's* narrative, which she told the *New York Times* was "completely false," and asserting an alternative, or rather the possibility of an alternative. It's not so much that there is one narrative that two people are fighting over or two narratives battling for primacy, but rather as if there's a space in the public forum where any number of storytellers might set up shop.

< 176 >

< 177 >

The business they're competing for in this metaphor is not just attention, but public opinion. Being written about is not the same as being thought about; the act of publishing is transformative. In a narrative space that is already contested, publication invites even more people to take sides, to offer their take. To be talked about, gossiped about, and judged is not the worst thing that can ever happen to you, but public opinion, gossip, and image are also not petty concerns one should just get over; how we're seen helps us determine who we are. "I don't want to be his literary object anymore," Hélène Devynck told the *New York Times* of her dispute with her ex-husband. "I just want to exist elsewhere." Similarly, after Knausgaard wrote at length about the dramas involved in the publication of his *My Struggle* books, his ex-wife, Linda Böstrom, wrote a novel about her experience with bipolar disorder and the end of their relationship, which Knausgaard had described from his perspective. "On a personal level I was really angry about the way he looked at me," Böstrom told the *Guardian*. "His view of me was so limited, he saw only what he wanted to see. It was as if he didn't know me at all. Reading it felt like suffering a loss." She said that in writing her novel, she was hoping "to be seen as a person and author in my own right."

In public relations and in common parlance, an injunction to "own it"—it being a flaw, a possibly unflattering story, an embarrassing detail, usually publicized—is an injunction to take agency, to avoid the possible shame that may come from the flaw by turning it into some kind of asset, "making it work." But that injunction also acknowledges that you can't get rid of whatever the flaw is—once it's publicized, it can't be destroyed, just manipulated. In pop psychology, to "own your story" is a self-help imperative: own your story before it owns you. Self-help shouldn't suggest paranoid readings—counterproductive—but the fact is that most stories involve more people than just the teller. The real danger is not the story owning you—that's just delusion, which can be enjoyable—but someone else owning your story. "Is there such a thing as the expropriation of intellectual property?" the narrator of Ingeborg Bachmann's 1971 novel *Malina* wonders, referring to an actress whose lover has written a novel about her. "Does the victim of such expropriation, should it indeed exist, have the right to some final difficulties in thinking? Is it still worth it?"

The suggestion, while presented as an absurd joke, is that to write about someone is to occupy their mind—in both senses. The author, in pursuing a radically different interpretation from events you both participated in, colonizes your mind with their own narrative. It's natural that you'd become fixated on this, on whatever space opens up between your interpretation and theirs. It's natural you might start looking for small business loans and try to set up shop there.

It would be awfully easy to note that these metaphors for one's relationship to the events of one's life are capitalist and that that says something about how we understand the world. Yet a better metaphorical framework does not appear. Crucially, Hjorth's novel *Will and Testament* is not only about the fallout from Bergljot's accusations; it's about a literal property dispute, the outcome of which it seems will determine who gets control of the narrative space. When Bergljot finally reads out her accusations to the family, she does so in front of their accountant.

THE TRUTH

The fictional "I" is always truer than it purports to be, and the nonfictional less. We can come up with a whole index of quotations that support this claim. That memory is fallible and deceptive is almost a

< 178 >

< 179 >

cliché; people also often simply lie. But there's a danger in leaning on the truism that nonfiction is less certain than it appears, and fiction more: really, it depends almost entirely on who's talking. Some people are thorough notetakers, are tireless in seeing clearly, and make sure to check their blind spots in their work. Others are incapable of telling the truth; they lack perspective in a self-serving way, a completely debilitating way, or both. This goes for readers as well as writers. The fear of being made public would probably be less existential if we could trust everyone to interpret texts in good faith. But there's a certain nihilism, or at least literalism, in expressing too much excitement about the claim that objectivity is impossible and truth a fiction. It's nice in theory, but in practice, it is the writer's responsibility at least to try. Actually, it's everyone's responsibility to try. By trying you can get surprisingly close.

THE FACTS

"Of course a properly done piece of narrative reporting requires imagination!—and a good deal of special technical equipment that is usually beyond the resources—and I don't doubt the interests—of most fictional writers: an ability to transcribe verbatim long conversations, and to do so without taking notes or using tape-recordings," Capote said in that same 1966 interview with George Plimpton. "Also, it is necessary to have a 20/20 eye for visual detail—in this sense, it is quite true that one must be a 'literary photographer,' though an exceedingly selective one."

While I don't like to make categorical statements, I'm almost comfortable saying that no one has ever had an ability to transcribe *verbatim* long conversations without notes or recordings, even before we became debilitatingly distracted by our phones and all the anxieties they give us. In one of the last pieces she published before her death, published in 2020, Janet Malcolm discussed, in retrospect, a journalistic "device" she used in her book *In the Freud Archives*: "the uninterrupted monologue in which characters made preposterously long speeches in impossibly good English." This was one of several devices, including the use of "composite characters" and setting certain scenes in locations where they did not actually take place, that were deployed by the great narrative journalists of the twentieth century—and according to those nostalgic for this era of journalism, these devices were what *allowed* these journalists to become the great ones. "Anyone could see that the speech had never taken place as such but was a compilation of what the character had said to the reporter over a period of time," Malcolm continued. "Not everyone liked the convention, but no one thought it was deceptive, since its artificiality was so blatant."

The rest of this essay is about what happened when Malcolm was sued by a subject for allegedly inventing quotations and libeling him. She eventually won her case—by presenting the jury with a monologue of her own on the use of the monologue technique—but discomfort about the possible deception in these devices hovers over her admission that "not everyone liked" it. Capote was allowed his delusion of a 20/20 eye for visual detail and savant stage actor's memory because *no one checked*. Although fact-checking was an institution in American journalism long before Malcolm's lawsuit—the best-named of the first fact-checking departments was the *New York World*'s Bureau of Accuracy and Fair Play, established in 1913—it was not quite as rigorous as it is today. Advanced recording technologies and the possibility of much wider audiences, and thus much wider networks of objection, online mean that as a journalist you can sometimes feel, as one friend told me, "like the police are going to come to your house because you wrote an essay about One Direction." Magazines

< 181 >

such as the *New Yorker* are known to put journalists through grueling, almost too-careful fact-checking processes; for a recent piece, *Harper's* told me they might have to call a bystander to a particular scene and ask them to confirm my observation that Gwyneth Paltrow's hair was kind of frizzy. (I had taken a photo, so the call was unnecessary.) "That Janet Malcolm rolled scenes together does not mean that the checking department at *The New Yorker* is a sham," one letter to the editor of the *New York Times* from 1993 reads. "I was a *New Yorker* checker for some 14 years, between 1974 and 1988. We checked nonfiction. We checked fiction. We checked poems. We checked cartoons. We checked cartoon captions. But we definitely did not check quotes; though we tried to make sure that the factual assertions folded into a speaker's poetry were accurate."

Today, the argument Malcolm used to justify her method—that something in a text presented as true may be so obviously fake that it doesn't constitute a "violation of the reader's good faith"—is applied chiefly to autofiction, most often to *My Struggle*. Of course Knausgaard can't remember conversations and feelings he had as a young child. If "whether or not it happened is not really important," as Elif Batuman had it, the backstage work to determine whether something is verifiably "true" is either impossible or not worth the effort. One must sometimes sacrifice such little details in pursuit of higher aims. But the reader does not tend to trust the autofictional author to determine the importance of "whether or not it happened"—hence the reason everyone hates autofiction and readers tend to assume that if some elements of an autofictional novel are verifiable, then all elements must be. Remember some of the benefits of fiction: it requires little from the author and gives him a lot. A journalist, burdened by proof, might naturally resent this. In bringing what was an autofictional story to fact-checkable reality—a legal dispute, reported in international news—Hélène Devynck did not just prevent Carrère from using her likeness in his autofiction; she prevented him from exploiting the ambiguity of the form. By contrast, the writer of nonfiction must earn the reader's trust. What's irritating about a writer of autofiction is that they seem not to care so much about being trustworthy—not only do they seem to live life as an unreliable narrator, by virtue of representing themselves as such, but they will also just take whatever they want from you, happy to make you into a character while remaining themselves the author.

YOU CAN'T MAKE IT UP

One of my favorite novels, *Mating* by Norman Rush, is narrated by a wayward graduate student in anthropology with a prodigious vocabulary and a pitch-perfect sense of irony. This narrator—her voice, her language, her challenging and versatile intellect—is the best thing about the novel. She is sui generis; she is also, Rush has said, significantly based on Rush's wife, Elsa—"pretty much a straight lift," he told the *Paris Review* in 2010. In 2023, I spoke to a journalist working on a story about *Mating*'s contemporary appeal—the novel has become a touchstone for youngish women and for anyone lusting after the good old days of books that feel like *actual novels* and not "wan little husks." During our interview, the journalist wondered if it wasn't a little disappointing that Rush had not totally imagined the narrator, but instead projected a real person into a different vocation and life stage than Elsa was in when the couple lived in Botswana, the setting of *Mating*.

I don't think it's disappointing. In literature, the fallacy that it's harder, and better, to make stuff up than it is to work with events that actually took place persists. Elsewhere, truth has value: it's disappointing to find that someone has embellished a really good story, and it's

< 182 >

< 183 >

particularly exciting to learn that some unbelievable detail is true and to be believed. Maybe it's all the ethical issues that elevate the status of pure fiction (doesn't exist) over autobiographical blends. Regardless, I will never meet Elsa. She exists only as an idea to me, so it really makes no difference for me whether the narrator is based on her; for my purposes, Elsa, Norman Rush's wife, is also a fictional character. The believability of the particular voice and mind, which comes from the narrator's closeness to reality, is exactly what allows one to suspend disbelief about other elements of the novel, to enjoy the unbelievability of it all. At one point, the narrator crosses the Kalahari Desert for a week, alone, to ingratiate herself with a man she has become intellectually and romantically obsessed with. It's a stupendously idiotic act and heroically impressive that she survives, despite beginning to hallucinate quite early on. She wonders, realistically, about this experience, how it is possible that she has done something so stupid, while also feeling proud that she has done it. Which is exactly what one would think if one had crossed the desert alone to pursue a man. I'm tempted to declare that Elsa herself obviously did not cross the Kalahari alone, under any kind of similar conditions. But that part of the novel is so well done that I am not sure that she didn't. We want life to be like a novel, and actually, it often is.

SCARCITY MINDSET

"When information becomes free and universally accessible, voluminous research for a novel is devalued along with it," Jonathan Franzen writes in 2018's *The End of the End of the Earth*. In view of the fact that anyone can google around for a few days and come up with a rich tapestry of researched narrative, the personal, the real, rises in value. During what Laura Bennett called the internet's "first-person industrial complex" in *Slate* in 2015, the "Internet's bottomless appetite for harrowing personal essays" encouraged young, usually female writers to sell their souls for about $150 in exchange for the possibility of a big break. Iconic examples of pieces published during what Jia Tolentino retrospectively referred to in the *New Yorker* as the "personal-essay boom" include "On Falling in and out of Love with My Dad" and "My Gynecologist Found a Ball of Cat Hair in My Vagina." When it ended, Tolentino wrote, "the online personal essay began to harden into a form defined by identity and adversity—not in spite of how tricky it is to negotiate those matters in front of a crowd but precisely because of that fact." The writers, spurred on by "friendly editors" and click-happy readers, were often being exploited to generate web traffic; these essays' failures—a lack of perspective, an oversimplified conclusion relating one's personal experience to a political issue—only encouraged more rubbernecking.

As the drawbacks to this economy became clearer, people became stingy with their anecdotes, their experiences. One night I was up late with two writer friends, swapping stories, deepening our bonds. One of the friends told an amazing story about her adolescence that was by turns hilarious, sad, and revelatory. A little while later, she asked me: Could I please not use the story in any piece of writing, as she intends to do so some day? Using it in this metanarrative way is, you see, a loophole. If she hadn't brought this up, I would have forgotten about the story, the way one lets things recede from the front of the mind. But I wouldn't have ever used it anyway. While people like to throw around T. S. Eliot's dictum that "good writers borrow, great writers steal," the unspoken code is to ask for permission before you fire up the Word doc, full of other people's ideas, and not to steal from other writers, particularly anecdotes in which they were actually involved.

< 185 >

But experience is only first dibs; once you exercise your first serial rights—that's what it's called when you excerpt a book in a magazine—your story is in the public domain. While writing her 2019 essay "Who Owns a Story?" the *New Yorker* critic Katy Waldman learned that publishing a personal story under your own name, for money, cannot even guarantee it's yours: the essay is about how Waldman came to suspect a novelist had taken inspiration from a very personal essay Waldman had published in 2015. When she noticed the novel in question seemed "connected in content, imagery, and tone" to her 2015 essay, she got angry. Whether this anger was justified is what she tries to parse in "Who Owns a Story?"

The moral of the personal-essay boom may be, simply, to try to get paid as much as you can for your writing, because once it's published you don't control it any longer. Is there something wrong with this? Art is one of the few commodities that allow the seller to retain any sense of ownership at all after it's been sold and paid for, and still artists expect total credit for everything we come up with. Yet the idea that the personal matters not at all—that it doesn't matter who writes what, or how many times, since we're all contributing to the repository of human knowledge—is a bit ruthless. "I write about these things not because they happened to me but because they happened, so they're not unique," Annie Ernaux has said. Her books might, in other words, be about anyone; they just happen to be about her.

The obvious retort is that Ernaux writes about what happens to her uniquely well, or at least in a unique way. "What I wrote almost mattered less than how I wrote it," Waldman noted. "Or maybe it is more accurate to say that I feel that I own my voice and thoughts more than I own the events that transpire in my life." What Ernaux writes about doesn't tend to be super uncommon—an illegal abortion, a wretched love affair, breast cancer. These experiences reflect The

Female Experience, you could even argue; the political point made in chronicling them is that they are not unique. Waldman, too, was able to see how the approach she'd used in her personal essay actually drew on tropes and archetypes that many other writers working on that topic—anorexia, another aspect of The Female Experience—use as well. (Waldman eventually called the novelist to ask her if her essay had played a role in her "creative process," and the novelist replied that she had read and enjoyed the essay when it came out in 2015, but the novel is "her own," in Waldman's paraphrase.)

Maybe they'd feel differently about the events of their lives if they had, say, fulfilled a lifelong dream by donating a kidney to a stranger, a much weirder thing to do. The viral *New York Times Magazine* story "Who Is the Bad Art Friend?" demonstrates the limits of this kind of transactional thinking. Published in 2021, the article details an interpersonal-turned-legal dispute between what one party would describe as two friends and the other would call, bitchily, two acquaintances. Years after Dawn Dorland, an amateur writer, and Sonya Larson, a slightly less amateur writer, met in a writer's workshop in Boston, Dorland fulfilled a lifelong dream by donating a kidney to a stranger. As we've seen, it's often not enough to do something; an experience is only complete once you have publicized it. Dorland formed a private Facebook group in order to tell her friends and family about her kidney donation journey, and she added a woman she thought was a friend, Sonya Larson. Larson eventually wrote a short story about a white woman who donates a kidney to an Asian American woman in a particularly annoying way. When Dorland learned of the story, she felt betrayed. When she learned that the story seemed to criticize the character obviously based on her, she became, I assume, embarrassed. When she learned the story utilized a sentimental letter written from the annoying donor to the recipient that was very simi-

< 186 >

< 187 >

lar to a letter Dorland had posted in the private Facebook group, she became litigious. In the US, we have only three stages of grief.

Throughout the article, it becomes clear that it was much easier for Dorland to give away one of her kidneys than to share the story. Why? Because she chose to give away one of her kidneys, knowing the risks and consequences. She was an agent. While she also chose to share the story, in the nefarious, social media sense of the word, she did not know exactly what that meant; nowhere in Facebook's terms and conditions does it stipulate that someone might take one of your precious posts and turn it into a mediocre short story. Never mind that, in using the anecdote, Larson has not prevented Dorland from writing about it later. If Dorland were to write about the kidney donation, she probably wouldn't come to the same conclusions about it that Larson did. Especially now—she could incorporate the whole saga into an even better reflection on attention and altruism. But her sense of betrayal and, I assume, embarrassment totally overshadows logic. It sucks to feel those things. If literary revenge seems impossible, many lawyers will happily take your money.

In terms of strategy, Larson made a mistake: she should have reworded Dorland's Facebook post so that she couldn't be accused of breaking a law, even as hazily nascent a law as transformative use of "private" social media posts. (I thought Facebook owned them!) "I think I'm DONE with the kidney story but I feel nervous about sending it out b/c it literally has sentences that I verbatim grabbed from Dawn's letter on FB," Larson texted her friends while working on the story. "I've tried to change it but I can't seem to—that letter was just too damn good. I'm not sure what to do . . . feeling morally compromised/like a good artist but a shitty person."

In terms of ethics, Larson did little wrong: she observed something in the world and wrote about it. You could even argue she was

involved. At one point, Dorland, seemingly seeking attention and ku-
dos, nudged Larson to acknowledge her act of generosity: "I think
you're aware that I donated my kidney this summer," she wrote to
Larson. "Right?" Whenever something that weird happens to me, I
put it in my "scenes for future novels" file. Another approach to convince the court that Larson's inclusion of the Facebook post falls under transformative use might be to blur the boundary between reality
and fiction: an auto- or metafictional commentary referring to the actual Facebook post, to Dorland's actual life, would suggest that using
the actual letter was critical to Larson's artistic project. This argument
would be better if Larson's story were a genius work of fiction, but
there are, will be, genius works of fiction that deserve the precedent of
leeway this story might set.

Outside the courtroom, what Larson was saying is that her work is
more important to her than Dorland's feelings. Hard-core or realistic?
If we attempted to put every acquaintance's feelings above our fiction,
no one would make anything. What's more, it would be a kind of
waste. When we hoard our material, our observations or our stories,
we prevent anyone else from finding something interesting in them.

YOU COULDN'T PUT THAT IN A NOVEL

Sure you could. The common criticism that you couldn't put in a
novel something especially apt or bizarre or absurd that really happened misunderstands both life and art. Our experience of life—our
expectations, our hopes, our fears—is colored by the art we con-
sume throughout it. Some people need a doomed protagonist like
Emma Bovary to understand this—again, fine. Life is like fiction
because fiction is like life—maybe because the same impulses drive
the desire to live an interesting life and to write an interesting novel,

< 188 >

< 189 >

maybe because the desire to write an interesting novel comes from living, or observing, an interesting life. The thing to criticize is not the content but the form. Because really you can put anything in a novel. It just has to be interesting.

The metafictional epic poem *Don Juan* by Lord Byron—left almost finished when he died in 1824—is the source of the phrase "stranger than fiction." In Canto XIV, the poet pauses the story of Don Juan and his possible lover, Adeline: "To leave them hovering, as the effect is fine, / And keeps the atrocious reader in suspense." He promises to get back to the will-they-or-won't-they drama in the next canto before warning the reader "to forbear / Anticipating aught about the matter"—Adeline, Juan, and even the poet himself, who "shall take a much more serious air / Than I have yet done, in this epic satire," will make fools of the reader who tries to predict what happens next. "'Tis strange,—but true; for truth is always strange; / Stranger than fiction; if it could be told, / How much would novels gain by the exchange! / How differently the world would men behold!"

If only he could tell the truth in fiction, he is saying, we could understand life through fiction better. Why must it be fiction? Fiction has that open quality that nonfiction does not; belief is easier to achieve when it must only make a story seem possible, rather than affirm what is. According to Catherine Gallagher's 2006 article "The Rise of Fictionality," we learned to read fiction this way recently. "In the early eighteenth century," Gallagher writes, "a likely fiction was still considered a lie by the common reader. While the only reliable 'operator' of fictionality was mere incredibility, believability was tantamount to a truth claim. As long as they did not contain talking animals, flying carpets, or human characters who are much better or much worse than the norm, narratives seemed referential in their particulars and were hence routinely accused of fraud or slander."

The rise of fictionality went through several iterations: in the early stages of fictional writing, authors used all sorts of narrative frames to suggest their lies were true. We are seeing something like the inverse with autofiction: writers' serious attempts to convince readers that their too-real tales are actually false. We have not yet learned how to read it alongside all the references—the frames—we have at our disposal. The autofictional form pushes to the limit "what we are all thinking" when we read a novel; the plausible deniability that fiction provides starts to fade. Yet the form insists on its fictionality even in the face of doubt. It insists that there is something to be gained from fiction. Isn't that nice? Isn't that wonderful?

COLLECTIVE OWNERSHIP

What comes after autofiction is a question that has nagged critics and authors since the form regained popularity. The works of Knausgaard et al. seemed to represent the end of a line: the extension of the personal as far as it could go without becoming memoir. Ernaux claims she has "never wanted my work to be seen as autofiction because even the term autofiction is turned in on itself, closed off to the world. I've never wanted the books to be something personal." Denial is better than even a whiff of self-obsession, in "these self-conscious times." What we've learned, or had to remember, through the personal issues of the past fifteen years is that it's impossible to make art without other people. So should the individualistic model of attribution change?

The idea that art is never the product of a singular genius but rather the result of collective external influence is another previously self-evident idea that has seen an attempt at overcorrection lately. In her 2021 essay "Fiction Detective," Sophie Haigney identified an anxious trend in fiction: bibliographies. She quotes the description of the

< 190 >

< 191 >

"Works (Not) Cited" page from the end of Miranda Popkey's 2020 novel *Topics of Conversation*: "This manuscript emerged in part from an engagement with and in some cases refers elliptically to the following texts, televisions shows, films, web series, works of art, songs, e-mail newsletters, and podcasts," Popkey writes before listing them. "It seemed to me at once overfull and inadequate, which of course it was, because how could it not be?" Haigney writes. "A works (not) cited list in its platonic form would be both systematic and infinite."

I've also wondered whether I should give unusual credit, beyond the acknowledgments section at the back of the book, to the people with whom I discuss my writing extensively, whose thinking contributes significantly to my own. Do these people deserve part of the eventual payment I will (hopefully!) receive for the work? I have come to feel that this devalues both the work and the mystery of writing, to suggest that sitting around—probably drunk!—having heated intellectual discussions, sharing references, is the same thing. If you hang out with smart people you will know that it is not that hard or rare to have publishable ideas, to come up with elegant interpretations and funny conceits. What is hard is making something out of them. It's not always fair; it's easier for some people than for others, for a variety of reasons, some nature, some nurture. But truth and beauty do not exist in a vacuum. Without life's unfairness, I don't think we'd be worrying about making art at all.

Over the past fifteen years, the "I" has been interrogated to the point of exhaustion, and it returns to discourse a little shaky, a little suspicious. No one trusts it, and it trusts no one. But when I use it here, nonfictionally, I mean something straightforward: that I am the one who is sitting here, in front of my computer, for hours and hours and hours, thinking and putting words and images and ideas together in what is often a quite difficult process. I am the one who decides what goes in and what gets cut; even the influences that I don't acknowledge or even consciously recognize as such—they're still mine, filtered by my mind. I am the one who must ultimately pull it all together and, after rounds of edits, catch the mistakes, and I am the one who will be criticized for missing something obvious. That many of a work's failures are the result of laziness—a quality that is often admirable in people and contemptible in writing—doesn't matter. I have help, various forms of it, throughout. But the final product is my own. The work of art creates a sphere of agency that is always separate from reality, inside which the artist controls everything that goes on. No one signs up for being born, but in art you get to choose.

And then you can choose to give it away. When I put my work in the world, I may earn some money for my trouble, and then anyone can do what they want with it (within the legal limits). My fictionalized friends can fictionalize me in return; they can give me an anecdote as a gift and then later log in to Twitter and say I stole one of their jokes. I can sue someone who plagiarizes me, and then I can write an essay about the trial. This is what life is all about: trust, contingency, misunderstanding, betrayal, taking, giving, going on, possibility. This is why we write in the first place: we take what's there and imagine something new or simply different. It doesn't matter whether it's about me or you, my ex-boyfriends or a woman who donated her kidney with ulterior motives—it just has to be interesting.

THE POWER OF VULNERABILITY

hadn't realized TED Talks were so short. On ted.com you can sort videos by duration; the last, longest option is eighteen-plus minutes. It seems impossible that I'd never watched one; I could imagine the big black stage, the suggestion of a projected slideshow in the back ground, the presidential hand motions of the speakers. I knew there were sometimes tasteful neon lights. But I didn't know the talks were so openly condensed, though of course it makes sense. They are not for people who want to have a lot of time to spare.

"The Power of Vulnerability" by Brené Brown is twenty minutes long and has more than sixty-two million views. Given at TEDx-Houston in 2010, it begins, as I seemed to have intuited many TED Talks do, with a self-deprecating personal narrative. When Brown was in graduate school, she says, a research professor told her class, "Here's the thing: if you cannot measure it, it does not exist." Brown loved that. She has many degrees in social work, she tells us: a bachelor's, a master's, and in this story she was working toward her PhD. Her motto, bolstered by this education, was: "Life's messy—clean it up, organize it, and put it in a bento box." Her mission was to understand "messy topics" and make them clean and neat so that other

< 193 >

people—and, we will find, she herself—could better understand and deal with them.

The messy topic she landed on, for her research, was shame: the "fear of disconnection," of not being enough. She spent years and years "deconstructing" shame, understanding what it is, how it works. At its root, she determined, shame is "excruciating vulnerability": the idea that, "in order for connection to happen, we have to allow ourselves to be seen, really seen."

She hated vulnerability, so she loved this finding. This was her chance to "beat [vulnerability] back with my measuring stick" and "outsmart it." By finding a way to eliminate shame, she thought, she could render vulnerability obsolete.

"As you know, it's not gonna turn out well," she says, to laughs.

"Data," she says. "Research." She wrote a book and published it. But something was wrong. She went back to her findings, eventually dividing subjects—no word on how or where she found them—into two groups: those with a strong sense of love and belonging and those who "struggle" for that. The difference between them was that the first group believed they were "worthy" of love and belonging; she calls them "Wholehearted." I assume the capitalization, as featured in her books and on her website, came later. She wanted to figure out what these Wholehearted people had in common.

Data, she says again. Research. She took her interviews about "worthiness" and performed an intense, "Jackson Pollock crazy" analysis over four days, trying to find a pattern. (Her husband and child had to leave town for this period. More laughs.) Among her unknown subjects, found according to who knows what criteria—buy her book to find out more—the "Wholehearted" had in common a belief that "what made them vulnerable made them beautiful." They embodied grand nouns—"courage," "compassion," "connection"—and "didn't talk about vulnerability being comfortable . . . nor excruciating . . . just necessary." They were willing, she says, "to do something where there are no guarantees . . . to breathe through waiting for the doctor to call after your mammogram . . . to invest in a relationship that may or may not work out." They said "I love you" first.

On admitting to herself that these were her findings, Brown had a little breakdown, or maybe a big one. (Again, laughs.) She felt she'd been betrayed: she had "pledged allegiance to research" in order to "control and predict"—and the research told her that the way to live is to give up controlling and predicting. Here was a turning point: a crisis, a reckoning.

As with many tales of vulnerability, this one is sponsored by a mental health professional with comedic timing. Brown sought a therapist—a tough one, who treated other therapists and was thus not easily manipulated—and told her that she had this vulnerability problem she wanted to solve. "No family stuff, no childhood shit," she told the therapist. "I just need some strategies." The therapist provided a wry, knowing response. The audience laughs again.

"It was a yearlong street fight, it was a slugfest," Brown says. "I lost the fight, but probably won my life back."

She went back to the Data-Research to determine what "the Wholehearted" know about vulnerability and what the rest of us have to learn. She presents her findings: "The problem is—and I learned this from the research—that you cannot selectively numb emotion," she says, whether through addiction or religion or perfectionism or withholding. "You can't numb those hard feelings without numbing the other emotions," such as joy, gratitude, and happiness. This initiates a vicious cycle. "The more afraid we are, the more vulnerable we are," she says. The more we attempt to avoid vulnerability, the more shame we develop. We must "love with our whole hearts" and "practice gratitude and joy in those moments of terror." She concludes her talk, and the crowd applauds.

* * *

I had never before felt compelled to watch a TED Talk because I had always figured they were stupid, and I reasoned that any culture-shifting idea they might promote would reliably make its way to annoy me in due course. This is what happened with "vulnerability": in the past few years, I began encountering it everywhere, in my professional life as a literary critic and my personal life as a young woman assumed to desire optimization in all my relationships. I thought I'd understood what it meant—it's a common word and fairly straightforward—but as time went on the word began to acquire a sticky sense of its own definition. It started to seem as if everyone was using the word to refer to ideas beyond what their preferred dictionary website might say. Someone had Talked about it, and slowly but surely, connotations were adhering.

The vulnerable version of this story would follow what Brown might call her "journey": I would do some research, purportedly in hopes of historicizing and then critiquing the concept of vulnerability in its contemporary usage but deep down in hopes of finding some relief from my cynical, soul-hardened shame. I would learn that Brown's vulnerability Talk is accepted as the source of the concept's contemporary popularity. I would put off watching Brown's Talk due to the aforementioned prejudices I have against the form and against people with many income streams who make even more money running corporate workshops, which Brown does. (She also offers a training program to deputize others to run corporate workshops.) When I eventually accepted that I had done all the research I could do without watching the speech, I would go to the TED website and feel my shock

< 196 >

at the shortness of the videos. I would wearily click play, thankful at least that it wasn't an hour of my life I was giving up for this. And then something magical—because this sudden change in perspective would indeed feel that way, light and unreal—would happen: I would find the introductory jokes charming. I would recognize in myself, and in the plans for this essay, Brown's desire to "outsmart" vulnerability. I would feel anguish in this recognition, embarrassment, but instead of defending myself against those feelings, I would accept them. I would let them wash over me. I would have an upsetting flashback to all the times I'd chosen shame and disconnection over vulnerability and love. All those negative book reviews I've written! I would reflect on them with remorse. Finally, I would cry a little, before concluding that vulnerability is essential to humanity, which I could now, at last, join.

But that's not what this is. I was right. TED Talks are stupid. Their content is so soluble that it's the kind of thing you don't notice has been in the tap water for years. I hate "Wholehearted," so much that I can barely bring myself to explain Brown's etymological doing here: it comes from "courage," which comes from the Latin *cor*, for "heart." Yuck, and I mean that.

In the years since Brown gave her Talk, vulnerability has come to be seen as a first principle of living, a quality without which one cannot have a fulfilling relationship to work, love, or friends. Between May 14, 2021, and May 14, 2022, the word "vulnerable" appeared in 3,494 articles on the *New York Times* website. On newyorker.com, searching "vulnerability"—rarer, less polysemic—turned up 101 results between March 3, 2022, and March 4, 2023. My preferred dictionary website's definition of "vulnerable" is "capable of being physically or emotionally wounded" or "open to attack or damage," but self-help and culture writing tend to highlight the emotional aspect, focusing on the openness and downplaying the possible harm, which, the idea is, you have no control over. The past decade has also seen a rise in awareness of what are often known as "vulnerable" populations, groups also referred to as "disadvantaged" or "minority": the poor and working classes, immigrants, refugees, disabled people, people of color, queer people, people with mental illnesses, women. "Vulnerable" was used to refer to those who were at higher risk of severe and long-term consequences from COVID-19. The phrase "vulnerable to" something—vulnerable to drug addiction, to domestic partner violence, to homelessness, to abuse—has contracted into a broad descriptor, usually an adjective but even, sometimes, a noun, "the vulnerable," though referring to groups of people using nominalized adjectives is now seen as dehumanizing. The title of Sigrid Nunez's 2023 novel *The Vulnerables* employs this new usage with only a light irony; the book follows an aging woman through the beginning of the pandemic, using her various experiences as opportunities to reflect on different kinds of vulnerability. The title comes from a conversation the narrator has with a "young friend" who chides her for spending too much time outdoors at the start of the pandemic: "*A vulnerable*, she called me. You're a vulnerable, she said. And you need to act like one."

By the end of the novel, Nunez makes clear that everyone, in our interconnectedness and concomitant dependency, is a vulnerable. "You start to care about all the animals, even the tiniest ones, you understand how highly vulnerable these animals' lives are, how vulnerable all lives are," Nunez writes, paraphrasing the observations of Craig Foster, the naturalist who developed a moving relationship with an octopus that became the subject of the documentary *My Octopus Teacher*.

You start to think about your own vulnerability and about death, your own death.

< 198 >

And in the hours and hours he spent exploring the kelp forest, he was stunned repeatedly by the intelligence—the genius—of what he calls the forest mind, a great underwater brain developed over eons, and the intricate work it does to keep everything balanced.

The term's use in computer programming is a reflection of this interconnectedness: a single mistake in code, or "vulnerability," can lead to a bug that compromises security and leaves the entire system open to hackers and other "malicious actors," not unlike the "bad actors" who prey on vulnerable populations in society. Software developers may operate using open-source code—meaning that the software is available for anyone to view, edit, and share—not only to offer models for similar projects or possible solutions to others' problems but also to strengthen their own code by allowing anyone to potentially identify and fix a vulnerability before a "malicious actor" gets to it. This is, broadly, how vulnerability is supposed to work in Brené Brown's formulation: when we open up the source codes of our hearts, our entire network strengthens. The seductive paradox at the heart of "The Power of Vulnerability" is the idea that it takes, and develops, strength to show weakness, or as Brown puts it, "vulnerability is not weakness; it's our greatest measure of courage."

There are many ways for an idea to be stupid. It is not the case that a stupid idea is always simply wrong. On its face, the value of vulnerability in our emotional lives is unobjectionable: of course, if you shield yourself from everything you fear and never let anyone see your flaws, you will live a sad, anxious, boring life. Of course, there are times in life—maybe many—when you need help. Of course, your relationships will be false and meaningless if you're never willing to expose your weak spots. This is either common sense or, if you like, a repackaging of a passage from Freud, who also acknowledged that what follows is "common knowledge." Describing "the way of life which makes love the center of everything" in *Civilization and Its Discontents*, translated here by James Strachey, he writes that a person with a love-oriented approach "clings to" the wider world and "obtains happiness from an emotional relationship" to it. This kind of person isn't merely aiming "at an avoidance of unpleasure" in an attitude of "weary resignation," but passionately "striving for a positive fulfillment of happiness." The downside is obvious: "we are never so defenseless against suffering as when we love, never so helplessly unhappy as when we have lost our loved object or its love."

Even withholding and avoidant people know this, somewhere in their sad, anxious, boring hearts. They probably know it best of all. But when a society agrees en masse that it must dress up a piece of common sense, or a nice bit of Freud, as a newly revolutionary idea, something not very revolutionary at all is usually going on.

* * *

I was hoping for some surprising etymology, specifically involving a relationship to "vulva," that would, in its obviousness, lead me to my argument. No luck. We're taking the long way. As detailed in the 2020 *New York Times* article "Why Be Vulnerable?" which is linked with the slug "/vulnerability-is-hard.html," vulnerability comes from the Latin for "wound," *vulnus*, which despite appearing both literally and metaphorically all over the *Aeneid* is not that complicated either. That the vulva has often been depicted as a wound, and wounds as vulvas, does not matter. That the vulva is referred to in niche, possibly not-that-utilized slang as a gash does not matter. There is no connection, etymologically. Patriarchally, sure. It's inarguable that vulnerability and weakness have traditionally been associated with

< 201 >

women. Gender is a reductive frame for thinking about dichotomies such as weakness and strength, emotion and stoicism, openness and reserve, but that's still how it works: weakness is understood to be feminine, strength masculine. If you are a "strong woman," as the cliché goes, you are to be lauded, because you are defying a stereotype. A man "in touch with his emotions" is similarly seen to be doing a kind of political work with his personal life.

Historically, these characters—the strong woman, the man in touch with his emotions—have always existed. In the *Aeneid*, one metaphorically and literally wounded subject is Dido, whose passionate love for Aeneas—brought on by Venus's orders to Cupid, who does the goddess's bidding disguised as Aeneas's brother—becomes a wound "that her heart's blood fed." Because of this maddening love, she eventually destroys her successful career as the ruler of Carthage, a city that by the way she also *founded*, and when Aeneas tells her he has to leave Carthage for Italy on instructions from the gods—it's his destiny to found Rome—she curses the Trojans, stabs herself (wound two), and sets herself on fire.

A cheap joke one might make in response to Dido's fate is a single word: "relatable." No one finds Aeneas relatable, even ironically, and he is not supposed to be—he is uniquely strong, honorable, heroic. Dido, too, should be out of our league, but in her vulnerability she becomes accessible. While both relatability and vulnerability ought to be relative—what is relatable or potentially wounding to me is not the same as what is to you, physical injuries excepted—today both words are used to assert that there exists a common or even correct interpretation of subjective experience. If I say that Dido is "relatable," I'm implying that many people will recognize and share her perspective and/or experience; I probably also mean that I related to her and thus want to suggest that I am like the many other people who relate to her. I both assert the existence of and join a group: those who find Dido relatable. In this way, "relatable" also has an exculpatory function—Dido is being kind of dramatic, but can we blame her? The gods meddled in her life.

None of this is what "relatable" literally means; to be able to be related to does not necessarily imply a close intuitive or experiential similarity. I can relate to something by being opposed to it. I'm related to a fourth cousin I've never met. All "relatable" establishes is a possible connection of some kind, not the type or strength of that connection. Thus, despite all contemporary tweaks to its meaning, to criticize something as not relatable also suggests that it is so unusual that it is basically alien.

The same logic applies to vulnerability in its contemporary usage as a measure of emotional maturity. Vulnerability is universal; someone who is invulnerable is an unfeeling robot. Everyone's default position is assumed to be weakness protected by guardedness; what we should all strive for is strength in our willingness to be hurt. What makes me feel anxious, embarrassed, or hurt is not the same as what makes you feel those things, but *vulnerability* has come to mean a very specific kind of emotional exposure: embarrassing feelings inarticulately expressed. Some people may respond to feeling threatened by lashing out and saying things they don't mean; others respond by making jokes; still others, by crying. But only one of these—the crying—counts as "being vulnerable." And when someone has been vulnerable, they're difficult to criticize: to do so would be to commit harm, against someone who is defenseless.

The ability to be related to and the ability to be wounded—what these qualities have in common is that they describe one's passive relationship to other people. They're also both associated with women. I'm generalizing again, but it's appropriate: what these terms do is

< 203 >

assert that the general or universal is female. (According to the T-shirt slogan, the future is, too.) Whether stated as "the power of vulnerability," in popular culture, or in terms such as "radical softness" or "tender," in niche queer and feminist spaces, everyone, regardless of gender, is encouraged to take off their "armor" and just be, flaws exposed, more like a woman. "'Feminine' Values Can Give Tomorrow's Leaders an Edge," a 2013 *Harvard Business Review* article claimed, citing vulnerability as one such value, while the widespread understanding that women are more "emotionally intelligent" than men undergirds conversations about how men need to "do better" both in romantic relationships with women and with each other. Studies and articles with titles like "Why Most Men Don't Have Enough Close Friends" demonstrate the coarser sex's inability to connect with others, a willingness to get vulnerable being a necessary quality in that connection. On International Women's Day in 2022, Sheryl Sandberg boasted that "no two countries run by women would ever go to war," echoing sentiments that had become popular in the liberal press throughout Donald Trump's presidency. If, under patriarchy, the male perspective was dominant, the norm now, today's feminist maxims proclaim, is that men are aberrant, and women ascendant.

These are political messages; their aim is to create an appreciation for women and a future that is equal. I'm not against this. I'm not arguing for a return to masculine values, to a time when men were men and could chop my firewood and kill my dinner; I do not fantasize about a mindless "tradwife" lifestyle of babies and dishes that I promote on Instagram as a pathetic hobby playing at fulfillment and corrupt financial independence. It's precisely because I find those fantasies not just personally uninteresting but repugnant that I am against the tyranny of vulnerability in emotional life. What I'm arguing is that the homogenizing universality inherent to terms like "vulnerability" reproduces the sexism it attempts to correct. While the calls for more vulnerability—or "radical softness as a boundless form of resistance," as the niche queer spaces like to put it—purport to be engaged in the project of creating a better world through the toppling of patriarchy, they also reinforce expectations that women be like women.

What's so wrong with being like a woman? Am I some kind of sexist or what? All things being equal, there isn't anything wrong with being emotional and dependent on others for help sometimes. But "woman" is a political category, and all things are not equal. The attempt to sell vulnerability to men and women alike helps explain why the reclaimed term is "vulnerability," not "weakness"; it also leads us to the power play at work in this rhetoric. On spurious quote aggregation websites and the shareable cards featuring inspirational lines found on social media, the translation of the most slogan-friendly aspect of the Freud passage quoted earlier is often slightly different from James Strachey's original work. While Strachey's "we are never so *defenseless against suffering* as when we love" is a pretty literal translation from the German ("ungeschützter gegen Leiden"), the internet alters the phrase to read: "We are never so vulnerable as when we love." Unable to acknowledge defenselessness or helplessness, no matter how beautifully or justifiably suffered—but don't mention the suffering either—the vulnerabilization of Freud reinforces the insistence that vulnerability is not just courage or strength, but the *greatest measure of it*. It has *nothing to do* with weakness. *Nothing!*

The elision of the drawbacks of vulnerability—you could get hurt—signals that someone is trying to sell you something. Let's return to the situation in which we're most vulnerable. On the NBC show *Parks and Recreation*, Rashida Jones's character, Ann Perkins, and Aziz Ansari's character, Tom Haverford, have a tendentious romantic relationship held together mainly by Tom's insistence that it continue. At the beginning of the episode "Lucky" from season 4, the two share a rare moment of genuine laughter, and Tom excitedly points out they've gone a full thirty hours without breaking up, though their record is forty-seven: "It happened when she was out of town for two days, and she forgot we were dating." By the end of the episode, he has ruined it, as he always does. "Hey, sweetheart. I'm not sure you're even aware of this, but we have now gone 48 hours without breaking up, shattering our previous record," he tells Ann, before handing her a wrapped anniversary gift. Ann is wary, and rightly so. The present is a sight gag: she pulls out a ream of condoms in different colors. "Forty-eight of 'em. Different flavor for each hour," Tom responds proudly.

ANN: Yeah, we're not dating any more, okay? Get out.
TOM: No, wait.
ANN: Get out.
TOM: Don't punish me, I took a risk!

A great joke, applicable to all sorts of situations, but especially relationships, where risk-taking has always had a romantic aura. The funniness of "Don't punish me, I took a risk!" comes from Tom's misconception that taking risks is always good and not the neutral, contextual enterprise it actually is. The fear of risk is the fear of failure; Tom's first mistake is in thinking that conquering the fear will be rewarded, that all difficult prospects are necessarily good. The absurdity of the scene—both the condom gift and the concept of the forty-eight-hour anniversary—is what makes it clear that this is a joke being made at Tom's expense.

The joke also gestures to the link between the feeling of vulnerability and the feeling of being under threat: a risk is not always an exposure to harm, but it almost always feels that way. If, classically, the romantic risk is a dramatic gesture—making potentially embarrassing public declarations, showing up outside the beloved's house with a boom box playing "In Your Eyes," or climbing the beloved's fire escape to woo her despite your professed fear of heights—the risks we're told to take in love now are more confessional, more directly revelatory, not least because today many of the iconic grand romantic gestures from film can seem invasive. Showing up at a woman's house unannounced, particularly if she has just dumped you, might be nerve-racking, a risk, but it is also an assertion of power: you will not be rid of me so easily, I know where you live. When any demonstration of vulnerability can be understood as putting the risk-taker in harm's way, it puts the risk-object in the power position, even if she is really not.

A woman who finds herself in this power position is expected to respect vulnerability, too: Can't she relate? Feminists would hardly argue that women's historical vulnerability to violence, exploitation, and crude jokes by men wanting to have sex with us was worth it because all of these experiences show us what it means to be human, though it is darkly, technically true. To be human is to be engaged in power dynamics, to be forced to actually acknowledge one's vulnerability through suffering. Yet the convenient avoidance of one's strength through denial is just as human an experience.

This rhetoric is, obviously, confused: it says that vulnerability is universal, human, but it also says that to be *a* vulnerable, a pawn in a structural game, as Dido is for the gods, is dehumanizing, as in alienating. Dido's only option to escape the torment of this powerlessness and reassert her humanity is to kill herself. While members of "vulnerable populations" might argue that the exposure to harm they experience as such makes them stronger—in her final act before death, Dido

< 207 >

curses the Trojans and ultimately causes the Punic Wars—it would only be a strength in context, a compensation: at least I have this, a rich experience that more privileged people don't understand. Or at least I can drag others down with me. Can you really put a price on perspective?

* * *

While it may seem strange that a concept so crucial to romance has also come to dominate conversations around human resources, vulnerability's popularity in the nebulous industry of management advice reflects its handiness as a negotiation tactic: when the powerful perform weakness, or "play the victim," they obscure their own position, making it more difficult to expect that they occupy it fairly.

Brené Brown has worked as a consultant with large companies such as Pixar and the Bill & Melinda Gates Foundation, and she has a team of "certified professionals" trained in her Dare to Lead program to conduct workshops in harnessing vulnerability to "embed the value of courage in your culture." The study of management is a study of manipulation: how to get one's "team"—it's always a team—to win at the never-ending game of results, growth, acquisitions, profit. An ambiguous concept such as vulnerability is hard to grasp, particularly when one is concerned with efficiency, as one always is at work; luckily, there are worksheets. "Sometimes I'll hear someone say something like 'How often should I cry in front of my team?'" Brown told an interviewer on *60 Minutes*. "That's not what I'm saying. Vulnerability is not about self-disclosure. I'm not saying you have to weep uncontrollably to show how human you are. I'm saying, Try to be aware of your armor, and when you feel vulnerable try not to Transformer up." If that doesn't make sense, remember that courage—which is vulnerability—is "a collection of four teachable, measurable, and observable skill sets."

As Brown suggests, the goal is to trick your employees into seeing you as human, just like them. "Having my team see me in a vulnerable state taught me that vulnerability doesn't have to be a weakness," Fidji Simo, the current CEO of Instacart, told The Cut in 2022, "and seeing me that way allowed my team to connect with me on a deeper level." Simo was discussing the period of time when, as a senior employee at Facebook, she had to go on bed rest for five months because of a difficult pregnancy, and she worried that she wouldn't be taken seriously if she didn't project her usual powerful image of control. She had "learned to lead" through posture, presence, and even, she mentions, wearing makeup; if she had to Zoom into meetings from beneath her duvet, how would she command the respect she needed to do her job?

As celebrities who participated in the "no makeup" ad campaigns of the past fifteen years know well, the ability to be seen sans concealer actually communicates confidence as well as, if you're a beautiful celebrity, natural beauty. Simo's comment that vulnerability need not be a weakness is more revealing than a naked under-eye. Technically, yes, all vulnerability is a weakness: it is the place where you are exposed to harm. What she is describing is not vulnerability, but the tactical deployment of what seems like vulnerability, which can actually fortify one's strength. Just as celebrities have all sorts of methods for maintaining their looks without makeup—being rich is great for the skin, as the saying goes—so too does the high-profile manager. If she has to conduct meetings from bed, the bed will be large, made with tasteful linens as well as some ergonomic pillows designed for particular sleeping postures. The message she sends, its bottom line, is still one of strength: even in bed, I am your boss.

One happy consequence of the success of "'feminine' values" in business has been that the gender of the individual boss has been proved to be mostly irrelevant—if more bosses are still men now, that

< 209 >

won't be true in a decade or so. Todd Field's 2022 film, *Tár*, offers a picture of this gender-neutral near-future. From almost the very first scene, a long, canny introduction to her (fictional) career via a talk at the New Yorker Festival, the world-famous conductor Lydia Tár is treated like a man in every way. Her list of accolades is parodically long; she somehow has both an EGOT (Emmy, Grammy, Oscar, and Tony) and a PhD in ethnomusicology, which she earned by spending five years studying indigenous tribes in Peru, as well as tenures at several major orchestras in the US, including the New York Philharmonic. When we meet her, she is the principal conductor at the Berlin Philharmonic, considered one of the best orchestras in the world. The occasion for her appearance at the New Yorker Festival is the publication of her book, the ridiculously titled *Tár on Tár*. Once her list of accomplishments is finally concluded, she gets to speak; she is almost incoherent, offering little depth beyond what Zadie Smith called in her review of the film in the *New York Review of Books* "eloquent but overly rehearsed bons mots." These include, when Tár is complaining about being called a *maestra* rather than a maestro, "We don't call women astronauts 'astronettes.'"

Of course, no one in the film will call Tár *maestra*; they will sycophantically suck up to her, quietly resent her, and let her pass through. We do not see her battling sexism or homophobia, nor do we get a sob story about how she once had to battle sexism or homophobia. She lives with her wife, Sharon, in the most notorious apartment in Berlin, the slick brutalist loft that is, in reality, the residence on the sixth floor of the Boros art collection, a Nazi bunker turned East German produce-storage facility turned hard-core sex club turned appointment-only private gallery. Except for its gender composition, the marriage is stereotypically heterosexual. An early scene represents the dynamic: home late after a business trip to New York, Lydia arrives back to that fabulous apartment to find all the lights on. She makes a dad-like joke about energy prices, only to find Sharon having an episode of heart arrhythmia and panicking—she can't find her medication. Lydia consoles her and locates a bottle of Sharon's beta blockers in the bathroom drawer, playing the stable husband to her constitutionally emotional wife. When Sharon tells Lydia that their daughter, Petra, is still being bullied at school, Lydia resolves to take care of it. The next day, we see her approaching the bully, another tiny girl child, in the courtyard before class. "I am Petra's father," she says to the girl, before threatening to "get" her if she ever harasses Petra again. Only once does Lydia identify herself as a woman, and she does it cynically, to win an argument. During Tár's master class at Juilliard, a self-described "BIPOC pangender person" says they don't like Bach because of the composer's misogyny, and this elicits the expected reaction in Tár. To communicate the credibility of her position in her debate against the student, who is a caricature of the specter of the woke teenager bent on convincing their elders of the virtues of identity politics, Tár engages with the student on their own faulty terms: she refers to herself as a "U-Haul lesbian" in order to legitimize her point of view that Bach's misogyny ought to be irrelevant in the context of his achievement as an artist. "The problem with enrolling yourself as an ultrasonic epistemic dissident is that if Bach's talent can be reduced to his gender, birth country, religion, sexuality, and so on, then so can yours," she tells the student. But Tár is not really a U-Haul lesbian; she is a jet-setting "Cultural Luminary," as Smith calls her, with what we're led to believe is a coterie of rotating young female lovers that supplement her relationship with Sharon. Tár has won, she is powerful, and she is literally on top.

When I first saw this movie, I found it irritating. I have a bias that I'm working on: I hate books and films that aren't realistic, that don't reflect the nuances of the real world, which I believe to be truly infinitely fascinating. So I saw the early scene of Tár at the New Yorker Festival, and I found it tedious: *This list of accomplishments is parodic!* I cried. As the film went on, it continued to be just a bit too much: the fabulous apartment, the "BIPOC pangender student." If Field had wanted to skewer "cancel culture" in the arts, as some critics believed was his intention, shouldn't he have depicted a realistic scenario? Why not just have the student call themselves a "nonbinary person of color," a phrase students actually use? I felt, by the end, that Field had made a compelling movie but shot himself in the foot by choosing these unrealistic details, which gave critics ammunition to say he had caricatured, and thus not really understood, the politics he was apparently trying to critique.

But then I couldn't stop talking about it; I realized—some vulnerability for you—that my initial interpretation had been all wrong. The entire film operates according to the logic of fantasy, and a particular one: What if women could act like men? We see Tár from rise to downfall, playing the man the entire time. We see her being called maestro; we see her getting fitted for a suit based on what a male conductor wore on the cover for his recording of Mahler's Fifth Symphony; we see her as Petra's father. Most important, we see her in this astounding, unrealistic career, which, in reality, a woman like her would never achieve. Not only because she is a woman, but because she is a woman who acts like a man: cocky, selfish, self-important, rude, on closer inspection a total fraud. To get ahead, women manipulate, too. But not the way men do it.

* * *

From the beginning of the film, the viewer gets an image of Tár's vulnerabilities: the very first image, which plays before the credits, which roll at the beginning, is a live video of Tár sleeping unattractively and unsuspectingly on a plane, taken by the young woman we can assume is her assistant, Francesca, who is broadcasting it to an unidentified interlocutor. In the following scene, we see Tár waiting in the wings for her New Yorker Festival interview, and we learn that she has facial tics and takes what we can assume is a beta blocker for anxiety. As Adam Gopnik, playing himself, introduces her to the crowd at the festival, we see her arm—the one not facing the audience—shake slightly; to begin his interview, Gopnik says he couldn't help but notice her "flinch" as he was reading her parodic bio, making reference to a very slight twitch of her mouth. She takes another beta blocker on a flight before opening a gift that agitates her more; back in her seat, she covers her mouth with her turtleneck to contain her disturbances as best she can. She washes and sanitizes her hands compulsively, she is occasionally overcome by debilitating anxiety, and she seems more than once to be on the verge of a nervous breakdown.

There is no doubt in the film about whether Lydia Tár is actually vulnerable; she is, as we all are, to varying degrees. Even wealthy, parodically successful people are vulnerable—if not to usurpers and journalists, then, at the end of the day, at least to death. The issue is whether Tár is herself actively *being* vulnerable, in the contemporarily sensitive way: whether she is willing to expose herself, to overcome her shame and connect with others. Obviously not. She does not want to let anyone else see any of these weaknesses; she wants to project an image of power, strength, and cold mastery. We learn in that early scene featuring Sharon's heart arrhythmia that the beta blockers Tár takes actually belong to Sharon; Tár pilfers them secretly. When Tár claims to find a spare bottle rattling around the bathroom drawer and relieves Sharon, it's an act; in the bathroom, guiltily frantic, Tár produces the same bottle from which we've seen her popping pills herself.

< 213 >

These little lies of persona grow and multiply as the film progresses. Later, when Tár trips on a concrete staircase running from a dog—a dog she encountered as she was pathetically running after Olga, a new cellist in the orchestra and her would-be young love interest—she smashes her face completely. She tells Sharon, and later her orchestra, that she was attacked, waving off Sharon's urging to go to the police. She tells the orchestra, in a show of bravado, "You should have seen the other guy."

There are other ways she could have handled the explanation of her mangled face. She could have told the truth, playing it off with self-deprecating charm: "You're not going to believe this, but I fell running up the stairs and hit my face on an iron railing. I'm an idiot!" Or she could have stuck with the lie but milked it: accepted the concerned pity of her wife and colleagues, lamented the dangers of being a woman in public, gotten a little teary. These are both ways of performing her womanhood: by being likable, relatable, ostentatiously oppressed, vulnerable. Tár chooses, instead, to project her masculine fantasy: while it's impossible for anyone to know whether she was allegedly attacked *because* she's a woman, what she can control is how she narrates her fictional reaction. She is tough, with no need for police or pity. She likes to hit the boxing gym when she's stressed.

As the film goes on, the viewer sees that Tár is quite vulnerable indeed, in both senses of the word: she has weaknesses, and she is in danger. In using a female protagonist stripped of all the social burdens of her gender, Field highlights the neutral nature of vulnerability: one might have anxiety that is warranted, one might be in danger and *deserve it*. Tár's former mentee and possible lover, Krista, has been writing frantic, desperate emails to Tár's assistant, Francesca, and it seems the two are in cahoots, or might be. We don't know for sure, though we can reasonably assume, that Lydia has done ethically questionable, possibly illegal, things in her "instrumentalization" (Smith) of the young women around her. When Krista dies by suicide, Tár panics; we see her deleting emails that suggest she had intentionally torpedoed Krista's career, painting her as emotionally unstable and nightmarish to work with to top orchestras around the world. Ultimately, we see that the fantasy Tár has been living in is not reality, which, the film suggests, has changed; the world of culture does not reward masculine values—rugged individualism, solitary genius, toughness, cockiness—any longer.

As Tavi Gevinson writes in her *New Yorker* review of *Tár*, "Lydia does not have to contend with other people's humanity—nor offer hers to them." Later, Gevinson writes that "embodying a persona protects Lydia from her own vulnerability, for a while." What punctures the fantasy, though, is not her failure to accept and embrace her own vulnerability so much as what vulnerability represents: the rise of "feminine values." The other feminine values represented in the film are collectivity—contending with "other people's humanity"—and gossip. As in many triumphant #MeToo narratives, what brings Tár down is a group of women, banding together, pooling their resources: as Krista's family is threatening to sue Tár for her involvement in their daughter's death, someone—presumably Francesca—posts online a heavily doctored video of that altercation with the BIPOC pangender student at Juilliard, making Tár seem wildly, definitely offensive, rather than debatably so. Meanwhile, Tár has been trying to hide the mounting controversy from Sharon; when the latter discovers what's been going on, she bars Tár from Petra and refuses to speak to her. During a deposition, it becomes clear that Francesca copied those guiltily deleted emails, which Krista's parents' lawyers now have. At the end of the film, Tár flees in disgrace to the Philippines, to become the conductor for a live performance of a Japanese video game called

< 215 >

Monster Hunter, with an audience of cosplayers, and we are to understand that this is her comeuppance, though it is really just another example of her instrumentalizing those more vulnerable than she. No longer able to manipulate the ambiguity of her womanhood as a power move in Berlin, Tár faces the stark reality of her power over the Filipinos she encounters, who themselves are ambivalent or amusingly blunt toward her, knowing their affect can't really affect their lives. The use and abuse of the country and its people by Western artists is established as a theme by a comment made by a Filipino guide; while touring a waterway by boat, Tár puts her hand in the water and is quickly told to remove it: the river is full of crocodiles. "Oh, I didn't think they'd be this far inland," Tár replies. "They escaped from a Marlon Brando movie," the guide explains—*Apocalypse Now*. All this makes Tár physically ill.

This is not a simple story about right and wrong, justice being served; it is about the ways people can and cannot exercise their power. I see no way that accepting her own vulnerability would have helped Tár, except she might have been more cautious about abusing her underlings; by performing vulnerability, she might have bought herself some time. But eventually the power structure at work finally reveals itself: while gender may provide the scripts, money is what talks. It's only once Tár reneges on an implicit quid pro quo with Francesca, and grants a coveted assistant conductor position to someone else, that Francesca releases to the media and Krista's lawyers the copious unflattering information she has on her boss. Of course, Francesca is, or was once, in love with Tár, too; we learn that in the very first scene, when she sends the live video of Tár sleeping to, we can later assume, Krista. In the accompanying text messages, Francesca self-deprecatingly admits as much. We are never so vulnerable as when we love, but that doesn't mean we're weak.

* * *

Richard Brody, the film critic on staff at the *New Yorker*, detested *Tár*. His gripes are many, and misguided. One in particular is noteworthy: "The movie scoots rapidly by the accusations that [Tár] faces; it blurs the details, eliminates the narratives, merely sketches hearings, leaves crucial events off-screen, and offers a calculated measure of doubt, in order to present her accusers as unhinged and hysterical and the pro-testers gathered against her as frantic and goofy."

This argument makes a mockery of the delightful verb "scoot." On one level, the film's intentional elisions represent Tár's resistance to being vulnerable; she is constantly performing, on stage and off, and she believes she is successful in hiding her weak spots, even from the viewer. But she isn't; she doesn't know we're watching, and she doesn't know her victims are watching, either. Most people I know who saw the film, and most of the reviewers, assumed that Tár did abuse her students and employees emotionally, and they assumed that she did conduct sexual relationships with some of them in order to accomplish her manipulation. We don't need to see the young women's sides of the story to make that assumption, and although, as one character in the film notes, most #MeToo accusations are presumed true by the same kind of liberals who wrote commentary on this film, here I think it's fair to say that, on the level of the film's plot, the allegations probably—key word—are true. We see the shamefully deleted emails; we see how Tár operates with beau-tiful young women, caddishly flirting with random fans as her dot-ing assistant looks on; we see the moony look Tár gets on her face when she's driving Olga home, followed by her pitiful attempt to return Olga's stuffed animal. We see a dream that involves caressing. "Probably" is how these stories of abuse, when publicized, work: we never get a true confirmation that what's alleged to have happened really did, and even in the rare case when allegations are meticulously detailed, we do not get to see what really went on between accuser and accused. This is why the slogan of the #MeToo movement was "Believe women."

But Brody wants to see it. Without a depiction of the actual ordeal the young women went through, it is as if the film did not acknowledge it at all. If a woman weeps in the forest and no one is around to hear her, was she even vulnerable?

The idea that vulnerable populations are expected to detail and relive their trauma over and over again in order to bring awareness to the injustices they face has a long history in feminist and anti-racist criticism. Called "misery lit" in the mid-2000s and derided for its cheap thrills—"Why are authors confessing their hurt so freely and do readers find morbid enjoyment in them?" wondered the BBC in 2007—today the pressure to perform or represent personal-political trauma is seen as another way women, queer people, and people of color are exploited to exchange tales of their lurid, morbidly enjoyable suffering for the illusion that it will help their political cause. There's little way to know for sure if this works—that's life—but, to use just one example, in the years since 2015's "#ShoutYourAbortion" campaign to encourage women to tell the stories of their abortions in order to destigmatize the procedure began, it can't be said that the pro-choice movement has had many wins; *Roe v. Wade* was overturned by the Supreme Court in 2022. Though critics like Brody can easily argue that "careful ambiguities . . . offer a sort of plausible deniability to . . . relentlessly conservative button-pushing," the valiant fight for mimetic justice in narrative art often feels like a justification for morbid enjoyment. Although one viral article published by The Cut expressed light bewilderment that "No, Lydia Tár Is Not Real," the expectation that the film show Francesca and Krista engaging in fraught imbalanced love affairs with the character reflects a hunger for reality that puts an undue burden on the film.

The popularity of signaling and celebrating "vulnerability" in art has risen in tandem with that of the "trauma plot," the narrative structure that Parul Sehgal described in a sweeping 2022 essay for the *New Yorker*. It's not hard to see why: to confess and recount trauma, in art or in a relationship, is, or ought to be, a risk. It makes one vulnerable—to rejection, denial, or painful memories. In art, however, vulnerability has come to represent the safer strategy. Trauma, which has become according to Sehgal "synonymous with backstory," functions in art as a neat explanatory device: motivations or actions that might be realistically mysterious, overdetermined, or ambiguous, are now eventually dispensed with in a gesture of completion that "reduces character to symptom, and, in turn, instructs and insists upon its moral authority." Far from eliciting cries of two-dimensionality, armchair psychologizing, and cheap sentimentality, though, the trauma plot offers the kind of satisfying sensational payoffs that audiences have always craved, with a modern political twist. It leaves space for no response but acceptance; it turns the audience into a passive listener, forced to empathize, and gives the character no space to be anything but a response to her pain. It "flattens," as Sehgal writes. This is especially a problem because trauma is associated with "vulnerable populations"; a sad story that relates to a political issue of the day but that lacks depth or complexity—because it can only relate to the political issue of the day—does the opposite of what the teller intends. Rather than raising awareness, to be vulnerable is to acquiesce to the expectations of the reader or viewer who thinks "the vulnerable" ought to be reduced to their demographics.

While the trauma plot has been most successful when it can be

< 218 >

< 219 >

linked to a political issue, we are all vulnerable when it comes to the trauma of everyday life. In Carrie Battan's December 2022 *New Yorker* essay "Jonah Hill, Selena Gomez, and the Rise of Celebrity Vulnerability," Battan considers "the idea that vulnerability is the highest of virtues" in "a moment in which public vulnerability is celebrated" through a review of two documentaries that purport to give the viewer an intimate look at the lives and mental health of celebrities, Selena Gomez's *My Mind & Me* (great title) and Jonah Hill's *Stutz*. If the previous era of media focused on the low-rent dramatic confessional—from weepy testimonials on reality television, to weepy personal essays that characterized online publishing's "first-person industrial complex," to weepy Instagram Stories and YouTube videos—this one might be about the controlled release of intimate details. Before, the purported aim was catharsis and, possibly, in the case of the many tales of abuse that characterized the genre, a latent bit of revenge; now, it's about a fantasy of collective growth. The virtual rubbernecking and commentary that always followed the drive-by viral essay are now seen as distasteful, exploitative, and cruel, so today we have to do our emotional exhibitionism and voyeurism under the auspices of helping others. Someone might see your story and relate to it; it might help them. "I've decided to make this because I want to present your tools . . . in a way that allows people to access them and use them to make their own life better," Hill says in *Stutz*.

The film is more a portrait of Hill's longtime therapist, Dr. Phil Stutz, who has worked with many celebrities, than a particularly revealing look at Hill's life, but the peek into the therapist's office draws on the recent popularity of media that lets viewers in on the intimacy of therapy sessions, such as the Showtime series *Couples Therapy* and the podcast hosted by the Belgian psychotherapist Esther Perel, *Where Should We Begin?* It's hard to imagine a serious problem, much less a trauma, that would benefit from such publicity, but exposing oneself helps untold others get their fix of other people's pain. That might be therapeutic.

Vulnerability is the contemporary iteration of one side of a long war in American culture: previous battles were fought between irony and sincerity in the 1990s and snark and smarm in the 2010s, with a skirmish between trash and twee somewhere in the middle. "Irony and ridicule are entertaining and effective, and . . . at the same time they are agents of a great despair and stasis in U.S. culture," David Foster Wallace writes in his 1993 essay "E. Unibus Pluram: Television and U.S. Fiction." Later in the essay, he sets the terms that would drive the New Sincerity movement into mainstream literary culture: The new "literary 'rebels,'" he suggested, might treat "plain old untrendy human troubles and emotions in US life with reverence and conviction" and "risk" accusations of banality, sentimentality, melodrama, credulity, and softness. As Anne Lamott puts it in her 1994 book *Bird by Bird: Some Instructions on Writing and Life*, "If something inside of you is real, we will probably find it interesting, and it will probably be universal. So you must risk placing real emotion at the center of your work. Write straight into the emotional center of things. Write toward vulnerability. Risk being unliked."

I love David Foster Wallace—vulnerability—but it's hard to forgive him for what he has wrought with these lines. These oppositions are, have always been, reductive, false: a complex work will almost always have both irony and sincerity, and it is possible to express sincere—or authentic, or true—feelings through irony, a rhetorical device that is useful when you want to represent the tension between two conflicting ideas at the same time. Snark and smarm are the opposing sides' derogatory terms for irony and sincerity, popularized by Tom Scocca's 2013 Gawker essay "On Smarm": the idea is to fight fire with fire, annoyance with annoyance. Trash, exemplified by the rise of *Vice* magazine, American Apparel, and ironic appreciation for political incorrectness in the 2000s, can be seen in opposition to twee's cute, innocent, and unthreatening aesthetic. But they are all the same thing: the nice guys believe they're fighting on the side of good against evil; the meanies think we're holding reality's ground against the encroachment of a ludicrous fantasy that everyone could ever just be nice.

What is contemporary vulnerability's enemy? At a time when we perceive, often not incorrectly, surveillance everywhere, it's clearly judgment: like a skittish animal that will retreat back into its burrow at the first sign of a threat, the vulnerable subject risks openness but is too fragile to handle whatever response that openness might elicit. "No judgment," but I think this is delusional. The Bible illustrates the relationship between vulnerability and judgment well: judge not, lest ye. But just as it is impossible for a person to be truly invulnerable—we are always being observed, always being seen, never truly outside or above ourselves—it's also impossible for a person not to judge: we are always observing, seeing, never truly inside ourselves either. If we did not judge, we could not survive. What's important is if and how we express that judgment. What we mean when we say "no judgment" is not that we aren't judging, but that we aren't holding our judgment against you.

Although critics whine constantly about the deleterious effects of millennial irony, which they claim to be straw-mannishly ubiquitous, vulnerability is the triumphant value in cultural criticism, and it is everywhere. While some instances of "vulnerability" published by the *New Yorker* in 2022 and 2023 draw on the word's political meaning—an article on Chinese spy balloons, some COVID updates—most are works of cultural criticism. A survey of the work of Rosemary Tonks in the magazine says that for the author, "love is its own thing, separate from both sex and its inverse, marriage, a dreaded vulnerability that could strike at any moment if one enjoys life a little too much." A review of *Magic Mike's Last Dance* describes Channing Tatum's hot bod as "a familiar symbol in the era of the nationwide-talent-search and dance-contest reality show: a spectacle of flamboyant heterosexual vulnerability, hidden, in plain sight, in the working class." "Vulnerability" also appears in pieces about, among other things, Jacques Rozier, Terence Davies, Claire Denis, *Batman*, and *Top Gun: Maverick*.

The idea that one should be vulnerable in one's life maps naturally onto prevailing ideas of art, which is often described, positively, in terms of its "humanity" or "human" qualities; the artwork must represent and reflect life as we know it, and it must be produced by a human and lifelike artist, from whom we cannot separate the art. The idea of the "art monster," a term that derives from Jenny Offill's 2014 novel *Dept. of Speculation*, is often theoretically invoked but never practically achieved, due to the pressures of patriarchy, allegedly; in *Dept. of Speculation*, the narrator sets up an opposition, for women, between being an art monster and marriage, and she gets married. That's fine; it's better to be human. Maybe the popularity of this "human" framework relates to growing fears about AI, which has for decades been idly threatening to take not only our jobs but our beauty, the way we make meaning. For some reason, I don't think the critics calling on vulnerability intend to refer to "teachable, measurable, and observable skill sets" that a work of art needs to demonstrate, yet the range of flaws and weaknesses a work may represent in achieving the goal of vulnerability is narrow. Being defensive and closed off is one of the most "human" flaws a person can have—that's what explains the explosive growth of this piece of common-sense advice—but it's the

< 222 >

< 223 >

opposite of being vulnerable; in a novel, according to the new critical rubric, any defensive, closed-off character must "grow" or "change" by the end of the story, or at least reveal the trauma at the heart of their bitter plotting, in order to become human, vulnerable, again. Anger, again unless felt on behalf of trauma, also doesn't count; nor does contempt, cynicism, nihilism, or any feeling that pushes others away, supposedly preventing them from seeing the real you.

When a word or tendency becomes a cliché it not only loses its meaning; it repels all meaning around it, like a shield, or armor. The critic praising vulnerability is only hurting himself: it's his job to judge, and the cliché of vulnerability forestalls all judgment. And anyway, critics have decided that it is no longer a risk to be sincere, soft, banal. It is completely safe.

* * *

I am, of course, in denial. What infuriated me about "The Power of Vulnerability" was not just its obviousness, but the argument's classically maddening structure, through which all objections to it, no matter how elegant or meticulously reasoned, can be funneled into its rock-bottom logic: my rejection can only prove its point. What Brené Brown does, in framing her intellectual work, her "research," as a personal journey of overcoming obstacles—in her books, we learn more about her background, which is full of hardship—is to force anyone who criticizes that work into a position of power they are abusing. By judging it "stupid," I committed a violation. Luckily, I only hurt myself, dragging my laughable attempts to outsmart a stupid idea further down the path of disconnection and shame. It's amazing I have any friends.

At the beginning of *Daring Greatly*, the *New York Times*–bestselling book that expanded on "The Power of Vulnerability," Brown explains where she got the book's title. It's an unlikely source for a text on empathy and love: a speech by Teddy Roosevelt. "It is not the critic who counts; not the man who points out how the strong man stumbles, or where the doer of deeds could have done them better," she quotes. "The credit belongs to the man who is actually in the arena, whose face is marred by dust and sweat and blood . . . and who at the worst, if he fails, at least fails while daring greatly."

This does not suggest, to me, a person who has overcome her fear of judgment or even of failure, but rather someone who has truly outsmarted them. An interpretation of failure that frames it as a success does not understand failure; it's a refusal to acknowledge what failure is. If we continue to see vulnerability as strength, then we never need to reckon with the difficulties of weakness, nor with the responsibilities of power. That's the strategy behind Roosevelt's more famous line on vulnerability: speak softly, and carry a big stick.

MY ANXIETY

want you to hold your jaw like a baby," the instructor said. She was a Greek woman named Angela who described herself as a dancer, choreographer, and yoga coach; she was also, incredibly, an actual dentist. At the union of these disparate professional areas was a passionate belief that the jaw had been neglected in the world of dance and that the rest of the body had been neglected in the world of dentistry. "Once you are grinding and pressing the teeth, your cranium and shoulders, hips, knees and feet are reacting to this pressure," her course description read, beneath a photo of her lying on her stomach, eyes closed somehow theatrically, cupping her jaw in her hands. "Once the skeleton is affected, also the organs are reacting. A chain reaction of organs and emotions is put in motion."

Officially this class, which meets semiregularly in Berlin, is known as the Jaw Release Workshop; I was calling it jaw yoga. What does one wear to jaw yoga? Yoga clothes, it turns out, though several people messed this up. "You need to wear clothes to *move!*" Angela cried. The women in denim were reluctantly forgiven; I snuck past in baggy black pants that were, secretly, also jeans. We sat in a circle on the floor and went around discussing our experiences with bruxism. A

Canadian, the only man there, had begun therapy during the pandemic, and a cascade of realizations followed, about the source of his physical ailments, in his hips, his knees, and especially his feet; at some point he had struggled to walk. A friend told him this problem could be solved only once he stopped grinding his teeth. When I said I had been doing so for eight or nine years, Angela pulled a dramatic facial expression and described my problem as "advanced disease." I was the most experienced person there.

Angela brought out a skull with its jaw detached and performed earnest acts of ventriloquism. This was serious. We learned the different parts of the jaw. She made us feel the place where the mandibular condyle pops out when you open your mouth. She made us go around in a circle and show her that we were pressing the correct spot. "That is not your jaw," Angela said, growing frustrated, over and over. She had been a little unclear about which part she wanted us to press, but we were in no position to object to her methods. We were pathetic. We had each paid twenty euros to go to jaw yoga. I moved my fingers to the correct spot. I experienced no epiphany; I was worried, in part, about preventing my right jaw from cracking as I opened my mouth. It doesn't hurt, really, but it could hurt, and it reminds me that I fear an inevitable future surgery. "Is that your jaw?" a man I was kissing asked once. Yes. We had kissed many, many times. It was always my jaw, at precisely the moment when the swell of feeling demanded a snakelike opening. It's a myth that snakes unhinge their jaws completely to eat. It just looks like that.

We turned to focus on the rest of the body. Jaw yoga was disappointingly like regular yoga, but easier. I wanted a body hack. I wanted one weird trick. A shoulder injury prevented me from engaging in partner-assisted stretching; Angela was visibly disappointed. I probably wouldn't have developed the shoulder injury if I didn't grind my teeth. I learned that from her.

< 226 >

At the end, as in regular yoga, we lay on the floor. This was a dance studio; the floor was hard and uncomfortable. Our inappropriate denim dug into our skin. We were told to close our eyes, and music began to fill the room. The song was, disastrously, "All You Need Is Love." Angela began to sing along. We were encouraged to join her; I mouthed a couple of words, let an uncertain warble escape, and then abandoned myself to waiting for it to be over. I imagined Angela looking down on me not singing, her jaw fully relaxed and free. "Love," she emphasized at the end, in her forcefully gentle speaking voice, "is all you need." As we all sleepily stood up, she passed around business cards that had the name of her company, You Are The Point, on them. We were encouraged to think more about ourselves and our well-being, as if we didn't do that all the time already.

* * *

It worked, for the night, though I think more because an hour of light yoga before bed relaxes the entire body than because jaw awareness results in jaw release. During the first year of the COVID-19 pandemic, Tammy Chen, a dentist, wrote an article for the *New York Times* about the illness's huge toll on the mouth. "I've seen more tooth fractures in the last six weeks than in the previous six years," she told a friend who was misguidedly concerned about a pandemic-driven dwindling of patients. The dentist recommended that grinders "wiggle like a fish" for a few minutes before bed each night. Like light yoga, this works. But the optimism that follows a single night of good sleep is eventually proven cruel. I find it difficult to commit to a nightly wiggle, though I do floss.

Until recently, I thought bruxism was more common than it is: only 8 percent of adults grind their teeth, according to the Sleep Foundation. It's more common in children and adolescents, which is

LAUREN
OYLER

sad. I am neither a child nor an adolescent, which is also kind of sad, but, thank God, not something I worry about. I worry about other things. I've been grinding my teeth since I moved to New York City in 2014 or maybe even before; I hadn't been to the dentist in several years by that point when a tan man in a linoleum hole informed me I needed a $700 mouth guard. Under the fluorescent lights, I panicked; I'm not exaggerating. I said that couldn't possibly be right; the little hole in one of my bottom molars, I was sure, hadn't come from a particularly violent unconscious gnash, as the dentist suggested, but from a conscious one: MDMA, you see. It makes you grind your teeth.

Unfortunately I am not a lively enough person to get into a fight with a cheap dentist about tooth damage caused by psychoactive drugs; I simply insisted with halting denialism that I didn't grind my teeth. Surely I would have noticed if I did. I learned from the *New York Times* article that this is a classic response. "'Oh, no. I don't grind my teeth,' is a refrain I hear over and over again," the hardened dentist wrote, "despite the fact that I'm often *watching* them do it." My cheap dentist was right, of course, and I should have noticed. I woke up with a headache every day. Tellingly, my teeth hurt.

When I left the dentist I went back to work—I sometimes attribute the bruxism to this job, though my anxiety has only gotten worse since I left it several years ago—and marched straight to Google, where I found a personal essay on the topic. The author, Leah Finnegan, wrote of falling in love with the drugstore mouth guard she purchased for much less than $700 "immediately" and so deeply that she began to wear it throughout the day: on the subway, in the shower, at her desk at work. It made her feel safe. At the time I was grateful that I didn't grind my teeth during the day, but things have changed; now I sometimes do. The mouth guard I wear at night is, like the author's, made of a gummy plastic you shape to fit your mouth

< 228 >

by dropping it into boiling water; it makes me look like a happy-go-lucky high school football player. I am absolutely not going to wear it during the day. Some dentists say the guards actually make bruxism worse, because they function like a chew toy.

Unfortunately, bruxism isn't the only issue I experience while trying to sleep. I could say that I'm sleeping badly, but it's worse than that—I'm sleeping incorrectly. When I lie down, I don't actually rest my head on the pillow; instead, I hold it slightly aloft, so that it touches the pillow but, instead of sinking into the soft material, remains hovering above it. To an observer I would seem to be lying down normally. Among other things, I'm worried I'll develop a thick neck, so it's imperative that I develop the ability to put my head on a pillow. I tell myself to relax, and when I do, I'm shocked at how much I had just moments before been not relaxing. *This is sleep,* I think to myself. *This is what going to sleep actually feels like.* But I soon find that my head has risen above the pillow again, and I must admit to myself that I do not know what going to sleep actually feels like.

When my ears began ringing at night, I dutifully went to an ear, nose, and throat specialist just to make sure I did not have a tumor or infection; I don't have a tumor or an infection, but I do have the hearing of an eighteen-year-old. The ringing is probably related to the bruxism, as is what's known as exploding head syndrome: I see flashes of light behind my closed eyes, as if there are fireworks outside my window, and when I wake up suddenly in the middle of the night, I hear mechanical or robotic sounds. Despite the spectacular name, the condition is "prognostically benign," accompanied by no pain or immediate threat to health. What is most alarming about this syndrome is that the hallucinations seem real—more so than my other anxiety symptoms, which I can at least recognize as such. The fear I experience along with these hallucinations inspires a series of worries followed by logical justifications: it's all in my head, which is of course exactly the problem. Though wouldn't it be funny if a doctor read this, and, cynically House-like, correctly diagnosed me with some rare disease causing this precise constellation of symptoms, rendering the entire exercise just that—an exercise?

From this, you would think I have difficulty falling asleep—not so. I am usually exhausted. If I fall asleep reading, I can often be found in the same position an hour or two later, holding the book upright, my arms erect and my grip tight enough that the book never falls from my grasp. I am usually awakened at some point by a tingling in my last two fingers, which I experience because I hold my arms tense in sleep with or without a book. I learned that this is caused by the ulnar nerve from a masseuse who observed my posture and guessed I had this problem; she also intuited that I had been born via C-section and was thus likely dealing with an original sense of having been forcibly removed from a warm place of safety. Is this the source of my constant dread—a fear, despite all evidence against it, that whatever security I build in my professional or personal life is going to be ripped away from me, leaving me with only lack? Probably not, but you never know; maybe that's the source, knowing you can never know. I wake up after about four hours and stay awake for two to four more (I'm *really* awake), which is supposed to be the way our ancestors did it, but our ancestors had different things to do in the mornings, and presumably no FOMO in the evenings. The eye mask does nothing; I usually take it off in a dream. Melatonin stopped working; it gave me surreal nightmares. Sleeping pills, no, never, or very rarely; I worry about dependency, and worse.

When you can't sleep it causes all sorts of other problems, or all sorts of other problems are made worse by being nauseatingly tired five days a week. While socializing I am cheerful, gossipy, and quite

< 231 >

fun until I'm sleepy, but sometimes I will notice myself doing artistic things with my hands and posture—fidgeting, wringing, clenching—even as I engage charmingly (I hope) with my interlocutors. Other times I will look down from a conversation and notice my fist is clenched; because I can laugh at myself, I hold it up to show my friend like it contains a surprise. I also shake, or even vibrate. I do not pick or bite my nails, but in groups or alone, at home or out, I cannot keep my shoulders down (large deltoids—almost as bad as a thick neck). Sometimes—as I write this, actually—it hurts too much to tilt my head backward, to look up at the beautiful sky or a particularly ornate ceiling. Twice now, at parties, men have come up behind me and attempted to physically correct my posture. One I knew; the other was a shirtless guru with a long beard who should have been turned away at the door. Never mind the cell phone addiction, the laptop that sits on the table so that I must look down on it, the ambient tension of contemporary life, when I must be on guard against men who come up to me and randomly correct my posture. No: they say my bad posture is the result of my failure to accept myself as a tall woman. I honestly don't think that's it, but the idea is that, until you've gone to therapy for some impressive amount of time, you can't know the sort of things about yourself that strangers can ostensibly observe just by looking at you.

Also the organs are reacting. I have occasionally fainted for no reason; no, I say, I did not lock my knees. I get sweaty, feel anxious about being sweaty—about the sweat becoming visible to others, disgusting them—and get sweatier. I have more than once broken out in hives from what could only be stress. After I go in the sun, I experience what I call sunburn neurosis, my skin burning and tingling, though I remain, due to anxious sunscreen application, white as a Victorian ghost; I haven't had a sunburn since I was a teenager. The sunburn neurosis can last for hours and is similar to the strange pains I sometimes feel in various parts of my body, just fleeting ones: in my arm and what I imagine are my lungs, though I learned during the pandemic that lungs do not have pain receptors, so when you feel pain there it is usually related to your heart, surrounding muscles, other organs, or the lining of the lungs. I find it difficult to eat and am often nauseated due to stress. Acid reflux can last for weeks and may be a cause of the misidentified lung pain; it's a huge problem if you like smoking and drinking, pastimes not unrelated to the stress that causes acid reflux.

I don't have any phobias, but I do feel afraid. I often sense movement out of the corner of my eye and jump, like a little animal preparing to fend off attack; there's nothing there. "You're always sighing," a new friend told me, and I had to explain: I had never thought about the expression "don't hold your breath" until an ex-boyfriend found it annoying that I could occasionally be found motionless, silent, not heeding it. "Stop your weird breathing!" he would say. Another boyfriend noticed the opposite: if I'm distressed, I will briefly hyperventilate. More cutely, I make little noises, sing little songs. Sometimes I perform feats of what might look from the outside like symptoms of very mild obsessive-compulsive disorder: checking that the front door is locked more than once or twice; changing the combination on a locker at the gym or a museum multiple times because I am afraid someone saw me set it; checking my bag for the presence of my phone, wallet, and keys despite having checked it for the same moments before. I am hesitant to even mention this one, knowing, because of my yearslong internet addiction—which I would attribute to, among other things, an attempt to escape my depressive, anxious, spiraling thoughts or maybe to externalize them—that if someone claims they "are OCD" about facts of life, such as cleaning the kitchen, people on the internet get

< 233 >

mad: perfectionism, neuroticism, and thoroughness are not OCD. On the internet, people mistake suffering for something valuable, because it is an easy route to the currency of the realm, attention; without an official diagnosis, you can't cash in your chips. Still, there are times when my ordinary neuroticism crosses over into irrationality; others notice, too. There are positive by-products of these tendencies; I have never locked myself out of my apartment, or lost my wallet, or had my valuables stolen out from under me at a bar. I believe that worrying about something bad happening helps ward off that bad thing from happening, not because of any supernatural phenomenon but because of the preventive measures I take in response to the anxiety.

My work suffers, of course. How could it not? If I have a meeting, or a phone call, or an appointment, or a plan—to say nothing of a date—I spend the whole day thinking, *I have a meeting, phone call, appointment, plan, or date*, accompanied by no other content or analysis; the fact that I have to be somewhere, doing something, at some time fixates me, and I get little else done. There are periods when I will respond to emails at a reasonable pace, and then there is the email about a potentially lucrative project that I ignored for months. I haven't even opened it; I don't know what it says. The things I do accomplish I put off until it is almost too late to complete them, and then I put them off a little more. The extremely boring hallucination I often experience illustrates my relationship to scheduling well: I look at a clock and see that it is a particular time. An eidetic image of the clock at that time forms. I become attached to this image. When I turn back later—not much later, obviously—it is about fifteen or twenty minutes earlier than the time I believed I had seen. In other words, I see the clock strike 1:45 when it is actually only 1:23, and when I turn back a few minutes later, certain that it will be 1:56 and my entire day will have been ruined due to procrastination, it's actually only 1:30.

NO JUDGMENT

Since I was a child I've had versions of the same dream, in which I am told to pack for some trip. I may have enough time to finish packing at the start of the dream, or I may already be too late; whatever the scenario, I am surrounded by clothes strewn chaotically around the room, and I cannot choose what to bring. Sometimes a family member looks down on me discouragingly, telling me I will not make it. It's never one of those dreams about physical impediments, in which you try to move but can't; the obstacle is always only my own mind, my own incapability, and that is the torment—that I have done this to myself. Occasionally I will be at the airport, sitting in anguish on the floor trying to pack, or I will go to the airport despite knowing that the timing is completely hopeless. Of course, I have never actually missed a flight. I am sadly not a perfectionist, but rather an avoider and a regretter who nevertheless manages somehow to "get it done." It is probably a reasonable enough fear of failure, or fear of failing to achieve the impossibly ambitious vision in my mind, that is my obstacle. Even worse is the possibility, floated by sanguine meditators and accepters of as-they-are things, that I may need the anxiety, and the promise of eventual relief from it, achieved only through doing and surviving the artificially dreaded task, to do anything at all.

What about panic attacks? I have never had the kind of panic attack people mistake for a medical emergency, though the other day I did have a minor one during which my arm started hurting; it was easy enough to reason that it was psychosomatic based on what I had been reading earlier that day: an article about the acronym to remember in order to determine whether someone is having a stroke ("A" is for arm). Sometimes I become very still, sort of unable to move, for, I don't know, ten to twenty minutes to an hour, and my muscles are sore the next day. There are the usual racing thoughts. Sometimes they are about whoever I am in love with, who does not love me back or

< 234 >

< 235 >

in the same way, or who may love me back and in a comparable way but possibly not for long. Sometimes it is that my hair is falling out; sometimes it is that I have squandered my potential as a writer and will never be able to earn money again. Injustices committed against me; chores. The internet addiction was appropriately distracting from all this; no matter how much I cared about what was happening online, about anyone who might have been saying critical things about or implicating me, it was, I see now that it's gone, safely distant. My ultimate anxiety is not that a certain fear will come true; all my fears are somewhat superficial, and when faced with an actual problem I am able to respond quickly and valiantly. I experience panic as mostly meta: the horror of being trapped, in this mindset, for the rest of my life.

Of course, I am not merely anxious; I am also very sad. The two are, for me, inextricable; I get anxious that I'll get sad and sad that I'm so anxious. The possibility of doing things I know will help relieve the anxiety, or at least distract me from it, vanishes into an imaginary realm to which I have no access. This inspires feelings of hopelessness, followed by mindlessness. By the middle of the day, I look forward to going to sleep, though as you know sleep is not a peaceful activity for me. It's harder to describe the deep dark depth and the fear of it, because fewer physical symptoms are involved. Weeping, that telltale sign of sadness, is usually cathartic, a response to a specific build-up of identifiable issues, and thus not involved in what I can't help but think of as the true suffering, which recedes and returns, recedes and returns. Painfully tearing up without actually crying, especially while doing chores or running errands, is more indicative. People often talk about being unable to get out of bed in the morning. What if you can get out of bed—after about an hour and a half of lying awake in it, thinking about how you should get out of bed? What if you can get out of bed but find it beckons you back throughout the day? What if you are, due to your difficulty sleeping, just tired? Which comes first, exhaustion or depression? Does it matter?

The best thing I have read about these feelings recently is Colm Tóibín's description of his mind on chemotherapy, published in the *London Review of Books* in 2019:

> It was easier just to lie on the sofa and think about nothing than have a friend offering drinks of water or checking to see whether I was still alive. It wasn't as though I was enjoying a period of inwardness and introspection. There was no inner self to examine or get in touch with. There was a surface self and all it could do was stare straight ahead. . . . All I really wanted to do was fall asleep and not wake up until it is over.

What's disturbing about my identification with this essay is that I'm not on chemo and do not have cancer, though of course I often worry that I do. Knowing that everyone worries they have cancer helps only a little bit. My mother had it twice. Once I dutifully explained my family medical history to a gynecologist, and the doctor replied, "Are you sure she's not dead?"

So I'm allowed to worry about getting cancer, though progress in genetic testing to date suggests I don't need to be, except inasmuch as it comes for about 40 percent of us at some point in our lives (another statistic I thought would be much higher than it is). This does not help with the hypochondria. It's strangely reassuring to fear you have two different kinds of cancer simultaneously, because although of course this can and does happen, and it means things have gotten very dire, odds are the double cancer you fear is just anxiety: you probably don't have two, so you probably don't have either. Distracting me while reading Tóibín's excellent essay about having cancer were thoughts about how much all his humane treatment would cost in the United States and how, although he surely has a good amount of money, from his bestsellers and movie adaptations and subsequent investments and so forth, it wouldn't have mattered if he had enough money, because he is Irish. They let him stay the night in the hospital while he is receiving five-day courses of chemo. Afterward, he enjoys his time with a physical therapist, and when blood clots are discovered he rushes back to the hospital immediately. In the US this would cost hundreds of thousands, if not millions, of dollars; with "good insurance," as we darkly refer to it, it would still cost, probably, tens of thousands of dollars. Medical pricing is intentionally opaque, as are insurance policies, and both are full of loopholes. For a while NPR was publishing a special series called "Bill of the Month," which included features on a $550,000 stay in the neonatal intensive care unit and a $1,012 bill for a doctor who didn't show up; you could write a bad political poem utilizing as a refrain the phrase "despite having health insurance." "The most terrible misfortunes are also the most improbable and remote—the least likely to occur," Schoepenhauer writes. "The rule I am giving is best exemplified in the practice of insurance—a public sacrifice made on the altar of anxiety." In the American medical system, we see how the improper application of things intended to relieve anxiety only makes it worse, multiplying the factors that can go disastrously wrong. I think about these things often, though I moved to Europe and do not intend to return. I once asked a boyfriend whether, when he thought about getting cancer, as we all think about it, what he feared was the possibility of death or the possibility of bankruptcy. He looked at me as though I were crazy. "Death," he said. He didn't realize that bankruptcy makes you wish you were dead. There are no conditions so bad they make you wish you were bankrupt.

* * *

There's something about these symptoms that allows them to both definitely exist and go unnoticed, the shading so gradual that you cannot see any line between what is "normal" and what is not, even knowing that "normal" is a nefarious construct, used to shame and control. I didn't realize until very recently, reading an essay by a friend who also suffers from bruxism, that I too have scars that run along the inside of my cheeks, an invisible Glasgow smile. More anxiety-producing: I don't know where to put the emphasis—not only when I say I have scars along the inside of my cheeks but also when I think about it myself. Is it the dramatic fact of the scars or the dramatic fact that one can have scars on, or in, one's body for years and not notice? Are the scars actually dramatic at all? Or is this just the sort of thing people walk around with? Should I think of myself as abnormal, or even unique, not just because of the scars, obviously, but for the whole possibly dramatic set of problems that I walk around with? They don't seem that extreme, even if they sometimes feel it, but feelings are subjective and reveal themselves to be an "is your color green the same as my color green?" kind of thing if you think too much about them. "You don't seem anxious," friends will say, surprised at my competent narration. Is the ability to competently narrate one's suffering a sign that it is not really suffering? Many of history's greatest writers want to know.

The comfort of believing you are normal is that you have company in misery and that the condition you suffer seems less likely to become worse. What is this logic? Well, statistically there are more people walking around who are normal than who are worse than normal; that is the nature of "normal," its harm and its solace. If what feels very bad is normal, this admittedly faulty logic suggests, the suffering you experience forms part of some greater aim, human life—though suicide is, as Camus writes, the fundamental question of philosophy, and for this reason, I assume, something most people have "thoughts of," as the public service announcements have it, even if they don't want to do it. Maybe it's not normal to be walking around thinking philosophically. In her short story "Five Signs of Disturbance," Lydia Davis writes of a woman who is "disturbed":

> she cannot always decide whether what seems to her a sign of disturbance should be counted as such, since it is fairly normal for her, such as talking aloud to herself or eating too much, or whether it should be counted because to someone else it might seem at least somewhat abnormal, and so, after thinking of ten or eleven signs, she wavers between counting five and seven signs as real signs of disturbance and finally settles on five, partly because she cannot accept the idea that there could be as many as seven.

As with anything that matters, the language we use to describe "mental illness" is all wrong. With things that don't matter, the language being all wrong is a relief, a tidy irrelevance unnecessary to worry about, but sufferers imagine their suffering might be ameliorated if only it could be named. Mental illness is "real," as real as a tumor, but not the same kind of real as a tumor. The effects are measurable, in blood pressure or hours slept, or noticeable, in weird hand gestures or an erratic mode of speaking or occasional bursts of tears, but mental illness has no shape or volume; its size cannot be conveyed through comparisons to fruits and vegetables (a grapefruit, my mother had the first time). (Still not dead.) It becomes real in the description of its effects, in the naming of everything around it, rather than in attempts to define or summarize it, though we have words and phrases that approach the task. "Disturbance" is funny, and accurate, because it refers both to the internal condition and what it produces: behavior that might unsettle others and oneself if one is capable of reflecting on it (maybe especially if one is *too* capable of reflecting on it). I become "nervous" in small-stakes situations of short or predetermined time frames; "nervousness" no longer describes the anxious disposition, as it did in the past, but the feeling of being anxious—I'll get to that one in a second—about a specific thing that is usually imminent. In old-fashioned parlance, I am also "neurasthenic" because I am a pale woman with thin, occasionally shaky wrists and "neurotic" because I know the basics of psychoanalysis and am a fast-talking big-city professional whose ability to spin out the implications of any anxiety-producing stimulus can be entertaining; I am all of these because I am well educated and earn a certain income. I am rarely, if ever, "hysterical"; that's sexist. (The psychoanalysts can tell you more about it.) My mother used to call herself, as well as me, a "worrywart"; to "worry" is to fidget with something in the mind. "Panic" is acute, "attack" is very acute, and a "fit" is a cute version of a "panic attack"; "throwing a fit" is what children do and what adults do when they are "freaking out" while simultaneously making childish demands of an observer or confidant—needing to be calmed down, reassured, or swaddled in a tight embrace. Like "freaking out," "going insane" is applicable as a joke in retrospect, though it became too popular on the internet a few years ago and lost its edge, particularly because the sort of people who said it were just the sort who ought to be arguing that the usage stigmatizes people with mental illnesses; similarly, among millennials and other internet users, "deranged" has become a common way to describe others' diabolically erratic behaviors, driven by some obvious, should-be-concealed motive. Because I'm actually, I think, "mentally ill," I could be justified in using either, but I don't, except in

< 241 >

casual conversation among friends, because these usages are now clichés, which means they mean nothing. I do indulge in "crazy," a classic. Because I'm not German, or a goth teenager, "angst" is also a joke, about a general condition of irritable despair. "Distressed" is the joke version of nervous, though someone "in distress" is being euphemized, as is someone "behaving erratically." "Stressed" applies to the inevitable anxieties of daily life that thus should not be overly concerning; they are truly normal and will pass quickly, to be replaced by new versions of the same things. A "crisis" is both intense and prolonged; a "spiral" is a crisis about one issue, characterized by repetitive and catastrophic thinking, and "spiraling" may feature prominently in crises, but in a slightly funny way. I fear having a true "breakdown," which suggests, to me, among other things, a failure of speech, but I also fantasize about having a true breakdown for the same reason. "Mental illness" is, of course, insufficient, though if a cold and cancer are both illnesses, then the range of psychiatric conditions that fall under the umbrella must also all fit; the problem is that I do not *feel*—I'll get to this, too—ill, though when I have seen other people in crisis I have thought I actually understand the term "mentally ill." These people are, I determined through observation, much less normal than I am, but what struck me, or most disturbed me, was the way they could describe their paranoias, delusions, and pain in terms that started with empirical reality; what I am saying is that these people in crisis took their ability to observe empirical reality as the basis for their extreme flights from it. "Disorder" is nice, for the implication that what it does is rearrange your mind and make it a mess. The concept of "mental health," did you know, comes from Plato, who said that it could be cultivated through the elimination of passion by reason. Today, good mental health means something like the absence of any variety of anxiety, cultivated through specific strategies, a working-through of one's problems or issues in order to *manage* them, and above all an elimination of both passion and reason.

The words I connect with are "stress" if its objects are rational and "fear" if its objects are irrational. Unless I'm about to appear onstage, in which case I am "nervous," I describe myself as "anxious" so that people know I'm serious: this is not a passing worry but a constant state, and if I were to seek a medical diagnosis I would get one, handily. The difference between anxiety and fear has been tracked for hundreds of years: fear, they say, has an object, while anxiety seeks one. Nevertheless: in the times I have been most anxious, it seems to me like fear, with a rapid cycling of objects, multiple per hour. Every interesting or exciting thing I've done in my interesting and exciting life has been accompanied by fear. I understand this fear to be irrational but know that, like the paranoias and delusions of those I've witnessed truly in crisis, it is close enough to a real threat that I can justify private anguish. I *could* be kidnapped in a taxi in a foreign country; my career *might* be ruined if I publish a particularly bad essay. And what if I cause damage in my rental apartment, injure myself exercising, or have depressing sex? The consequences, the unforeseeable consequences. When asked by a friend to describe what I'm anxious about, any list I come up with is immediately revealed to be, if not ridiculous, then at least manageable, and I ultimately reply that I can't describe it because it's just an oppressive atmosphere of dread and foreboding that I understand to be irrational. If I am presented with logical reasons why what I fear will not come to pass, I can only agree with those reasons; I am even capable of coming up with them myself. But agreement and acceptance are different from belief. While philosophically supported, my discomfort with language may merely be another symptom: everything presented to me is wrong, not enough.

A friend replies to a description of my problems: "Would you say your anxiety is . . . generalized??" "Well, you have generalized anxiety disorder," says another, though I've never told her I have generalized anxiety disorder because I've never been diagnosed with it. The question "Why not?" naturally arises. The answer is that I am one of those people who don't like to go to the doctor, for the personal-historical reasons implied above and for the sociocultural reasons made explicit below. The DSM-V has a list of six symptoms for Generalized Anxiety Disorder, including one symptom with six subsymptoms. I experience all but one: "The anxiety, worry, or physical symptoms cause clinically significant distress or impairment in social, occupational, or other important areas of functioning." I don't know what "clinically significant distress" means; if I suffer more of the listed symptoms when I am doing my job—writing articles for magazines, say—does that mean I am suffering clinically significant distress in my occupational area of functioning? It would be hard to argue otherwise. So in fact I suffer all the symptoms.

In medicine, the problem of language is a problem of classification; I do not seek a diagnosis, probably, because I do not want to be trapped in a single term. Like almost everyone else's, my mind dabbles in an array of mental illnesses to create a bespoke product, and I find all the terms I know either ludicrously broad or ludicrously specific. I learned from Scott Stossel's distressingly thorough 2014 book *My Age of Anxiety: Fear, Hope, Dread, and the Search for Peace of Mind* that the term "generalized anxiety disorder" was conceived at a dinner party held among members of a task force working on the DSM-III in the mid-1970s. They were all drunk, wondering how to classify a colleague who "didn't suffer from panic attacks but who was worried all the time . . . just sort of *generally* anxious," a psychiatrist who was there, David Sheehan, writes. "For the next thirty years," Sheehan continues, "the world collected data on" the group's drunken musing.

The point of this anecdote, Stossel establishes, is not to say that the generalized anxiety disorder diagnosis is totally whack, but to demonstrate how somewhat arbitrary decisions made by powerful people can shape how we see ourselves. I also don't mean to suggest that the ideas that we have drunk are bad—more that drunkenness can give us an admirable economy and frankness, and encourage us to just pick something and go with it, which some of us really struggle to do.

* * *

Where does all this come from? Famously, it's overdetermined. First, my parents, surely. They passed down bad genes, and then they didn't raise me right. Not a very satisfying conclusion. To go further I'd have to discuss the particular genetic issues that may or may not be genetic at all, or may be related to the ways my parents weren't raised right. Then I'd have to discuss the particular ways they didn't raise me right, and while, like everyone, I have a list of these in the Notes app on my phone, and I update it every few days when a new injustice committed against my past innocence reveals itself, through relentless reflection and healing,* I am hesitant to go down this path, which narrows to a tunnel, which is eventually pitch-dark. I am the way I am because my father did this, or my mother didn't do that—someone who attributes their issues to a single cause so confidently always seems to have fallen into a trap from which it is unlikely they will be able to escape.

From my parents, I do know some illuminating stories. When I was an apparently very impressionable age, my class took a field trip to Safety Town, a small theme park designed to teach children various principles of traffic and lifestyle safety. The day began with educational videos about what to do if you smell smoke in your home or

---

* I'm kidding.

< 244 >

< 245 >

see a strange car parked outside your house for a long period of time, and these were followed by a demonstration using glitter about how germs can spread. The trip culminated in a session driving little cars around a little track to learn to follow traffic rules. Driving was not a relevant threat to me at age five or six, but I began to believe that a house fire was a common experience, almost a rite of passage, and that it was thus only a matter of time before it happened to me. I was so concerned about this that my mother eventually bought me a collapsible, fireproof ladder that I could toss out my window to escape the inevitable blaze. Returning from school one day, I found a babysitter watching an episode of a daytime talk show—maybe *Oprah*, maybe *Maury*—featuring multiple victims of kidnapping, all of whom were of course about my age when they were taken. In my memory, the episode culminates with a large group, maybe twenty children, coming together in a silent chorus of lost girlhoods. When I expressed to the babysitter my natural fear that I too would be kidnapped, I could not be reassured. To be prepared for my eventual kidnapping, which I believed would take place in my bedroom, I pretended to be asleep and made my babysitter lift me—gently, gently, like a kidnapper would—to see whether I would wake up if/when it happened to me. Remember the recurring packing dream: I clearly felt my home was *unsafe*.

My childhood sense that the things I feared were common did not come out of nowhere: I made reasonable assumptions—the way children do—based on what I and many children of my generation were being told. We're now in our thirties and forties during what is accepted to be a nationwide "mental health crisis" by 90 percent of Americans, according to a 2022 poll conducted by CNN and the Kaiser Family Foundation.

The second probable cause of anxiety, mine and yours, has nothing to do with my parents, except inasmuch as they, too, are sadly shaped by forces beyond their control: society. It's so fucked up! In the early 2000s, a group of academics in Chicago formed a collective called the Feel Tank—an alternative to the think tank, though of course they also oppose "the facile splitting of thinking and feeling." According to their manifesto, they sought "to understand the economic and the nervous system of contemporary life" by being "interested in the potential for 'bad feelings' like hopelessness, apathy, anxiety, fear, numbness, despair and ambivalence to constitute and be constituted as forms of resistance." The most concise way to convey their message is with one of their early slogans: "Depressed? It might be political!"

Here the concept of normality truly collapses: what is normal—financial precariousness, an inability to plan for or expect a future, war—is not good at all. "Norms" is shorthand for everything you want to destroy in identity and sexual politics. In the years since the Feel Tank was established, this approach to understanding emotions as shaped by and constitutive of power structures—in the academic humanities, it's called affect theory and has been a dominant mode of analysis since the "affective turn" of the 1990s—has become wildly influential, though it's not new. The concept of Americanitis, popularized by William James in a book review published at the end of the nineteenth century, described "the high-strung, nervous, active temperament of the American people," according to an 1898 issue of the *Journal of the American Medical Association*. The causes—advances in technology and accompanying pressures of capitalism—were much the same as they are today. Whenever your contemporary occurs, anxiety and depression are now seen as natural reactions to it, and performances of profound mental discord in response to the news will be familiar to anyone on social media. Female rage, for example, was the subject of multiple successful books in the years following Hil-

< 247 >

lary Clinton's defeat in the 2016 election; the phrase itself implies the books' message, that women are angry in response to their status as women under patriarchy. But anytime you hear someone on the news talk about the "national mood" or describe the "atmosphere," or even "vibe," of a work of art or a party, what they're talking about is affect.

There is something a little simplistic about the way one can attribute all feelings of negativity, disconnection, or anxiety to what amounts to a higher power, as anyone who's read those social media laments will know. Doesn't this encourage more bad feelings: solipsism, nihilism, futility? Looking for something to blame may feel better than beating oneself up, but it doesn't feel *good*. In the introduction to her 2012 book *Depression: A Public Feeling*, Ann Cvetkovich describes the aim of the Public Feelings Project—the Feel Tank members described themselves as a "cell" of this larger group—as an attempt to "depathologize negative feelings so that they can be seen as a possible resource for political action rather than as its antithesis" but without suggesting "that depression is thereby converted into a positive experience; it retains its associations with inertia and despair, if not apathy and indifference, but these feelings, moods, and sensibilities become sites of publicity and community formation." If conventional understandings of mental illness tend to make it about oneself—because of the chemicals in one's brain or the particular contours of one's life—this interpretation wonders whether you can harness its power for good.

Cvetkovich develops her arguments using personal experience. In the first section of the book, "Going Down," she describes spraining her ankle while rushing around campus as a graduate student about to go on the academic job market. "Fretting" about the big and small concerns involved in applying for these jobs, as well as a "troubled romance" and what she's just witnessed at a protest advocating for divestment in South Africa, she steps off a curb funny and falls. Hours later, she goes to a party, apparently having suffered only embarrassment. It is only when she almost passes out and looks down to see her ankle swollen to twice its usual size that "the visual evidence forced me to actually feel the pain and to realize that I could no longer walk." Up until this point, she has described, in retrospect, her own depression and anxiety as troubling because they were both constant and seemingly endless, keeping her "fixated on the immediate present" and "unable to think about other things"; she writes that she would express wistfulness about "the things normal people could do." Yet it was only when it became physically measurable that she could realize how not normal she was.

The structure of this story, in which a reckless achiever ignores her problems until they force a reckoning, has become a classic in the genre of self-help, offering as it does a lesson in the importance of paying attention to the body, the mood, and the vibe: don't wait for psychic pain to cross the dualistic barrier. Although it's a valuable lesson, such narratives are almost always boring or irritating, and this one is no exception. The tension they offer is always underdeveloped. A few years later, the cycle repeats. Although Cvetkovich "appeared to be a successful junior faculty member with all the conditions in place for finishing her book"—a tenure-track job, a fellowship "in Connecticut" (at the prestigious Wesleyan University), an article accepted for publication (with no revisions!)—she "was actually about to crash harder than I ever had before."

Hearing a successful person describe how they felt total abjection but somehow managed to achieve success—the sort of success that the vast majority of people will never achieve due to some combination of bad luck, bad attitudes, and bad work—always lends the narrative of our anxiety an unreal quality, even when the accounts are true. (When

< 249 >

we meet her in this state, Cvetkovich is trying to work on a book chapter about melodrama.) Less successful people will always read about the suffering of the winners with bitter envy and a sense of the unjust distribution of fates; if only they had the advantages the successful anxious person has, they would be perfectly content and therefore manage life better. This is why the interpretations that compete directly with the idea of collective feeling and collective resistance, conservative narratives of bootstrapping and hard work and conviction in one's talents, are so compelling: they make a lot more sense.

As my fixation on health insurance ought to show, I am more sympathetic to the left's understanding of suffering than the right's ignorance of it. But I am also a pragmatist; I have noticed how the encouragement to understand our suffering as determined by external conditions does not seem to ease it. Explanation is deceptive; if it doesn't work as a cure, it might be due to some fault in the logic, one more thing to obsess over. The simplicity that is often the sign of a solution might be suspicious.

Until the revolution that would be our relief comes, we must "do the work" to get better ourselves, as the internet phrase goes. It's palliative, but it's what we have. The doctors and healers and organizations who profit off our anxiety tell us that our suffering is special, and that it requires the purchase of products or adoption of nonintuitive frameworks to alleviate. Let's get out of the way the Instagram apps, which I have been served relentlessly since I started writing this essay; no serious person would believe the answer to psychic pain lies inside the iPhone, but the advertisements for these are so funny and so bizarrely, classically advertisements, speaking directly to the consumer in bold, selling language, that I just want to list a few. I endure so much; please allow me this simple pleasure. FitMind, "THE APP THAT REWIRES YOUR BRAIN," informs me that "50-YEAR-OLD MEDITATORS

HAVE THE BRAINS OF NORMAL 25-YEAR-OLDS, ACCORD-ING TO HARVARD RESEARCH." BetterSleep promises "SLEEP IN SIX MINUTES with this sound [emoji] [emoji]" and urges us to "try to feel your brain smoothing itself out [emoji]." Just a few years ago, "smooth brain" was a Reddit-style insult, meaning idiot, and a person without care or worry might ironically celebrate her own smooth brain to convey the idea, a partial joke, that she has abandoned thinking too much about all the upsetting information and people she encounters (usually also on the phone). The Tapping Solution claims "You Can Reduce Your Stress & Anxiety by 41% with Tapping in under 10 min-utes"; Tapping, capitalized, is also known as the Emotional Freedom Technique (EFT), and is just what it sounds like: tapping specific parts of the body, according to principles of Chinese medicine. An ad for CBT Thought Diary features a smartphone screen that reads "What unhelpful thought do you have?" and a response underneath it, being typed by someone whose pink manicure is growing out: "Everyone hates me." A testimonial for the Breethe app reads: "It's like they turn my brain off for me. I highly recommend it." My favorite ad is one for the Calm app, whose mission is "to make the world healthier and hap-pier"; like Headspace, it has wide name recognition in the "sleep and meditation" space. It's easy to see why it's so popular; they know what they're doing. The ad I get features a black-and-white photo of, I think, a thumb playing with a fidget spinner, but calmly, and reads, in sans-serif font: "Are targeted ads convincing you that you have a disorder?"

Many of these apps offer inspirational wisdom on topics best left to professionals, such as childhood trauma. "Have you tried talking to someone?" people ask me when I mention my various problems. Are you that somebody? No: they mean I should go to therapy, which is invoked in this euphemistic way when the person who should go to therapy seems resistant to the process, potentially so sensitive that even the mention of professional help might harm them. Otherwise, therapy is mentioned so frequently in popular culture that it's become a meme: men will literally [*insert something totally absurd*] instead of going to therapy. Therapy has come to be understood as the baseline for a functional social existence; without it, you are seen as volatile in your lack of self-knowledge, unable to form meaningful relationships, and tormented by patterns you can barely identify, much less break. In the summer of 2023, special issues of both the *New York Times Magazine* and the *New Yorker* focused entirely on the subject; not a single article in either was critical of the practice wholesale, though specific approaches did receive scrutiny.

I have tried talking to someone; it's fine. The responses I get when I utter the magic words "my therapist" are more thought-provoking than any of the personal revelations I've uncovered with him so far, though the idea is really that you need to do it for years in order for the benefits to accrue. "I'm proud of you," friends say. As if it is so difficult to think seriously about myself for hours a day—as if that weren't what I was doing with my anxiety anyway. These friends will talk about my problems with me endlessly, as long as I am "in therapy," "doing the work"; if I am not, or if I express my doubts about the possibility of transcending the workings of my own mind by paying someone to guide me through the process, because I am currently engaging in it as honestly as I can and finding it merely fine, the response is unanimous: I must find a new therapist, someone who is "right for" me. They wonder, gently, gently: is it possible that I, so high-achieving, am unconsciously telling the therapist what I think he wants to hear, deceiving him and myself by being adequately emotional, apparently reflective, in order to give true self-knowledge the slip? Should I not find someone meaner, nicer, female, more intellectual, less intellectual, someone who will not fall for my tricks?

Although we have mostly abandoned this framework for talking about lovers or life partners, acknowledging that there is no such thing as a soulmate, with mental health professionals we are told that out there somewhere we might find the one. I must try a different therapeutic approach, ideally the one that the friend I'm talking to has found helpful. A bit of research quickly reveals an overwhelming expanse of options; the project of finding the therapist who is right for me could effectively distract from my anxiety, if it weren't adding to it. Somatic experiencing therapy, cognitive therapy, behavioral therapy, cognitive behavioral therapy, dialectical behavioral therapy, integrative therapy, holistic therapy, gestalt therapy, humanist therapy, existential therapy, psychodynamic therapy, art therapy, exposure therapy, shock therapy, couples therapy, family therapy, feminist therapy, trauma therapy, queer affirmative therapy, anti-racist therapy, and biofeedback. I could go on. There are many schools of psychoanalysis; some sound like cults, others like literature seminars. At a wedding, I was strongly recommended EMDR, or eye-movement desensitization and reprocessing therapy, which is supposed to retrain the brain to respond to trauma using eye sensors and is advertised online as "scientifically proven," the hallmark of something that is scientifically proven. Sometimes it might be called counseling, which feels more targeted, like less of a commitment; sometimes it might be called coaching, which is less clinical and less accredited, though, like the issues therapy is supposed to treat, accreditation for mental health professionals is mainly an issue of naming. Some of these styles of therapy are more or less the same thing, just with different names, but given the nature of the enterprise, you have to assume that the selection of one name or another, or a combination of names, indicates subtle differences in approach that surely multiply, butterfly-effect-like, to create different outcomes. Whether you're supposed to

< 252 >

< 253 >

think about outcomes is a key differentiating factor in therapeutic approaches. You can do it on the phone, on the couch, over Zoom, over text messages. A friend has suggested that, if I do not want to pay, I might benefit from filling out anxiety worksheets you can find online. There's also an app, Bloom, that promises to help you "become your own therapist": "Self therapy is new but proven to be effective!"

A psychiatrist might prescribe medication, a fraught topic. It is hard to write about it without having taken it oneself, which I have so far resisted, though I have often wondered whether I should give up that fight. I have tried a couple of popular pharmaceuticals recreationally, a handful of times in total, and find I am more afraid of them than I am of illegal club drugs; they really work. While I have no idea what it's like to be on psychiatric medication long term, no one else can say what it's like, either; the medications famously interact with each person differently, so there is no way to understand them as an experience except through trial and error. If I were to criticize what seems to be a craven policy of overprescription of psychiatric medication for what were once considered normal problems, someone would respond with some version of "Wellbutrin saved my life." *It's not about you*, one wants to reply, gently. *Or me!* But here is the great trick of declaring outsize anguish, of being publicly clinically wrecked by one's feelings: once you do it, your feelings set the limits, and no one wants to hurt them.

The reasons for the growing sense that medications for psychiatric illnesses are overprescribed are the same reasons I, personally, don't want to go on them: they have drawbacks, sneakier than those of, say, cocaine and MDMA, which are much discussed and implicit in their illegality, and ideally consumed rarely. With legal drugs, prescribed by a doctor, the period of trial and error daunts; the possible side effects are just as bad as the symptoms the medication is supposed to alleviate, and those side effects can themselves inspire the same anxiety and depression again. The process of stopping these medications, which many patients want to do, is criminally understudied and requires a painful period of weaning that comes with prohibitively horrifying side effects, too. (To start antidepressants is to sign up for some future moment when you won't want to take them anymore, and to have to decide whether you want to experience what are called "brain zaps" in order to stop.) My problem is also not urgent, I think. It might always be environmental, situational; once I finish this book or the next one, I will surely feel better.

At the same time, it's tempting. There are many possible medications and dosages, and they sometimes work. At the end of Sheila Heti's 2018 novel *Motherhood*, the narrator begins taking antidepressants, and all her problems—primarily her vacillation about the question of whether to have a child, which constitutes the entire novel, and a debilitating, weeping sadness around her period—are suddenly solved, with what the critic Willa Paskin called a "Lexapro-ex-machina." The abruptness of the conclusion is itself a comment on the role psychiatric medication plays in North American life, but this plot point, one of the book's very few, also demonstrates the way philosophical searching—let's say that the decision to create life (or not) is a second fundamental question of philosophy, along with whether to end it, as Sally Rooney wrote in her review of the novel—ceases when the anguish that propels it is no longer there. The medication allows Heti's narrator to ignore the upsetting reality that she could go on trying to decide, or regretting, forever; there is no point to get to, and if there were, it's certainly not her, or me, or you.

I'm told I should smoke more weed, which I don't like, or else "do something nice for yourself," which I like so much that I do it every day; the issue is possibly that I do too many nice things for myself and have become a decadent millennial with no values or principles except expertly curated consumption. What about cold showers? I should take one every day. What about exercise? I can't help but feel insulted by this suggestion; I am visibly fit. I am also not going to latch onto a hobby whose specificities I can analyze to regulate my emotions and think about "the body"—contributing to the literatures of swimming, running, yoga, etcetera—or to read my way out of my problems by selecting the right novels. The best medicine, laughter, must also be questioned, critiqued, and reintegrated into a theory of my problem: a sense of humor in a sad individual is often said to be mere mechanism, coping or defense. What's more, as Lauren Berlant and Sianne Ngai note in their 2017 article "Comedy Has Issues," it is not enough to say, "as so many other theoreticians have noted," that comedy lessens anxiety; it also "produces it"—"risking transgression, flirting with displeasure, or just confusing things in a way that both intensifies and impedes the pleasure." Too bad. Occasionally someone will suggest pretending to try religion, just to see whether it works. Barring that, I should pay someone to teach me how to sit quietly for some amount of time every day.

A resistance to helping oneself is often a simple denial of reality: I don't want it to be true that I need help, not because I would like to imagine myself as strong and never in need—this is a common explanation, blah blah—but because I do not want to have these problems that are notoriously difficult to solve, about which there is no professional agreement. I do not want to embark on a yearslong project dedicated to my own mind. I have other things to think about; I hate thinking about these, which feel forced on me.

* * *

A final worry: Am I being confessional? The confession is a simple form of writing; it does not contextualize, illuminate, or complicate;

its main purpose is not the creation of aesthetic beauty out of the materials at hand (life, pain), but selfishness: relieving the confessor's desire to confess. That one usually confesses to having done something bad doesn't help the case. The confession travels in one direction, from me to you, offering no path to analysis, critique, or, God forbid, argument. This is why feminists have denounced the tendency for critics to refer to women writing about their lives as confessional: the "merely" is implied, as are the accusations of narcissism and self-obsession.

My list of symptoms creates a picture of me, an incomplete one, but one. On its own, it might emphasize the lesson from the jaw yoga instructor's business card: I am the point. This is wrong, or not what I intend. The experience of intense anxiety or intense sorrow creates the illusion of uniqueness not through the feelings themselves but through their intensity: I often think, in horror but perverse pride, that if many people were walking around feeling the things I was feeling—that if what I feel were *normal*—life could surely not go on. But at the same time, there are people for whom it doesn't, and I am not one of them. One yearns for the breakthrough, the epiphany, that will make sense of it all, and thus cure it; the reader here is just like me, waiting for some obvious climax and resolution. But catharsis for me is boring for you.

TK KICKER

t's over! Almost. How will it end? I wish I knew.

Patience is an issue; I deal with it a lot. I want to know what will happen in advance, not so much because I want to plan for it—I hate planning—but more because I like to prepare myself emotionally. Foresight is no antidote, but a solace: if something bad is going to happen, at least I was cunning enough to see it coming. I often want to skip to the end, unless of course the middle is entirely fun and the end is nowhere in sight. At the same time, I would hate to not see the end coming, the fun suddenly spoiled and me embarrassed for not realizing that of course it couldn't last forever. I don't want merely to anticipate, which is not for me a pastime but a counterproductive expansion of time. I want to be sure, which is different from anticipation. I am told, as everyone is, all the time, to live in the moment, but I feel that living in the moment is blinkered, unrealistic. The past is not even past, and it is also prologue, we know, and the future is exciting or threatening or hanging in the balance. Under such conditions, how could anyone possibly take things day by day?

I've heard about people who take this fretful approach to movies, television, books; they won't go into it without knowing what happens.

They use Wikipedia, Reddit, reviews, and friends to learn the shocking twists and dramatic scenes in advance; they know he dies, she dies, he gets the girl, she walks into the ocean. They love spoilers and feel that, when viewed in terms of plot, many narratives seem to justify advance notice. In 2018, Jenna Wortham wrote in the *New York Times Magazine* that "losing myself in a film almost guarantees an anxiety attack" and called spoilers her "virtual Xanax," the thing that allows her to "keep watching." The ease with which we confuse what we read and watch with reality is what led the humor magazine the *National Lampoon* to use the term "spoiler" in an issue from 1971: "with the country a seething caldron of racial, political and moral conflict, the average American has more excitement in his daily life than he can healthily handle. (Remember what the American Heart Association says about excess nervous tension.)" They were joking, but the effects were real: anyone who went on to read the next few pages would find succinct descriptions of what happens at the end of nearly one hundred films and works of literature. "There was a telescreen behind the picture, through which the Thought Police had watched them all along."

The article's headline—"SPOILERS," in a gratifying period typeface—acts as a sufficient alert for anyone hoping, on the flip side, to preserve their innocence, an approach that has grown in popularity over the past five decades. One would think that now, when the average shot time in film has shrunk to between 2.5 and 4 seconds, so much happens in a movie that any one spoiler couldn't possibly actually spoil things. On television, too, things keep moving; within a season, each episode ends with a question or even a cliffhanger, so that the network TV viewer is eager to tune in the next week and the streaming customer has no choice but to let the content continue to flow. But no. While studies show that being exposed to spoilers has no effect on an audience's enjoyment of a story, studies often fail

< 259 >

to represent the most extreme views. Online in particular, haters of spoilers range from mildly annoyed to vicious defenders of audience rights. In a 2010 interview with the *New York Times*, a mystery writer called spoilers, whether on Wikipedia or in conversation, "the self-aggrandizing vandalism of another person's potential pleasure." For the artist who works with suspense, they are particularly threatening. "Please don't give away the ending," Alfred Hitchcock said of *Psycho*. "It's the only one we have."

To some, the idea that there is only one ending may seem a retrograde notion about filmmaking. In recent years, sequels, prequels, franchises, and remakes have proliferated alongside the idea that for a critic or social media user to discuss the details of a plot without warning is somehow immoral. To conceive of multiple or alternate endings, endless possibilities, is not to end at all. In 2019, *Radio Times*, the British television listings weekly, examined the top twenty highest-grossing films worldwide every five years going back to 1983 and found that the number of "reboots, remakes, spin-offs and prequels" among the hits increased by 700 percent. Of the top twenty highest-grossing films in 2018, sixteen were what is known as "unoriginal." Potentially infinite iterations of movies and television series mean audiences never have to face a fear of spoilers; the escapism of entertainment never has to end.

As a critic, I have never minded spoilers; Nabokov famously said there was no such thing as reading, only rereading, and I tend to believe it's not possible to understand a work until you've taken into account its end. Surprise distracts; you miss stuff on the first round. If I want to have fun, entirely, I tend not to seek out spoilers, and I can see why one might view them as a slippery slope. Any advance knowledge of a work alters your perception of it. For years, I had heard that *The Sopranos* begins with a mafia boss having a panic attack and seeking therapy—the show's iconically funny conceit. By the time I watched the series, though, I had totally absorbed the premise of a mob boss with clinical anxiety, and I didn't delight in it the way I probably would have if I hadn't known about it for years. Like a relatively recent development in the history of women's rights that has nevertheless always been a part of my life—bank accounts, 1974!—the remarkable idea in the show was only intellectually interesting to me, not emotionally exciting.

The projection of fictional narratives into the nonfictional world through fan fiction, fandom discussions, and the fantasy of "shipping," or the desire to pair two characters or real people in a romantic or sexual relationship, is another manifestation of the fear of spoilers; the more dimensions possible to a story, the less likely any one development matters. These derivative creative pursuits seemingly allow audiences to take the narrative into their own hands, wresting control from the author, but because their status as fictional, as creations, always remains at the forefront of any interpretation, which is part of "fanfic culture," there is no real escape from the reality of the story's fictionality. Unlike traditional fictional worlds, in which we may "lose ourselves," the work of fan fiction is always interpreted according to the terms set by the inspiration: whether this character would really fall in love with that one, whether that one would really say such a thing. The blog *longlivefeedback*, dedicated to "discussing feedback culture in fanfiction," takes as a given that fan fiction is just as much about community participation in a story as the story itself.

This is where the disproportionate hatred of spoilers begins to make sense. A flamboyantly theoretical argument to make would be that a fear of spoilers is a fear of death; we don't want to know how it ends because we'd like to imagine it won't. If we become too invested in a work—if we find it "too real"—we identify too much with the

< 261 >

characters, and confuse the fictional world with our own. If we give in to that confusion, we must acknowledge, on some level, how little sway we have over the director or author, the megalomaniacal figure controlling the fates of his characters, who are us. A belief that spoilers are unethical is rooted in a desire to control—if the fictional narrative you eagerly await is out of your hands, you can at least chastise fellow mortals for talking about it incorrectly.

But putting strict rules on how and when we can discuss works of art robs them of their power to indeed go on forever, through discussion, interpretation, revisiting, dissent. This is another kind of potential pleasure. At some point the credits roll, but a great book will last you, as we suggest when we're getting to know each other, on a desert island, until you're dead.

FURTHER READING

The following is a list of some of the works consulted and cited in *No Judgment*.

EMBARRASSMENT, PANIC, OPPROBRIUM, JOB LOSS, ETC.

Abrams, Brian. *Gawker: An Oral History*. Kindle Single, 2015.

Blumenkranz, Carla. "Gawker: 2002–2007." *n+1*, no. 6 (Winter 2008).

Deuxmoi. *Anon Pls.* New York: William Morrow, 2022.

Donegan, Moira. "I Started the Media Men List." *The Cut*, January 10, 2018.

Galtung, Johan, and Mari Holmboe Ruge. "The Structure of Foreign News: The Presentation of the Congo, Cuba and Cyprus Crises in Four Norwegian Newspapers." *Journal of Peace Research* 2, no. 1 (1965): 64–91.

Garton Ash, Timothy. "Yearning to Breathe Free." *New York Review of Books*, May 11, 2023.

Gluckman, Max. "Gossip and Scandal." *Current Anthropology* 4, no. 3 (June 1963): 307–316.

Hardwick, Elizabeth. "Its Only Defense: Intelligence and Sparkle." *New York Times*, September 14, 1986.

Holiday, Ryan. *Conspiracy: Peter Thiel, Hulk Hogan, Gawker, and the Anatomy of Intrigue*. New York: Portfolio, 2018.

Mahler, Jonathan. "Gawker's Moment of Truth." *New York Times*, June 12, 2015.

McKinney, Kelsey. "Gossip Is Not a Sin." *New York Times*, July 14, 2021.

Meyer Spacks, Patricia. *Gossip*. New York: Knopf, 1985.

Radtke, Kristen. "Letter of Recommendation: Gossip." *New York Times Magazine*, June 29, 2021.

Read, Max. "Did I Kill Gawker?" *New York Magazine*, August 22, 2016.

Roiphe, Katie. "The Other Whisper Network." *Harper's*, March 2018.

Rose, Phyllis. *Parallel Lives: Five Victorian Marriages*. New York: Vintage, 1983.

Smith, Ben. *Traffic: Genius, Rivalry, and Delusion in the Billion-Dollar Race to Go Viral*. New York: Penguin Press, 2023.

Staley, Willy. "What Was Twitter, Anyway?" *New York Times Magazine*, May 3, 2023.

Trotter, J. K. "Tommy Craggs and Max Read Are Resigning from Gawker." *Gawker*, July 20, 2015.

< 264 >

< 265 >

MY PERFECT OPINIONS

Adler, Renata. "The Perils of Pauline." *New York Review of Books*, August 14, 1980.

Austerlitz, Saul. "The Pernicious Rise of Poptimism." *New York Times Magazine*, April 4, 2014.

Baumgartner, Karin. "Travel, Tourism, and Cultural Identity in Mariana Starke's *Letters from Italy* (1800) and Goethe's *Italienische Reise* (1816–17)." *Publications of the English Goethe Society* 83, no. 3 (2014): 177–195.

Brooks, Van Wyck. *America's Coming-of-Age*. New York: B.W. Huebsch, 1915.

Colbert, Benjamin. "Mariana Starke." *Women's Travel Writing, 1780–1840: A Bio-bibliographical Database*. Univ. of Wolverhampton, 2014–2020. btw.wlv.ac.uk.

Hale, Kathleen. "Catfish." *Kathleen Hale Is a Crazy Stalker*. New York: Grove Press, 2019.

Hardwick, Elizabeth. "The Decline of Book Reviewing." *Harper's*, October 1959.

Herford, Oliver. "Say It With Asterisks!" *Neither Here Nor There*. New York: George H. Doran Company, 1922.

Lorentzen, Christian. "Like This or Die." *Harper's*, April 2019.

McGurl, Mark. *Everything and Less: The Novel in the Age of Amazon*. New York: Verso, 2021.

Militello, Paolo. "Mariana Starke and the Grand Tour in Europe,

Italy, and Sicily between the Eighteenth and Nineteenth Century." *Interdisciplinary Studies on the Mediterranean* 1 (2023): 13–31.

Moore, Lorrie, and Heidi Pitlor, ed. *100 Years of the Best American Short Stories*. Boston: Houghton Mifflin Harcourt, 2015.

Orwell, George. "Confessions of a Book Reviewer." *Tribune*, May 3, 1946.

Pickford, Susan. "Mariana Starke, Letters from Italy (1800)." *Handbook of British Travel Writing*. Berlin: De Gruyter, 2020.

Ruby, Ryan. "A Golden Age?" *Vinduet*, April 25, 2023.

Sanneh, Kelefa. "The Rap Against Rockism." *New York Times Magazine*, October 31, 2004.

Scorsese, Martin. "I Said Marvel Movies Aren't Cinema. Let Me Explain." *New York Times*, November 4, 2019.

Starke, Mariana. *Letters from Italy, Between the Years 1792 and 1798* (2 vols.). London: R. Phillips, 1800.

Starke, Mariana. *Travels on the Continent: Written for the Use and Particular Information of Travellers*. London: John Murray, 1820.

Stendhal (Marie-Henri Beyle). *The Charterhouse of Parma*. Translated by C. K. Scott-Moncrieff. New York: Boni & Liveright, 1925.

Stilman, Whit, dir. *Metropolitan*. Rialto Pictures, 1990.

WHY DO YOU LIVE HERE?

Abish, Walter. *How German Is It: Wie Deutsch Ist Es*. New York: New Directions, 1980.

< 267 >

Baldacci, Cristina. "Ephemeral Bodies: The 'Candles' of Urs Fischer." *Bodies of Stone in the Media, Visual Culture and the Arts*. Amsterdam: Amsterdam Univ. Press, 2020.

Benson, Michaela, and Karen O'Reilly. "Migration and the Search for a Better Way of Life: A Critical Exploration of Lifestyle Migration." *Sociological Review* 57, no. 4 (2009): 608–625.

Bishop, Elizabeth. "Questions of Travel" (1956). In *Questions of Travel*. New York: Farrar, Straus & Giroux, 1965.

Chayka, Kyle. "Welcome to AirSpace." TheVerge.com, August 3, 2016.

de Kerangal, Maylis. *The Cook*. Translated by Sam Taylor. New York: Farrar, Straus & Giroux, 2019.

Durastanti, Claudia. *Strangers I Know*. Translated by Elizabeth Harris. London: Fitzcarraldo, 2022.

Garzon, Sara. "If It's Called the Tourist Season, Why Can't We Hunt Them?" *Arts of the Working Class*, May 2022.

Gregory, Alice. "In the Shadow of Geneva Eating Dry Bread." *n+1* (February 8, 2016).

Guo, Xiaolu. *A Lover's Discourse*. New York: Grove Atlantic, 2021.

Latronico, Vincenzo. *Le Perfezioni*. Translated by the author. Milan: Bompiani, 2022.

Lerner, Ben. *Leaving the Atocha Station*. Minneapolis: Coffee House Press, 2011.

Lewis-Kraus, Gideon. *City of Rumor: The Compulsion to Write About Berlin*. Readux, 2013.

FURTHER READING

Nabokov, Vladimir. "A Guide to Berlin" (1925). Translated by Dmitri Nabokov. *New Yorker*, February 22, 1976.

Twain, Mark (Samuel Clemens). "The Awful German Language." *A Tramp Abroad*. Hartford, CT: American Publishing Company, 1880.

Walser, Robert. "Berlin and the Artist" (1910). In *Berlin Stories*, translated by Susan Bernofsky. New York: New York Review Books, 2012.

Wordsworth, William. "The Brothers" (1800). In *Poems*, vol. 1. London: Longman Hurst, Rees, Orme & Brown, 1815.

I AM THE ONE WHO IS SITTING HERE, FOR HOURS AND HOURS AND HOURS

Amis, Martin. "Nabokov's Natural Selection." In *The Rub of Time: Bellow, Nabokov, Hitchens, Travolta, Trump: Essays and Reportage, 1994–2017*. New York: Knopf, 2018.

Bachmann, Ingeborg. *Malina* (1971). Translated by Philip Boehm. New York: New Directions, 2019.

Bennett, Laura. "The First-Person Industrial Complex." *Slate*, September 14, 2015.

Boström Knausgård, Linda. *October Child*. Translated by Saskia Vogel. New York: World Editions, 2021.

Byron, George Gordon, Baron (Lord Byron). *Don Juan* (1819–1824), edited by T. G. Steffan, E. Steffan, and W. W. Pratt. London: Penguin Classics, 2005.

Franzen, Jonathan. "Ten Rules for the Novelist." *The End of the End of the Earth*. New York: Farrar, Straus & Giroux, 2018.

Gallagher, Catherine. "The Rise of Fictionality." In *The Novel*. Vol. 1, *History, Geography, and Culture*, edited by Franco Moretti. Princeton, NJ: Princeton Univ. Press, 2006.

Haigney, Sophie. "Fiction Detective." *The Drift*, no. 4 (April 29, 2021).

Heti, Sheila. *How Should a Person Be?* New York: Henry Holt, 2012.

Hjorth, Helga. *Free Will*. Translated by Anne Bruce. Independently published, 2021.

Hjorth, Vigdis. *Will and Testament*. Translated by Charlotte Barslund. New York: Verso, 2019.

James, Henry. "The Art of Fiction" (1884). In *Partial Portraits*. New York: Macmillan and Co., 1888.

Knausgaard, Karl Ove. *My Struggle*. Translated by Don Bartlett and Martin Aitkin. 6 vols. New York: Archipelago, 2012–2018.

Kolker, Robert. "Who Is the Bad Art Friend?" *New York Times Magazine*, October 5, 2021.

Kunin, Aaron. *Character as Form*. London: Bloomsbury Academic, 2019.

Lerner, Ben. *10:04*. New York: Farrar, Straus & Giroux, 2014.

———. "The Storyteller." *New York Review of Books*, October 21, 2021.

Malcolm, Janet. "A Second Chance." *New York Review of Books*, September 24, 2020.

———. *The Silent Woman: Sylvia Plath and Ted Hughes*. New York: Knopf, 1994.

Nabokov, Vladimir. *Lolita*. New York: Putnam & Sons, 1955.

Rooney, Sally. *Beautiful World, Where Are You*. New York: Farrar, Straus & Giroux, 2021.

Rush, Norman. *Mating*. New York: Vintage, 1991.

Tolentino, Jia. "The Personal-Essay Boom Is Over." *New Yorker*, May 18, 2017.

Waldman, Katy. "Has Self-Awareness Gone Too Far in Fiction?" *New Yorker*, August 19, 2020.

——. "Who Owns a Story?" *New Yorker*, April 17, 2019.

Winter, Jessica. "Our Autofiction Fixation." *New York Times*, March 14, 2021.

THE POWER OF VULNERABILITY

Angell, Katherine. *Tomorrow Sex Will Be Good Again*. New York: Verso, 2021.

Battan, Carrie, "Jonah Hill, Selena Gomez, and the Rise of Celebrity Vulnerability." *New Yorker*, December 19, 2022.

Brody, Richard. "'Tár,' Reviewed: Regressive Ideas to Match Regressive Aesthetics." *New Yorker*, October 12, 2022.

Brown, Brené. *Daring Greatly*. New York: Penguin, 2015.

——. "The Power of Vulnerability." TED talk, TEDxHouston, June 2010.

Field, Todd, dir. *Tár*. Focus Features, 2022.

< 270 >

Foster Wallace, David. "E Unibus Pluram" (1993). In *A Supposedly Fun Thing I'll Never Do Again*. Boston: Little, Brown, 1997.

Freud, Sigmund. *Civilization and Its Discontents*. Translated by James Strachey (1930). Boston: W. W. Norton & Co., 2010.

Gevinson, Tavi. "What 'Tár' Knows About the Artist as Abuser." *New Yorker*, November 24, 2022.

Nunez, Sigrid. *The Vulnerables*. New York: Riverhead, 2023.

Scocca, Tom "On Smarm." *Gawker*, December 5, 2013.

Sehgal, Parul. "The Case Against the Trauma Plot." *New Yorker*, December 27, 2021.

Smith, Zadie. "The Instrumentalist." *New York Review of Books*, January 19, 2023.

Virgil. *The Aeneid*. Translated by Robert Fagles. London: Penguin Classics, 2010.

MY ANXIETY

Berlant, Lauren. *Cruel Optimism*. Durham, NC: Duke Univ. Press, 2011.

Berlant, Lauren, and Ngai, Sianne. "Comedy Has Issues." *Critical Inquiry* 43, no. 2 (Winter 2017): 233–249.

Camus, Albert. *The Myth of Sisyphus*. Translated by Justin O'Brien (1955). London: Penguin Books UK, 2005.

Cvetkovich, Ann. *Depression: A Public Feeling*. Durham, NC: Duke Univ. Press, 2012.

Davis, Lydia. "Five Signs of Disturbance." In *Break It Down*. New York: Farrar, Straus & Giroux, 1986.

Finnegan, Leah. "Clenching the Night Away." *The Morning News*, January 23, 2013.

Heti, Sheila. *Motherhood*. New York: Henry Holt, 2018

Stossel, Scott. *My Age of Anxiety*. New York: Knopf, 2014.

Tóibín, Colm. "Instead of Shaking All Over, I Read the News. I Listened to the Radio. I Had Lunch." *London Review of Books* 41, no. 8 (April 18, 2019).

Watts, Madeleine. "The Year of Grinding Teeth." *Paris Review*, January 21, 2021.

TK KICKER

Cohen, Noam. "Spoiler Alert: Whodunit? Wikipedia Will Tell You." *New York Times*, September 17, 2010.

Kenney, Doug. "Spoilers." *National Lampoon* 1, no. 13 (April 1971).

Kermode, Frank. *The Sense of an Ending*. Oxford: Oxford Univ. Press, 1967.

Nabokov, Vladimir. "Good Readers and Good Writers." In *Lectures on Literature*, edited by Fredson Bowers. New York: Harcourt Brace Jovanovich, 1980.

Wortham, Jenna. "Letter of Recommendation: Spoilers." *New York Times Magazine*, February 14, 2018.

ACKNOWLEDGMENTS

Thanks to my agent, Alia Hanna Habib, for the usual support and beyond, and to Sophie Pugh-Sellers at the Gernert Company. Thanks to my editor, Rakesh Satyal, for patience, confidence, and getting it, and to Ryan Amato at HarperCollins.

Thanks to Beatrice Monti della Corte and the Santa Maddalena Foundation for offering me space and time, at the last minute, when I really needed it, and for friendship that will last longer than that. Thanks to Rasika and Manju for providing a completely unrealistic experience. Thanks to Matteo Colombo and Naoise Dolan for all the great conversation, which is surely reflected here.

Thanks to Adam Dalva and Elyse Walters for speaking with me at length about Goodreads and its discontents. Thanks to Gabe Habash for gamely answering my strange fact-checking questions.

The essays in this book have benefited from conversations with, readings by, and advice from at least the following people: Dom Amerena, Kris Bartkus, Kevin Brazil, Carleen Coulter, Sloane Crosley, Hannah Froehle, Monica Heisey, Martin Jackson, Jeffrey Kirkwood, Leigh Clare La Berge, Vincenzo Latronico, Christian Lorentzen, Huw Nesbitt, Ellena Savage, Josie Thaddeus-Johns, and Alex Wells. Thanks to Ben Mauk for letting me come up with my own title this time, and for everything else. Thanks to Dave Wingrave, my first reader, for answering mostly promptly all emails with the subject line "do I sound crazy?" and for apparently providing me with a lot of inspiration. And thanks, finally, to Thom Sliwowski, for not minding when I just need fifteen more minutes and we're already late for our sauna appointment, for teaching me about Exploding Head Syndrome (among many other things), and for sitting on the couch with me for hours and hours and hours. I don't know how I would have done it without you.

ABOUT THE AUTHOR

Lauren Oyler's essays on books and culture appear regularly in the *New Yorker*, the *New York Times*, the *London Review of Books*, *Harper's Magazine*, and other publications. Her debut novel, *Fake Accounts*, was published in 2021. She lives in Berlin.